I0803493

Praise for *Manifesting by the Moon*

"Jen Sankey has written a completely new and original take on how to connect with the moon. . . . Practical, inspirational, and fun, this is my new go-to lunar magic book."
—**DEBORAH BLAKE,** author of *The Eclectic Witch's Book of Shadows*

"Filled with helpful information and an expansive list of exercises, this book is a must-have for anyone who loves lunar lore and would like to bask in the beauty of moon magic."
—**MONICA BODIRSKY,** divination artist, author, and modern mystic

"A user-friendly workbook that makes working with lunar energy accessible and enriching. Jen Sankey guides you through each step with warmth and wisdom, blending personal insight with fascinating lunar facts."
—**STEVEN BRIGHT,** author of *Tarot: Your Personal Guide* and *The Oracle Creator*

"This book offers clear tools, rituals, meditations, tarot spreads, and more to align your spirit, mind, and body with each moon phase. Whether you're new to moon magic or looking to deepen your practice, this book is a beautifully accessible companion."
—**ETHONY DAWN,** author of *Become an Exceptional Tarot Reader*

"A luminous repository of everything your moon magick practice craves: history, correspondences, spellwork, and practical wisdom woven with heart and intention. Jen Sankey has created a guide that is both enchanting and essential."
—**DANIELLE DEACY AND DINA ROSENBERG,** co-owners of Amityville Apothecary

"A gentle, powerful guide for anyone seeking to personalize their lunar practice to divine real-world change through creative intentions, devoted will, and acts of magical transformation."
—**MARIA MINNIS,** author of *Tarot for the Hard Work*

"Jen Sankey provides a wide array of methods and approaches to working with the Moon in all arenas of life."
—**IVO DOMINGUEZ, JR.**, lead author of the Witch's Sun Sign series

"A beautifully accessible guide to lunar manifestation, perfect for anyone who wants to deepen their magical connection with the moon's cycles. Jen Sankey's practical rituals, creative spellwork, and insightful tarot techniques make working with moon energy feel as natural as the night sky."
—**THERESA REED,** author of *The Cards You're Dealt—How to Deal When Life Gets Real*

"I love that this book includes both history and lore, and I especially appreciated the enchanted pen exercise. This book is a great resource for more magical understanding about the power of the moon."
—**LILITH DORSEY,** author of *Tarot Every Witch Way*

"A must-have manual for enchanted rituals and inspired spellwork. Jen Sankey has created a sacred treasure trove that will inspire you for many moons to come!"
—**SASHA GRAHAM,** author of *Dark Wood Tarot*

"A tool for tuning your intuition, mind, and body to the lunar current. This is how you optimize ritual work with change. Empowering and truly special."
—**BENEBELL WEN,** author of *I Ching, The Oracle* and *The Tao of Craft*

"An incredibly insightful book. Jen has each page packed with information that is not only practical but also underpinned by a wealth of knowledge."
—**JANE MATTHEWS,** Director, World Divination Association

"A luminous, heartfelt guide that weaves the moon's radiant energy into a transformative journey of manifestation. Brimming with practical exercises, it ignites the magic within us all, guiding beginners and seasoned seekers alike to bring dreams within reach."
—**TONI SAVORY,** The Card Geek, Founder of World Divination Association

"Jen Sankey shares her spiritual insights and an elegant ritual for every phase of the moon cycle. Readers will learn more about setting intentions, the meanings of the lunar phases, divination, and meaningful suggestions for lunar magic."
—**ASTREA TAYLOR,** author of *Intuitive Witchcraft* and *Inspiring Creativity Through Magick*

"A wonderful array of resources for any magical practitioner, energy worker, or witch who wants to power up with our closest celestial partner. The real prize is the large collection of exercises, journaling prompts, spells, tarot spreads, and correspondences."
—**THOMAS WITHOLT,** author of the *Seaborn Kipper* and *The Hermit's Book of Moon Spreads*

"A practical and insightful guide to harnessing lunar energy for manifestation. Perfect for beginners as well as seasoned practitioners, it offers easy-to-follow rituals and guidance."
—**AMY ZERNER AND MONTE FARBER,** authors of *The Enchanted Tarot* and *The Vision Board Oracle*

MANIFESTING BY THE MOON

About the Author

Jen Sankey, an author, professional witch, and tarot reader, is dedicated to teaching the mystical arts. Her work has been featured in numerous publications, and she has been a sought-after speaker at various events. Jen is a two-time gold COVR award winner, recognized both for her insightful interviews with peers in the metaphysical community and for the self-publication of her three-time award-winning tarot deck, Stardust Wanderer Tarot. She is also the creator of Enchanted Forest Felines Tarot and Goblin Whispers Tarot, the latter in collaboration with Llewellyn Worldwide. As the director of the World Spiritual Association on social media, Jen plays the honored role of connecting spiritual practitioners from all over the world.

When she is not writing, teaching, or creating new magical projects, Jen may be exploring the Florida Keys or hiking in the mountains with the Fae, flitting through these spaces with immense gratitude for the enchantment woven into the world. Jen's love of nature, whimsy, and the unseen realms continually inspires her craft and creations, infusing them with wonder and a deep reverence for magic. You can follow her journey and upcoming projects at www.stardustwanderertarot.com, on Instagram @ stardustwanderertarot, or at linktr.ee/stardustwanderertarot.

MANIFESTING BY THE MOON

A Guide to Lunar Magic

JEN SANKEY

LLEWELLYN
WOODBURY, MINNESOTA

First Edition
Second Printing, 2026

Cover design by Kevin R. Brown
Editing by Laura Kurtz
Interior art by the Llewellyn Art Department
Tarot cards are from Tarot Original 1909 Deck © 2021 with art created by Pamela Colman Smith and Arthur Edward Waite. Used with permission of LoScarabeo.

Library of Congress Cataloging-in-Publication Data
Names: Sankey, Jen author
Title: Manifesting by the moon : a guide to lunar magic / Jen Sankey.
Description: First edition. | Woodbury, Minnesota : Llewellyn, [2026] | Includes bibliographical references. | Summary: "Offers a guided journey into manifestation using the moon's phases as a tool for personal transformation. Includes phase-by-phase workings with deity, energy, crystals, and more. Also includes meditations, tarot, and recipes"-- Provided by publisher.
Identifiers: LCCN 2025041069 (print) | LCCN 2025041070 (ebook) | ISBN 9780738781402 paperback | ISBN 9780738781563 ebook
Subjects: LCSH: Moon--Miscellanea | Magic | Crystals | Tarot
Classification: LCC BF1623.M66 S265 2026 (print) | LCC BF1623.M66 (ebook)
LC record available at https://lccn.loc.gov/2025041069
LC ebook record available at https://lccn.loc.gov/2025041070

Llewellyn Publications
A Division of Llewellyn Worldwide Ltd.
2143 Wooddale Drive
Woodbury, MN 55125-2989
www.llewellyn.com

Printed in the United States of America

GPSR Representation:
UPI-2M PLUS d.o.o., Medulićeva 20, 10000 Zagreb, Croatia
matt.parsons@upi2mbooks.hr

Dedication

To my forever love, Jay: Thank you for being my biggest fan and loving me through every phase of our lives. I love and appreciate you more than words can ever say.

To my boys: Tyler, Ryan, Jason Jr., and Justin: Thank you for choosing me to be your mom. It has been the most incredible honor of my life to watch you grow into the fantastic men you are today. I'm endlessly proud of each of you.

And to my younger self: Little Jen, you did it. Every step, every struggle, every dream was worth it.

Contents

Spells, Rituals, Exercises, and Activities

Disclaimer

This book is intended to provide information and guidance related to metaphysical practices involving the moon. The content of this book is not intended to replace professional, medical, psychological, or legal advice. Consult a professional before practicing anything in this book if you have medical conditions, mental health concerns, or legal questions. If you plan on trying any herbs, oils, or practices you may not be familiar with, consult with the appropriate professional beforehand. The author and publisher of this book have no liability arising directly or indirectly from the use of the information or practices described herein, including but not limited to any adverse effects, outcomes, or consequences.

FOREWORD

There are very few things in life one can truly rely upon in a world that consistently finds new ways to surprise us. The moon, however, is one of those things which offer us a sense of grounding and stability. She may grace the night sky in a different way, waxing and waning in her dance through light and shadow, but she's always there—listening, offering her quiet magic to those who respect her wisdom.

She teaches us to follow her journey: that the full moon is never far behind the darkness. Yes, the night might seem bleak at times; Luna needs her days to rest too. And in honoring her own shifts and cycles, she shows us how to do the same. We watch her be her full self and learn that authenticity doesn't mean sameness. It means understanding there are different parts of us that will appear at different times, each one worthy. Not only are your *phases of self* valuable but when embraced fully, can teach us how to be successful in a way that is uniquely our own.

I, like so many others, have gazed affectionately at the moon since childhood. I didn't know anything about moon phases or moon manifestations back then, only that when I looked out my window at night, the moon was right there, staring back at me. It wasn't until many years later that I discovered Luna had so much more to give than simply being a night light for a shy little girl.

I stumbled into spirituality the way I've stumbled into most meaningful things in my life—clumsily, curiously, and without a clear plan. One of the first spiritual practices that truly felt like home was working with the moon phases. Flowing with the moon became a ritual that nourished me, comforted me and helped me grow in ways I never knew were possible.

But then life happened. I found myself in a spiritual place that wasn't very spiritual at all—at least not in the ways that truly matter. It shattered my confidence in healers and spiritual teachers. It showed me an ugly side that truly broke my heart and I found myself turning away from spirituality completely. I wanted nothing more to do with crystals or herbs or the moon or sabbats or goddesses. I didn't feel safe or supported, even though the moon had always been something sacred for me.

This continued for a year, until one day I felt so hollow it brought me to tears. I felt lost and confused, afraid, and deeply depressed. I couldn't tell you why but that tearful day inspired me to take out my watercolors and paint. I didn't have a plan, just an ache to create something. The first thing that came to mind was the moon phases. So, I painted. And suddenly, I felt an overwhelming urge to work with the moon again. In fact so much so, that I went from having no spiritual practice to speak of to diving back in head first. I even got the idea to start a moon-based apothecary, where every creation was inspired by her. I have not looked back since.

At some point, I paused the time to reflect upon this journey and I realized that yes, life did indeed become dark and bleak. That I couldn't connect with the moon in an obvious way, and yet—she was still there, waiting for me. The light returned, and I felt whole again.

In truth, I didn't know how to trust in the moon back then. I wish I'd had a guide like the one you're holding in your hands now. One that taught me how to understand myself by understanding the moon. One that offered me a framework to revisit when I experienced those dark nights as well as bright ones. Jen's approach is structured in a way that feels practical and easy to follow, yet leaves ample room for you to embody the moon's lessons in the most authentic way possible.

What I love most is that she doesn't paint this work as fluffy or easy; she lets you know that this is work that will bring up nerves and challenges. It will require you to be clear and confident—and to remember that manifestation is, at its heart, an inside job. This book will force you to ebb and flow, but it will also reward you for your efforts.

The world would have you believe life moves in a straight line—that the only way forward is, well, forward. But as you work with the moon, you'll discover that life so rarely—if at all—moves in just one direction or that you go through a cycle and when it ends, that phase is gone forever. When the reality is that, you'll return to the same places again and again, finding new ways to harness the energy Luna has to offer.

Let *Manifesting by the Moon* be your trusted companion as you revisit each cycle. This book isn't just a book; it's a guide to your homecoming. It's a treasured tool that will help you experience manifestation, yes—but more importantly, to deepen your understanding of yourself using the moon phases as your framework. This guide will help you to incorporate all of the phases of self into your life in a way that feels honest and supportive.

It's only when we know how to truly be ourselves—no matter what version of us appears—that we find a success that's not just meaningful, but deeply, soulfully our own.

~ Lorriane Anderson

INTRODUCTION

Who would not want to confidently curate their best life and embody their magic? You can accomplish this and more by harnessing and working with the moon. When you become fully present in your spirit, mind, and body, you open a new door to your magical potential and awaken a power within that has been waiting for this moment.

The moon presents herself as a manifesting mystical advisor as you take this journey of self-discovery and unlimited potential. She lights the way for your manifestations and creates a cosmic roadmap for you to move forward with grace and conviction.

My Journey with the Moon

As a teenager suddenly thrust out alone with no resources, I experienced a life-changing epiphany. I had always loved to be outside late at night, sitting in the moon's company. Although I wasn't sure why at the time, I soon realized that the calm, direct power the moon shared with me always kept me moving in the right direction.

Things were looking a bit dire for me as a homeless teen, so I turned to the moon. After trying a few different ways to work with the phases to manifest what I needed, I discovered that incorporating and dedicating my whole self—spirit, mind, and body—yielded the most consistent results. Being fully present in my intuition and magical practice brought me a sense of power and control when everything else in my young life was unstable.

I did not fully understand the magic the moon held for me until I started actively incorporating her energy into my developing magical work, eventually creating a practice of which I am proud. The moon was my companion in a confusing and difficult part of my life, and I am forever grateful. When I realized that I could use the moon's phases to manifest and develop my innate power, I began to hone the practice to guide others so that they wouldn't have to go through the hardships I did.

As I became more experienced in my practice, I started to include these moon manifesting strategies in tarot readings for clients. I taught the people I read for to become more mindful of their magical capacity as well as how to change their lives on their terms. Returning clients were often excited to share their experiences with moon manifesting. At that point, I could smooth the edges of this magical moon-manifesting practice to share with others.

After teaching clients one-on-one using this method, I then began to teach it to larger groups, and it has been the subject of many conferences I have attended. Through all these situations, I have led people to recognize and step into their magic while learning to incorporate the magic of the moon for success. Nothing makes me happier than speaking to clients or students and hearing about their excitement for successfully manifesting and creating their fulfilling practice.

The Beginning of Your Journey

This book is for those who want to understand themselves fully, step into their magic, discover their inner and outer worlds, define their paths, and be fully present in their lives by creating a powerful practice of moon work to bring clarity, peace, and change.

Using the techniques in this book, you can reframe your thinking and mindfully combine your spirit, mind, and body magic to manifest successfully. Just as the moon phases change, so do the seasons of our lives. By working with this powerful lunar energy, you can confidently align your practice to these ebbs and flows of life while effortlessly adjusting to changes. Whether you are just starting on your journey or well-established in your practice, there is something in this book for all skill levels.

With the moon's guidance and the energy she freely gives, you can more concisely amplify your wants and needs to the universe. Focused action and knowing how to use your magic and the moon's energy will help you create successful manifestations and a feeling of power you may not have experienced before.

As you begin this exciting and life-enhancing journey, first imagine yourself as a magnet of magical manifestation; whatever you practice and focus on, you will attract. When you harness this flow and synchronize your manifestation process to this lunar rhythm, you will open your magical self to expand and heighten all your abilities. And if you practice mindfulness, you will feel the dynamic cycle of expansion. Set forth as if your intention has become a reality. When manifesting with the moon's phases, you'll be guided to keep your intention, energy, and manifestations focused.

Building a Practice

Under the guidance of the moon phases, you will build your own unique magical practice. As you get to know yourself better throughout the cycles, you will also be able to build a strong and satisfying spiritual base to enhance your abilities and deepen your knowledge of the world around you. Building a strong spiritual base will help you understand others' emotions and actions in a more empathetic way. Incorporating all facets of yourself and your energy into your magical practice will help you decide who to cultivate relationships with and identify exactly what kinds of energy you want from others.

You'll incorporate your inner and outer worlds and bring in the energy of the moon phases to reveal a clear path to success. This moon energy will give you the guidance and focus you need to produce a successful outcome.

I will introduce you to each moon phase and teach you many ways to incorporate them into your manifestations. You will use techniques such as meditation, journaling, and affirmations to create a successful mindset for your magical practice, divination, and spell work. As you become more comfortable with moon work, utilize the additional techniques and suggestions I have included to build on your new practice. By working on the incorporation of your spiritual, mental, and physical self and threading it through your moon manifestation practice, you will create your mystical tapestry of manifesting success.

While you can skip around and use the information however it suits you, this book has a structured framework for your moon manifesting practice. I encourage you to work through it in order. As you become more comfortable, you can use it as a reference guide. At the end of each chapter, I include correspondences that you can change up depending on what you plan to manifest during each moon cycle.

In part one, you will learn the foundations of magical practice and start building your own. Here is where you will discover your innate abilities and how to use them with the moon phases. In part two, you will start to use the moon manifestation method, set your intention for the lunar cycle, and create your new reality. We will begin at the new moon. Each chapter introduces you to the next moon phase and provides examples of how you can incorporate it into your lunar spirit, mind, and body. This structured practice creates a fully encompassing experience for successful manifestations. You will first be prompted to do activities for your lunar spirit, followed by your lunar mind, and finally to bring your moon phase practice together with your lunar body.

When you have mastered magical practice and feel comfortable trying something different, see the chapter on advanced moon work to further your moon manifesting. It also covers lunar eclipses and the zodiac.

The Moon Awaits—Let's Get Started

There is a vast amount of information out in the world about manifestation and moon magic. Any subject can become overwhelming when there is an overload of tips, tricks, and "make it work faster" promises available. This book will help you create a magical framework while allowing you room to find what resonates with you. As you learn more about yourself throughout this process, staying consistent is vital. It will take work, so read the following pages carefully—they contain all the necessary information to establish a successful moon manifestation practice.

It is expected to be a bit nervous when starting something new, but that energy also accompanies new possibilities, as you will discover in the chapter about the new moon. Taking advantage of the advice within these pages can help you move through those very real and important feelings. Let the moon be your advisor as you ebb and flow through your inner world, grounding and anchoring your magical self to reach beyond your greatest expectations, break through limiting beliefs, and become the best version of you.

Imagine having a clear, focused vision of the life you want and confidently taking steps to make it a reality. With the moon, you can do just that. Discovering yourself can make you mentally stronger and more confident. By stepping into this all-powerful energy, you will be more present in your life.

By understanding yourself and how to use the energy of your lunar spirit, mind, and body, you develop an innate knowledge of this energy, the possibilities and manifestation methods available to you. And more importantly, what resonates with you as you build your practice.

Manifesting has become a buzzword online. I want to show you what it can be—not some fluffy version involving wishes and waiting. Consider this book your moon manifesting charcuterie board; the moon manifestation method is all laid out before you in these pages, and you can choose your own path and create an abundant, easy-to-do moon manifesting life.

PART ONE

PREPARATION

As with any new journey, learning the basics is especially important. In this section you will receive the basics of moon manifesting magic, learning about your lunar spirit, mind and body and how you will integrate these components to create a successful and fulling moon practice.

CHAPTER ONE

LUNAR WISDOM

In this chapter, you will learn about the moon itself. A deeper understanding of *la luna* will create the foundation for your manifestation practice and strengthen your use of the moon's magic during the lunar phases. You will dive into the history of moon worship, how those practices have changed throughout the centuries, how the full moon came to have so many special names, and how the people of times past honored the moon and its energy.

Even in a magical practice there is a bit of science. You will see how scientists have incorporated the history and lore of the moon into their findings, as well as how the tides are affected by the moon's phases. Finally, you will be introduced to the phases of the moon and what the energy of each phase brings.

Moon History from Long Ago

People have been using the moon's guidance for thousands of years. Long ago, humans looked to the moon for practical things, such as knowing when to harvest and fish and celebrate their seasonal gatherings or other holidays. Ancient people used the moon to mark the passage of time and the changing seasons.

Cave art and bone carvings from ancient peoples lead us to believe they tracked the moon, time, and seasons using the resources in the areas in which they lived such as animal bones or herbs for paint used in cave drawings. Similar cave drawings of deer, cows/oxen, stars, and the moon were found throughout caves from western Europe to Africa. These early civilizations had no straightforward way to communicate with each other across cultures, so it seems incredible how they all represented the moon similarly in their stories.

In some ancient cultures the moon deities were male, as with the Egyptian moon god, Khonsu, or the moon god of the Babylonians, Sin. In Hindu culture, the moon god Chandra rides across the sky in a silver chariot drawn by antelope. In other cultures, the moon deity is female, one of the more famous examples being the Greek goddess Artemis. Because Greek moon goddesses are most familiar to Western audiences, you will work with a few of them throughout the moon phases later in this book. Chapter 5 provides information on creating a goddess practice for your moon manifesting magic.

In some cultures, it is said that the more names something has or how many generations a name is used, the more important it is. For example, in Lakota and Navajo tribes, someone with multiple names reflects their achievements and unique abilities.[1] The great Lakota holy leader, Black Elk, was so named for his ability to bring native tribes together in peace. He was also the fourth man in his family to hold that name, considered an honor, since having this family name was said to carry special achievements from the generations down to help guide the current name holder.[2]

In ancient Babylon, deities often had several names representing their different traits and authorities. For example, the goddess of art of medicine went by the names Bau, Gula, and Ninisinna.[3] Over time, the moon has collected so many names that it would take pages to list them all, proving how important it was to various cultures.

Many cultures also associate animals with the moon. Some examples of these animals include the eagle moon in the Cree nation, the moon

1. Vine Deloria Jr., *God Is Red: A Native View of Religion* (Fulcrum Publishing, 1992), 202.

2. "Black Elk," *National Park Service*, last updated August 31, 2020, https://www.nps.gov/people/black-elk.htm.

3. Samuel Noah Kramer, *History Begins at Sumer: Thirty-Nine Firsts in Recorded History* (Doubleday, 1956), 80–82.

hare in Chinese culture, the ibis in ancient Egyptian culture, and the lizard in Hawaiian cultures. Animals with long tusks play many roles in myths about the moon, as seen in the Indus Valley civilization.

In folklore, you will find bears, bees, moths, night birds, wolves, swans, geese, frogs, silvery fish, snakes, crabs, and crayfish in ancient moon stories. One of my favorites is the Navajo tale of the moon and the coyote. In this tale, the moon is represented by a beautiful woman. The coyote, known as a trickster, falls in love with the moon and tries using his antics to impress her. But these tricks are in vain; the moon does not take notice. Soon Coyote starts to play tricks on other animals, and the moon eventually does see him trying to gain her attention. Slowly but surely, she acknowledges him and a bond forms between them. Coyote learns from this that a strong relationship takes time and patience.[4]

Some gods and goddesses that represent the moon also had animal companions. The Roman goddess Luna had a white horse, and Greek mythology's Hekate had her black hounds. Cave art of lions and the moon have been found in the United Kingdom that may be among the oldest depictions of the lunar phases.[5]

Naming the Full Moon

Ancient cultures often used the moon to predict the weather and track their celebrations, hunting seasons, planting, and harvesting. Cultures that utilized the moon's energy would name each full moon to differentiate between them. For example, in the northeastern United States, the Algonquin tribes considered April the month of the Pink Moon, because when that moon showed itself in the sky, a certain early blooming pink flower appeared. When they saw this flower, they knew spring was on its way

4. Richard Erdoes and Alfonso Ortiz, eds. "Navajo Stories of the Moon and Stars," in *American Indian Myths and Legends* (Pantheon Books, 1984), 140.

5. Bob Yirka, "Cave Paintings Show Ice Age Hunter-Gatherers Used a Lunar Calendar," *Phys.org*, January 5, 2023, https://phys.org/news/2023-01-cave-ice-age-hunter-gatherers-lunar.html.

and would prepare for the new season. People from different regions used names suited to where they live.

Today many people still rely on the moon phases for their everyday plans. Farmers pay attention to the moon to decide when to plant or harvest their crops. *The Farmer's Almanac*, an annual guide for a wide variety of agricultural information including weather forecasts, planting, gardening advice, moon and sun cycles, and more, is a popular resource even though we have modern technology at our fingertips. I purchase one yearly and it is an important part of my moon manifesting toolbox.

Many of us have heard the plant and animal names for the full moons throughout the year. These are also included in *The Farmer's Almanac*, which I love to mention because it holds so much magical but practical information.

Even though the full moons are usually named, their energy does extend into the entire moon cycle. What I mean is the full moon energy hangs around like a shadow. For example, if you decide to manifest with the harvest moon in September, you'll experience the energy of gathering and making space during that cycle. Refer to the following list to see moon names to incorporate their energy into your practice. Just note that since the moon cycles do not strictly follow the Gregorian calendar, there may be more than one moon energy present in your moon manifesting cycle. With this information, you can document how the energy feels for you and use that to create your moon phase action steps.

Moon Names and Energy by the Months of the Year

The following names for the full moons are taken from *The Farmer's Almanac*.[6] The following names are taken from Indigenous sources—mostly Algonquin—as well as early colonial sources and other traditional North American heritage sources.

6. Catherine Boeckmann, "A Guide to Traditional Full Moon Names and Their Meanings," *The Old Farmer's Almanac* website, last updated March 12, 2025, https://www.almanac.com/full-moon-names.

JANUARY: WOLF MOON

The Wolf Moon was named for the howling of wolves in the middle of winter. Other names for this moon in the Algonquin tribes are the Ice or Old Moon. The energy of the Wolf Moon wants you to tap into your unknown potential. What is hiding under the surface that you can start to thaw and give attention to?

FEBRUARY: SNOW MOON

Due to the cold snowy weather in the northern hemisphere, the Algonquin tribes named the February full moon the Snow Moon, which they also refer to as the Hunger or Storm Moon. Here we want to adjust energy in our lives to make room for expansion. This can mean curbing limiting thoughts, unhealthy habits, and overthinking to a point of inaction.

MARCH: WORM MOON

Worm Moon refers to the worm trails seen on the ground as the snow thaws and the ground becomes visible. The Algonquin peoples also called this moon the Chaste Moon or Sap Moon due to the tapping of maple trees for syrup. It is also called the Crust Moon, which is interesting to me because the name refers to the last remnants of snow still around in March. When this moon comes around, prepare for new higher vibrations to come your way. What can you nurture to bring about new opportunities and change?

APRIL: PINK MOON

This name refers to a specific pink flower that starts blooming at this time of year, an indication that spring is on its way. Other names given by the Algonquin tribes are the Egg Moon, Fish Moon, and Sprouting Grass Moon, all names that describe the same thing—a new growing season is coming. During this month you will want to tap into your true potential and discover ways to expand it that will align you with your higher self.

MAY: FLOWER MOON

Blooming May flowers give this moon its Algonquin name. It can also be called the Milk Moon, Hare Moon, and Corn Planting Moon. This blossoming moon energy calls you to focus on what is going well for you right now and how to best stay in this energy as you change and grow through the year.

JUNE: STRAWBERRY MOON

For the Algonquin tribes, June is strawberry harvest season. This moon is also called the Rose Moon or the Hot Moon due to rising summer temperatures. This time of year is about tapping into the energy of appreciation as well as focusing on the benefits of your successes. Look to what else is around the corner and navigate through the month with higher energy and integrate your abundance.

JULY: BUCK MOON

The Algonquins called this the Buck Moon because male deer start to grow their antlers back in July after shedding them earlier in the year. Other names for this month's moon include the Hay Moon to mark the hay harvest and the Thunder Moon for the summer storms. When this energy shows up you may be in the middle of abundance and receiving, and you need to be able to navigate this expansive new energy in a way that will benefit you best. Here learning and patience is the key to success.

AUGUST: STURGEON MOON

The Algonquin observed that sturgeons are most active during this time of year, hence the name. It also goes by the Grain Moon, Green Corn Moon, and the Red Moon for the reddish tint it takes on during the humid summer months. This moon energy wants you to step fully into your abundance and show extra gratitude not only to the universe but also to those who helped you along the way.

SEPTEMBER: HARVEST MOON

The Harvest Moon is so well-known there are even songs about it. Both Algonquin and Sioux tribes use this term for the September moon. It marks the autumn equinox and when crops are harvested. It is also called the Barley and Corn Moon. This moon is high and bright in the sky, allowing farmers to work longer to gather their bounty for the year. The Harvest Moon asks you where you need to trim back, where you need to expand, and how you will go about taking steps to prepare for the month ahead. Wherever you shift your focus, stepping into your magic fully is important for your next level of expansion.

OCTOBER: HUNTER'S MOON

After the harvest is collected, fox and deer are unable to hide in the tall grass, so they are easily hunted. This moon is high and bright in the sky, giving hunters an advantage over their prey. It is also referred to as the Dying Grass Moon and Travel Moon. This moon is the last push as the year winds down. Here you should focus on how you can best support and prepare for your next endeavors. You are sowing seeds for the next year or starting to harvest what you have been working on already.

NOVEMBER: BEAVER MOON

The Algonquin named this moon for the beavers observed building and securing their winter dams at this time. Another name is the Frost Moon. This moon's energy is all about preparation and building the base of what you desire. Planning and setting energetic intentions now will benefit you later.

DECEMBER: COLD MOON

This moon's name relates to the long cold nights and winter settling in. The Algonquin also called this moon the Oak Moon as well as the Long Night Moon. The full moon in December is about your internal self. Now is the time to dig into the stories you tell yourself and how they affect what you want to manifest. Maybe it's important to use this time to build a more stable magical practice, or you could explore what your magical practice means for you. Use this quieter time to reflect and clear anything that will not serve your moon manifestations. Releasing thoughts, feelings, and old ideas are especially important right now as you prepare ahead for a whole new year with its experiences, learning, and opportunities.

> **Tip:** One way to effortlessly incorporate the full moon's energy into your own magical workings is to add an item related to the moon you are working with on your altar. For example, incorporate strawberries if it is the Strawberry Moon. (You can use artificial berries or even a picture.) If you want to use real strawberries, try using dried ones as they keep longer without spoiling and will not attract pests. We certainly don't want you waving away fruit flies during your moon practice!

Moon Science

In Charles Darwin's classic work, *Descent of Man*, he wrote, "Man is subject, like other mammals, birds, and even insects, to that mysterious law, which causes certain processes, such as gestation, as well as the maturation and duration of various diseases, to follow lunar periods."[7] Darwin observed that the moon influences us even more than was previously believed, a notion that gives us further encouragement to harness the moon's energy to create the life we desire. In a recent publication from the scientific journal *Frontiers in Neurology*, scientists studied the effects of the moon on humans as it relates to time. While the moon may not physically influence people and their behavior, the human psyche has been conditioned to believe it does, something we can certainly consider when working with moon energy and tapping into the innate belief that the moon guides us.[8] In fact, we can condition ourselves to believe anything is possible.

Because we are made up of about 60 percent water, it may not be surprising that the gravitational pull of the moon affects us just as it affects the

7. Charles Darwin, *The Descent of Man, and Selection in Relation to Sex*. 1st ed. (John Murray, 1871). Last updated October 2022, https://darwin-online.org.uk/converted/published/1871_Descent_F937/1871_Descent_F937.1.html.

8. Florian Raible, Hiroki Takekata, Kristin Tessmar-Raible, "An Overview of Monthly Clocks and Rhythms," *Frontiers in Neurology* 11, no. 8 (2017): 189. doi.org/10.3389/fneur.2017.00189.

tides. Sleep studies have been done specifically in relation to moon phases to see if the new and full moon cycles affected sleep patterns. In these studies, it was proven that volunteers fell asleep faster during new moons but during full moons, deep sleep decreased; it took participants on average five minutes longer to fall asleep.[9]

Outside of formal studies, many people do believe the phases of the moon affect us physically and mentally. In 1995, a survey was sent to 325 people in New Orleans, asking if they believed the lunar cycle affected humans. Nearly half believed it did, and what is interesting about this study is that out of that 50 percent, a sizable number were nurses, doctors, and service people.[10]

One myth that has been debunked by science is that the menstruation cycle synchronizes with the moon phases. The theory was that a woman's cycle was correlated to the gravitational pulls during the moon's phases. Some studies showed that when women calculated their cycle by the synodic month (the lunar cycle rather than the regular Gregorian calendar), especially those aged thirty-five and under, it aligned with the new and full moons. This was not always consistent but seemed to align often in the women who participated in this 2001 study.[11]

Research psychiatrist Robert Ornstein believed different sides of the brain were affected by the electromagnetic forces of the sun and the moon and posited that we are these days taught to ignore the lunar side that focuses more on everyday tasks and survival, things that ancient peoples relied on. Ornstein states, "There can be no further biological evolution

9. Leandro Casiraghi et al. "Moonstruck sleep: Synchronization of human sleep with the moon cycle under field conditions," *Science Advances* 7, vol. 5 (2021): 1–8. doi:10.1126/sciadv.abe0465.

10. Martin Röösli et al. "Sleepless night, the moon is bright: longitudinal study of lunar phase and sleep," *Journal of Sleep Research* 15 (2006): 149–53. https://blog.surf-prevention.com/wp-content/uploads/2012/01/Sleepless-night-the-moon-is-bright-longitudinal-study-of-lunar-phase-and-sleep.pdf.

11. Charlotte Helfrich-Förster et al, "Women Temporarily Synchronize Their Menstrual Cycles with the Luminance and Gravimetric Cycles of the Moon," *Science Advances* 7, no. 5 (2021): eabe1358. doi.org/10.1126/sciadv.abe1358.

without conscious evolution."[12] We as a society need to start tapping into our conscious selves; practicing magic and working with the moon facilitate learning and growth—something that everyone needs to engage in, regardless of how they choose to do it. We are at a standstill because we may be too "busy" to give magic our time. Working with the moon to manifest and harness your unique magic adds to the collective energies as well, and that benefits not only you but everyone around you.

As you move through this book and the included prompts, you will activate the lunar side of your brain and incorporate your whole self, combining spirit, mind, and body just as those before us did. You will be guided to fully embrace aspects of yourself and tap into your magical manifesting abilities.

The Moon's Phases

The moon phases are a scientific phenomenon caused by the moon orbiting around Earth. As it does, the moon is slowly rotating and always keeps the same side facing our planet. The moon and sun orbit around the same center of gravity, called the barycenter, which is in constant motion because both the sun and moon are in constant motion. Because Earth is bigger than the moon, it "pulls" the barycenter closer to itself than to the moon. The barycenter is located below Earth's surface about three thousand miles from the center of the planet.[13]

What do moon phases look like in the sky? Read the following here to learn what each phase looks like. And as you move through the chapters, you'll find more in-depth information on each one.

Moon Phases Visual Explanations

New Moon: It is not visible to the naked eye.

Waxing Crescent: Those in the Northern Hemisphere will see a sliver of light on the right. For those in the Southern Hemisphere, it will appear on the left.

12. Robert Ornstein, *The Evolution of Consciousness: The Origins of the Way We Think* (Simon & Schuster, 1991), 2.

13. Kim Long, *The Moon Book: Fascinating Facts about the Magnificent, Mysterious Moon*. Johnson Books, 1998, 1.

First Quarter: Half the moon is illuminated; right side in the Northern Hemisphere, left side in Southern Hemisphere.

Waxing Gibbous: Three quarters of the moon is lit.

Full Moon: The whole moon is illuminated.

Waning Gibbous: The moon is three-quarters of the way darker now.

Third Quarter: In the northern hemisphere the left half of the moon is illuminated, and the right side is lit for the southern hemisphere.

Waning Crescent: Now just a sliver of light is visible on the left side of the moon in the Northern Hemisphere and the sliver of light is on the right for the Southern Hemisphere.

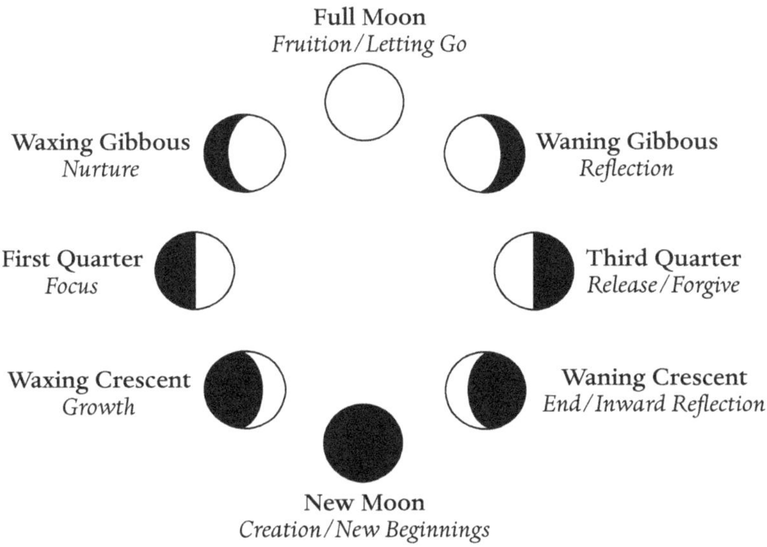

Moon Phase Graph

These are the phases you will be working with. Take some time to look at the phases closely and notice how each one makes you feel. Visualizing the moon phase you are currently working with helps establish a deeper connection and understanding of these emotions.

Moon Wisdom Meets Moon Magic

When you understand the science behind the moon phases and how your body reacts to them, you can use this information during your moon manifestations. Bringing your awareness to the present moment at every moon phase—especially when feeling a new physical sensation—is a good way to work on the body exercises included in each chapter. Being aware of how you feel will help you to incorporate the spirit and mind practices as well. Following your own rhythm and learning how to work with this powerful internal flow will lead you to become a masterful manifester and create a confident practice. In doing the work you are joining a long legacy of moon magic practice and communing with the moon. You will also be learning to incorporate your lunar anima—your lunar spirit, lunar mind, and lunar body—for a fully encompassing moon manifesting experience.

When I started manifesting with the moon, most of what I read was focused on the intuitive practice of manifesting. After trying that for a couple of moon cycles, I realized I wanted my practice to incorporate all aspects of self, not just the spiritual aspects. Performing my moon magic in a way that allowed me to tap into all the energy my whole self had to offer was important and, as I came to discover, extraordinarily successful. Playing off the concept of the Celtic cauldrons within the body, I applied this to my moon manifesting and was excited to see how it turned what can be a stale, monotonous practice into a lucrative, full-spectrum moon manifesting blueprint.

The concept of the three cauldrons is based on "The Cauldron of Poesy," a medieval Irish bardic poem that speaks of the three metaphysical "cauldrons" contained in the physical body.[14] In the article "Tending to Your Spiritual Cauldrons," author Laura Zakroff, explains these metaphysical cauldrons and how they work in your magical practice. The first cauldron is the Cauldron of Warming, located in our pelvic region, the area of basic needs and the energy we need to live. The second cauldron is the Cauldron of Motion. This cauldron sits near your heart center and connects you to inspiration. The last cauldron is the Cauldron of Wisdom, located near/above your head and is related to the spiritual self.[15]

14. John-Paul Patton, *Lightning Bolts and Dew Drops: A Cauldron of Poesy* (Independently published, 2015), 72.

15. Laura Tempest Zakroff, "Tending to Your Spiritual Cauldrons," Llewellyn website, May 22, 2017, https://www.llewellyn.com/journal/print.php?id=2629.

I applied the cauldrons to each moon phase as follows:

Lunar Spirit

Igniting your higher self through meditation, activations, and moon devotionals.

Lunar Mind

Bringing your intention to the forefront of your mind by journaling, practicing gratitude, and practicing affirmations. This will bring your awareness and intuition into your manifestation practice for added energy.

Lunar Body

Incorporating your physical self as well as having space to focus on and create a daily physical practice. Use other divinatory tools for extra guidance and support.

In doing this work, you will be cultivating a practice that encourages personal transformation. Each phase you go through will create a better individual understanding of self. You are more like the moon than you realize; just like it, you move through phases—light and dark—but both of you will always cycle through these times and have the chance to start anew.

CHAPTER TWO
YOUR LUNAR SPIRIT

Awareness of the present is an essential tool in a moon manifestation practice. This chapter covers mindfulness, how to achieve it, and ways to start working your intuitive muscles. Here you will begin to define your lunar spirit. I will also cover meditation and igniting your intuition, all of which can be life-changing when you regularly tap into this side of yourself. As you prepare for your moon manifesting journey, use the next few chapters to learn, practice, and settle into these new methods, or review them if you are a seasoned practitioner.

Mindfulness

Mindfulness is defined as being active and open to the present moment. It is a state of observing one's thoughts and feelings without judgment. When you fully emerge in the present moment, you gain a clearer perspective on your thoughts, feelings, wants, and needs. When focusing on circumstances that cannot be shifted, you energetically push yourself out of receiving abundant energy because you are too attached to the outcome. By learning to quiet those thoughts and be present in the here and now, you can focus on your magical intentions and know which of your current action steps need attention.

Another vital piece of mindfulness is accepting what is without judgment. Mostly regarding yourself. Self-acceptance prevents you from becoming energetically stuck. When you refrain from judging your thoughts and feelings, mindfulness will allow you to open yourself to active listening, which can help you really talk to others. When you listen actively, you pay more attention to what someone is saying. Practicing mindfulness will also help you to pick up nonverbal cues you may miss if you are too worried about thinking about what to say next.

When we practice mindfulness, we remind ourselves how important being in the present moment is not only for our own self-care but for the benefit of everyone we interact with. Align this practice in your moon manifesting and you'll have a clearer picture of what you want and how you can achieve it.

EXERCISE: MINDFUL BODY

Being aware of your body is a fantastic way to incorporate mindfulness into your everyday routines.

What you need:

Your daily shower
Notebook
Pen

What to do:

As you shower, whether in the morning or at night, look at each part of your body. Think about what this part does for you every day. After you have set your thoughts about each body part and what it does for you in motion, send thanks and love to each of these body parts. You can do this as quickly or slowly as you like but dig deep and genuinely feel gratitude for each part.

Take a few deep breaths and continue with your shower. When you leave, look in the mirror and say three good things about yourself, and be sure you say them aloud.

Continue with your day. See how you feel after doing this for at least a week. If you noticed anything has changed, write in a notebook on your experience.

EXERCISE: INTENTIONAL PAUSES

An intentional pause is a moment of stillness you incorporate into your day. Yes, I want you to choose a few minutes in your day to do nothing. Doing this will help break the cycle of being on autopilot and bring your awareness front and center. You will notice how refreshed you begin to feel after practicing intentional pauses for a few days.

What you need:

Cellphone or alarm to schedule your mindfulness exercise

What to do:

Choose several times during the day for an intentional pause. If needed, set a reminder alarm on your phone. When the time for an intentional pause arrives, stop what you are doing.

Now it is time to just sit—just be in the moment. Look around you, listen to the noises outside, or close your eyes. When your minute is up, take a deep breath and continue with your day.

Intuition

Intuition is like a muscle, and any muscle needs to be used to stay strong and helpful. You will be using your intuition daily as you go through this moon manifesting process; before you realize it, you will come to trust your intuition without a second thought. In a magical sense, using your intuition or inner knowing can help you to determine your true feelings if something is not sitting right with you. This sense develops when you understand how your body receives and processes information.

In her book *The Secret Psychic*, author Angela Wix explains that inner knowing comes from our energetic senses: clairvoyance, clairaudience, claircognizance, clairempathy, clairolfaction, clair gustance, and clairtangency.[16]

Clairvoyance is the ability to receive intuitive messages through your psychic vision. When you receive messages this way, they come through

16. Angela A. Wix, *The Secret Psychic: Embrace the Magic of Subtle Intuition, Natural Spirit Communication, and Your Hidden Spiritual Life* (Llewellyn Publications, 2021), 78.

your mind's eye, not your physical eyes. For example, picture your kitchen in your mind's eye. Look at the counter and envision what is there. Doing this uses your clairvoyant sight.

Clairaudience relates to your intuitive hearing, not just your physical hearing. Think of a time when a song played on repeat in your head or you thought you heard someone speaking to you but no one was around. That is your intuitive hearing.

Claircognizance is the gut feeling you get when you just *know* something. You know deep down that you are right or need to do something immediately even if you are not sure why.

Clairempathy is the ability to tap into or feel others' emotions. For example, say you are in the checkout line at the store and a wave of anxiety suddenly washes over you but you do not understand why. But then as you talk to the cashier, they tell you it is their first day alone on the register and you realize you were noticing their energy.

Clairolfaction and clairgustance refer to the intuitive ability to receive messages through smell and taste. For example, think about your favorite meal. Can you smell the delicious aromas? Is your mouth starting to water? That is your intuitive sense of smell and taste.

Clairtangency can also be known as psychometry. This way of receiving intuitive messages is through touch. For example, some mediums like to touch a picture of the deceased or an object they owned to receive messages.

When you feel comfortable, you can start to work on the clair senses that do not come as quickly to you. Once you gain some experience, you will be surprised with how much easier it is to use all of them.

Unfortunately, as a society, we are taught not to trust our intuition and instead solely rely on cold hard facts. Has your gut ever told you to do one thing but you went the other way because it was deemed the "right" thing to do? That gut feeling was your intuition. But do not fret, you can start practicing right away. Trust yourself and try not to overthink things. Do not be afraid to go with the first choice that comes to mind. Avoid second-guessing that gut feeling; instead, believe it is the best decision. Keep trusting your first instinct until it becomes second-nature and you'll reach a point where you no longer question it. Even though trusting your intuition takes some time to achieve, it is not impossible. Once you have worked on this part of yourself, it will amaze you how quick decision-making becomes. It is very freeing to let your innate self-decide something without questioning or needing to validate your choice.

Will our intuition always be correct? No, but it tends to guide us where we need to be even if we do not realize it. Strengthening your intuition will become easier as you start using all your magical tools and the moon to manifest. Use the guidance of the moon's energy and trust in the universe as well as yourself to become the strong magical person you've always hoped you could be.

Meditation

When many of us think of meditation, we visualize a person sitting in lotus position or cross-legged with incense burning and chimes ringing around them. The meditating person typically looks like they are serenely contemplating life for hours at a time. This movie-style visual has made people decide that meditation isn't for them. Fortunately, this is not how a meditation practice needs to look. Start with shorter meditations—only five minutes a day—if you are completely new to them. Slowly work your way up to at least fifteen minutes a day as you become more comfortable.

Meditation is a practice that trains your mind, body, and spirit to focus. As you work through the moon phases and incorporate your lunar practice, meditation will help improve your ability to focus your energy where it is needed.

There are many ways to meditate that do not involve sitting still for extended periods of time. Trying different methods is encouraged to see what works best for you. For example, walking meditations are useful for anyone who has trouble sitting still. I encourage you to experiment with different methods at various times of day to see which work best for you and your schedule. A quick internet search will show you tons of walking meditations made specifically for movement. I suggest trying guided ones to get a feel for how they work.

Another way to meditate is through dance. Putting on music for whatever feeling you are trying to tap into and moving however your body wants is such a fantastic way to clear your mind. You can adapt any meditation to fit your schedule, but I do encourage you to carve out time for longer meditations when you feel the need to refocus and balance your lunar mind, body, and spirit.

As you move through the moon cycles and learn to work with your magic and hone your moon manifesting practice, you will create a lot of energy. Meditation is a great practice to step into any moon phase's energy with a clear, open mind and help balance this new energy. I have included a short meditation in each moon phase chapter. Use these whenever you feel the need to center and tap into the moon's energy in a direct way.

When you do these meditations, be sure to give yourself time to record your experience in a notebook afterward and nourish your body physically. That notebook can be dedicated to meditation work or become your moon journal, something covered in chapter 3. Drinking water after meditation is important—it helps leftover energy leave the body and hydrates your cells for fresh, new energy.

When you feel ready, I encourage you to start creating your own meditations. Intuitively creating your own meditation is like curating a self-love spell that focuses its energy right where it is needed. Always keep in mind that your practice can be as simple or involved as you like; there is no right or wrong way, and the magic is just as effective.

EXERCISE: SIMPLE RELAXATION MEDITATION

Being able to clear your mind is one of the most productive ways to tap into your intuition and allow it to blossom, so try the following to simply relax at any time of day

What you need:

A quiet space

Notebook and pen

What to do:

Find a comfortable position somewhere you will not be disturbed for a few minutes. Imagine in your mind's eye the place where you have felt most peaceful in your life.

Imagine you are now in this space. What do you hear? Smell? See? Take a moment to activate each of your senses. Breathe slow and steady. Then take a long, slow breath in, letting it out just as slowly. As you take another breath in and slowly release it, picture all your muscles relaxing as you let that breath go.

Looking around your peaceful place, you notice a small body of water with a stream of water that runs from the top of your head into a pond. Gaze at this water and notice that any negative thoughts turn into fish and swim to the stream. Watch as the fish disappear from the stream as they reach the pond. Know they are now being repurposed for your great good and will not return. Breathe steadily as you do this and take as long as you need until you feel every fish swim away. When you are finished, you will feel a sense of calm and relaxation fill you and restore you.

Take a few more minutes to sit in your peaceful place. Know you can come back here anytime to feel replenished. Take another slow deep breath in and out, then open your eyes. Record your experience.

EXERCISE: DANCE IT OUT MEDITATION

There are times when movement is the best way to bring focus and balance to our spirits, minds, and bodies. You may feel silly when first trying this exercise but ignore your ego and enjoy it. Try doing this dance meditation under different phases of the moon to see how the energy changes. You do not need to go outside, but if you can, give it a try.

What you need:

A few songs that make you want to move or put you in a soothing flow, depending on your mood and a means to play them

Plenty of space to move around

Notebook and pen

What to do:

Be barefoot if possible. Turn on the music. Stand still for a moment and focus on your breathing. Close your eyes if you are comfortable.

Now bring your awareness to the music, the rhythm, the beat. Where are you feeling the music in your body? Start moving that part any way you like. You do not have to follow the rhythm; create your own. Move and flow to the music using your whole body. Make sure to breathe.

If any thoughts come into your mind, shake your body and bump them right out of your head. Get lost in the music and your movements. When you feel you are done, slow your movements until you are still. Close your eyes if you want and take a few breaths. Release.

Write in your notebook about your experience, including the songs you played. If you want to recreate this meditative space again, refer to your notebook.

Daily Practice

Mindfully tapping into all your senses daily helps your sixth sense, or intuition, become stronger. For example, as you eat your next meal, focus on the taste and how that affects you. What thoughts about these tastes come up? How does texture affect the taste? Decide how the smell enhances the taste of your food. It may seem a bit extra to bring so much awareness to your food, but igniting these senses and using them on a mindful level allows different thoughts, feelings, and ideas to surface for you. Following are some other ways to easily establish a daily practice.

Meditation

Meditation is a terrific way to kick up intuition. If you can sit and refocus your thoughts, a sitting meditation may work well for you. If focusing on your breath in a quiet space is not your cup of tea, try a walking meditation. Play your favorite music and give it all your focus, letting any thoughts float away with the notes of the song. For those who have trouble sitting still, dance it out, only focusing on the rhythm of the music. Going outside is always a great option.

Being Creative

Be creative and tap into your artistic self even if it is not your strong suit. Our creative brain is rich with ideas and inspiration. When you create mindfully, your intuition also learns how you receive messages best. You can even color in a coloring book or rearrange a space in your home, adding creative touches. Grab a piece of canvas and paint. Just let your imagination go as you intuitively choose colors and shapes without worrying about the outcome.

Dream Journal

Keeping a dedicated dream journal is a low-effort way to receive and keep track of intuitive messages. When you are settling in for the night, set the intention you will receive a message from your higher self. As soon as you wake up, write down whatever comes to mind. I have found some of my best insights this way. I suggest recording your dreams either in a journal or on a voice recorder right as you wake up before you even move. Make sure to record your feelings as well as the events, places, and situations in a dream; don't worry about them being in order.

Body Awareness

Do not just use your thinking brain; start relying on your body's sensations and feelings. You may physically feel your intuition in your core, which is how the phrase "trust your gut" became so popular. If you do not sense it in this place (which is completely fine), notice how and where you feel it in your physical body when you receive an intuitive nod. Some examples of gut feelings include a flash of a thought or emotion not related to what you are doing, a tightening or tensing in a certain part of your body, goosebumps or a prickling sensation on the skin, sweaty hands or flushed skin, and not being able to get someone out of your mind. There are so many ways your intuition could show up and it is different for everyone, which is why it is so important to practice mindfulness so you can determine when your intuition is calling.

Removing Blocks

Release any resistance or expectation when building your intuition. If you are harboring expectations, they will quickly block your intuitive flow. When these thoughts of what should happen come up for you, do some grounding and say to yourself, "I'm releasing all expectation." Saying this affirmation will help to condition your subconscious and let go of expectation.

Keeping Records

When you feel you have received an intuitive message, write it down. If you can do this consistently for at least a week or two, you will notice how often you receive intuitive hits when you give this message a little extra attention. I suggest sitting down after a week or so of record keeping to see if there are any commonalities in your notes and decide what the message could be.

EXERCISE: BODY SCAN

For the following, you will be using your intuitive senses to check in on the energy of your body. Take your time. I like to do this right before I go to sleep or upon waking, when I know I will not be disturbed. Practicing bodily awareness will help you pinpoint how you perceive your intuition and how different energy shows up physically for you.

What you need:

A quiet space
Notebook and pen

What to do:

Take a few breaths and come into the present moment. If thoughts are nagging you, imagine in your mind's eye all these thoughts going up in smoke and floating away.

Starting at your feet, imagine what they look like. Focus your energy on them and decide how they feel energetically. Do your feet feel achy? Warm? If they feel unbalanced, send some balancing energy there.

When you feel your feet are balanced, move up to your legs. Be sure to breathe. Notice if there are any areas of tension in your legs. Send balancing energy where needed.

Move up to your hip and groin area. This area tends to hold a lot of emotion and energy, so give it extra time. If you start to feel overwhelmed, take a few deep, cleansing breaths and give loving energy to this area.

Proceed to your torso. How is the energy here? Visualize your organs, not in any order, and send balancing energy where needed. Move to your heart and send calm, soothing energy there.

Now move to your upper chest and throat. Feel for any blocked energy and clear it away in your mind's eye like clearing away cobwebs. Balance as needed.

Now focus on the back of your neck and head. There tends to be a great deal of energy held in these spaces. Balance where needed, use your energy to open space, take a few deep breaths, and release.

Imagine in your mind's eye you are rising above your physical body. Look down on yourself and see all the energy in your body as colors. Does everything look balanced? If not, send energy where it is needed until you see it balance. Send love to your physical body.

Return to your physical body, take a breath, and wiggle your fingers and toes. You are now fully aware of the present moment again.

If you are able, write in a notebook about this experience and how you perceived the energy with which you were working.

EXERCISE: COLOR INTUITION

The following color intuition exercise will help you become aware of your intuitive energy, be able to use your intuition every day, call upon your intuition quickly, and build confidence in your abilities. As you start your moon manifestation journey, this exercise will help you as you work through the moon phases.

What you need:

Your color of the day and how you will incorporate it into your day (outfit, jewelry, etc.)
Notebook and pen

What to do:

When you wake up in the morning, set an intention for your day. For example, "Today I will drink eight glasses of water." When you get ready and before you get dressed, think of a color to support you during the day. Do not question what color comes up, even if you dislike it. Now incorporate this color into your daily outfit any way you like. Look at this color and say your intention for the day.

Notice throughout the day when and where this color shows up for you. Make sure to do an action related to your intention as this color shows up. At the end of the day, write in a notebook on how this color showed up and how it helped guide your intention.

As you start to cultivate your moon magic practice, make use of your intuition, practice mindfulness, and centering yourself with meditation during each moon phase, you will merge the spirit, mind, and body of your lunar magical practice and make it stronger.

CHAPTER THREE

YOUR LUNAR MIND

In each moon phase chapter, you will be guided to write about your experiences. Even if it seems like a menial task, documenting this process is incredibly important because it helps to define your true wants and needs. Following a gratitude practice is something we all need to do more often because as you start to receive in this high-energy space, it will become a vital step in manifesting success. Actively saying aloud what you want for yourself really does help it become real. The more you hear it, the more you can see it happening, therefore making it easier to manifest. When you start manifesting, you may not believe what is out in the world waiting for you; affirmations help to slowly let your subconscious know these things are available.

Your lunar mind refers to the everyday creative work you do using the practices of gratitude, affirmations, and journaling as they are brought into your moon manifesting process. When you do these practices, you build a moon practice foundation and reframe your mindset for success. By instilling gratitude, affirmations, and journaling into your manifesting practice, you are opening pathways of intuition you may not have tapped into before. The lunar mind part of this practice can become more demanding as you harness your true wants and needs and work to bring them into your new reality.

Journaling

Journaling is a terrific way to help you process your feelings as you tap into your magic. You obviously cannot be positive every minute of the day, and I certainly do not recommend trying to be as it will cause guilt and frustration. You need to give your thoughts and feelings some space, release them, and create a new frame of thoughts for your moon manifestations. As you are working through these emotions and strengthening your energetic base, situations and thoughts you may not want to deal with will creep in. Stowing them away may seem like the best course of action, but please do not avoid them altogether; you may miss some incredible insights and growth.

Physically writing down observations, thoughts, and feelings when working through the moon phases is akin to a magical spell for me. Putting this information down on paper helps make it real and is a productive way to call the universal flow for a manifesting journey. Documenting your thoughts, feelings, and insights also helps to develop your magical practice. Journaling can help you organize your intentions along with your action steps.

Sometimes you may go to journal and no words will come to mind. If that happens, start doodling, write your intention repeatedly, or close your eyes and let your pen roam over the page. Creating new affirmations to use at some point in your moon manifesting journey can open your energetic flow. Journaling is not always about what is written; a lot of the time it is more about the act of writing itself and the physical movement of energy. Do not judge yourself or worry about what goes on the actual page. Do not read what you wrote until the moon cycle is complete. This activity aims to move unneeded energy that can block you in your manifesting and make space for improved thoughts.

Picking Out Your Journal

Journals, notebooks, and pens make me a happy witch. With so many pen styles and cute notebooks to pick from, it is sometimes hard for me to choose. This is when I let my intuition decide for me. Interestingly, I've noticed that I tend to pick out a journal or notebook that goes along with the intention I want to set.

My higher self knows what is right, and it knows how to bribe me! The first journal I had was a diary—you know the kind, with the little lock on the side. As a child I would sit in my room late at night and write poems, songs, stories, or about everything going on. It was a wonderful escape, and even then, I would write about my dream life. Having that safe space to just be and create anything I wanted was magic. Try stepping into that childlike energy as you sit down to journal next time.

EXERCISE: ENCHANT YOUR PEN

Your newly dedicated moon manifestation journal should also have an enchanted pen to go with it. You can use any writing implement you like, but for this exercise, I recommend a pen. Buying a pen specifically for magical work is a fantastic way to focus on what you are working, plus it's fun to do. You have magic all around and within you, and "enchanting" favorite objects for a purpose creates a wonderful bridge from the mundane to your magic, blending it into your everyday life.

What you need:

A blank sheet of paper

A pen (or any writing tool) you want to enchant for use in your moon manifesting practice

½ C sugar (any type)

1 tsp cinnamon powder (or powdered ginger or a brown marker)

Crystals of your choosing or rocks found outside you chose mindfully

What to do:

Gather your items and bring them into your sacred space. Take a few moments to breathe and start focusing your energy toward enchanting your pen. Next, place the blank sheet in front of you. Take the to-be-enchanted pen and draw a circle big enough to fit the pen inside. Place the pen in the circle.

Now pick up the sugar and carefully place the sugar around the hand-drawn circle. As you do so, say, "I enchant this pen for my moon manifesting practice. May it guide me to stay in gratitude and a positive mindset." Look at the sugar enclosing the pen and imagine its sweet, pure, giving energy being infused into the pen.

Now take the cinnamon and carefully create another circle outside the sugar circle. If you didn't use cinnamon, use the ginger powder or the brown marker to draw the circle. Say, "I enchant this pen to help me discover my magic within and to dive into deep truths for my greatest good." When you are done, sit back and imagine the cinnamon infusing the pen, giving it some spicy energy.

Now pick the pen up and hold to your heart center. See in your mind's eye your own loving energy infusing with the pen. Say, "I enchant this pen to be able to help me express my desires for the best outcome."

Write around the top of the circle, "This pen is enchanted for my moon manifesting and will guide me to define what I most want." Take a breath and write "And so it is" three times at the bottom of the circle.

Place the pen in the middle and place your crystals and rocks around the cinnamon and sugar rings. Say, "This pen is now enchanted for my own magical use, and so it is."

Leave your pen here for a few hours as the crystal ring strengthens the enchantments you bestowed upon it. Redo as needed when you switch pens or do a bunch at once!

EXERCISE: NEW JOURNAL RITUAL

One of the best parts of journaling is picking out the journal you will write in. Make this a big deal and dedicate a journal just to your moon manifesting magic. Your journal can be the notebook that you've already used in earlier exercises or a new one devoted solely to the work going forward. You may even want to do a ritual to welcome your journal into your exciting new space. Here is a ritual that you can follow.

What you need:

A journal or notebook that makes you feel abundant when you hold it

4-inch purple taper candle plus a candle holder or firesafe dish, and a lighter or matches

Pen

What to do:

Sit in a quiet, comfortable spot. Take a few breaths and settle into this space. Pick up your journal and take a moment to really look at it. Turn it around, flip through the blank pages, smell it (yes, really), and notice any imperfections it may have.

Still holding on to your journal, pick up your purple candle. Hold both items to your heart and send love and gratitude to them. Envision filling those pages with success and seeing in your mind's eye all your manifestations as if they have happened. Do this until you feel the journal and candle are filled to the brim with love.

Now set your candle in the candle holder or warm the candle's bottom and press it onto your firesafe plate until it is secure. Light your candle and pick up your pen.

Open the front cover of your journal and write a note of thanks to yourself and an intention on what you and your journal will achieve during your time together. When finished, write "so it is" three times at the bottom and sign your name. Close your journal and hold it to your heart again. Send some last-minute love to it.

Put the journal down and focus on the candle flame. Take another few breaths and snuff it out. Now you and your journal are magical friends. You may light the candle for extra magic when you journal throughout the moon cycle.

Journaling Tips and Advice

- Find the best time during the day for you to dedicate to journaling. For some, first thing in the morning works best, and others like to journal before bed. If you incorporate journaling into your practice, it does not matter what time you do it.

- When following the journaling prompts for the moon phases, be honest with yourself. Do not just write what you think you should. This will not create a beneficial flow for you and your intention.
- If you feel stuck, try pulling a tarot card to get you writing.
- When creating what you want in life, come at it from your future-thinking self. This will also help you decide on action steps for each phase.
- Be creative and have fun with it. If you are too serious, journaling may cause anxiety. Loosen up and let your imagination run wild.
- Set the tone for your writing; turn on some music. I like to listen to binaural beats as I journal. Light a candle or some incense if they help you focus.
- Take a few minutes away from social media and silence your devices.
- Go outside if you can. This is one of my favorite places to journal, even at night. I just grab a flashlight and go.

Gratitude

Gratitude is an essential step in successfully manifesting. It's important to show genuine gratefulness for simple things such as a bird sitting on your windowsill, finding a penny, or hitting all green lights on the way to work (my favorite). When you notice these things happening to you, say thank you and count it as a win for the day, no matter how trivial it may seem. As your energy increases, higher vibrational occurrences also begin to happen to you daily. You will start to notice and recognize these subtle signs from the universe as gentle nudges, telling you that you are on the right path.

In the book *Thanks!: How Practicing Gratitude Can Make You Happier*, Dr. Robert Emmons, a leading psychology expert in the study of gratitude, explains that the word *gratitude* is derived from the Latin *gratia*, meaning "favor," and *gratus*, meaning "pleasing."[17] These Latin root words convey the ideas of kindness, receiving something for nothing, and the beauty of giving and receiving. Gratitude can help motivate you and inspire you to have more appreciation for everything that comes your way, especially when manifesting.

When you create a practice of gratefulness, you will work that feeling into your life overall. Making gratefulness a part of your magical practice strengthens it, and you will realize anything is possible.

Gratitude Practice Suggestions

Try adding some of these suggestions to your moon manifestation practice.

- Be genuine; only express thanks for things you truly feel grateful for.
- Practice gratitude every time something good or not so good happens. I say thank you aloud all the time. My kids used to think I was a bit crazy, but I've noticed it's rubbed off on them.
- Make it fun. Express gratitude in ways you normally would not. For example, every time you say thank you, give yourself a gold star.
- Sit quietly in gratitude and get to know how it shows up for you, so when you express it you can tap into the energy quickly.
- If it is difficult to express gratitude at a tough time, backtrack a bit and start with something that is easier to be thankful for and work your way up to it.
- You are allowed to be grateful for everything in your life and for things on the way. Do not be afraid to embrace this idea.
- Give back. When we help others, we open ourselves up to receiving gratitude, and that is just as important as giving it.

17. Robert Emmons, *Thanks! How Practicing Gratitude Can Make You Happier* (Houghton Mifflin Harcourt, 2008), 4.

EXERCISE: GRATITUDE IS MY ATTITUDE

In the following exercise, you will be mindfully practicing gratitude for events that you usually do not give much attention to. This exercise will prompt you to be mindful and thankful for the little things in your life.

What you need:

An open mind
Your journal or the Notes app on your phone

What to do:

Anytime something annoying or unexpected happens to you, say thank you aloud. If it does not feel genuine, say it one more time. Note in your phone or in your notebook how this makes you feel. Continue this throughout the day.

At the end of the day, take a moment to reflect on this gratitude practice and see how it may have changed your outlook. Do this practice whenever you feel you need to refresh your gratitude experience.

EXERCISE: FILL THE AIR WITH GRATITUDE

This exercise uses candle magic to create a beautiful vortex of gratitude to return to during your moon cycle manifestation practice.

What you need:

4 of your favorite flowers (fresh or dried, stems optionally removed)
A small bowl filled with ½ C water
4-inch taper candle of any color, a medium firesafe dish, and matches

What to do:

Sit in your sacred space and get comfortable. Take a few deep breaths and start to think about being grateful and what that means to you. Now take a flower and hold it to your heart center. Think of one thing you are grateful for and see that energy infusing with the flower. Place the flower in the water and repeat with each flower.

Once you are finished, light your candle near the bowl of flowers. Close your eyes, take a deep breath, and see the gratitude energy in the flowers fuse with the candle in your mind's eye.

Open your eyes and stare at the flame. Your loving, grateful energy is filling the room and being raised into the universe. Say "Thank you" three times and sit in this energy as long as you want, then snuff out the candle.

Leave the flowers in the water for twenty-four hours, then return them to the earth if possible by disposing of them outside. If you cannot do that, drain the water and throw them away, imagining the flowers eventually returning to the earth.

Anytime you want to revisit the concentrated energy of gratitude, relight the candle and sit for as long as you need to.

Affirmations

An affirmation is a practice of repeating phrases to empower and motivate you. When you have a regular affirmation practice, you are creating new neural pathways in your brain and using more magical brain power.[18] Creating affirmations is a fun and effortless way to incorporate your intentions into your life. Affirmation suggestions for each moon phase are included in their own chapters, but feel free to make your own.

When creating your affirmations you first must decide what you want—and what you want your future to look like. When starting a moon manifesting practice, you will come across this question many times. The key to finding out what you want is to discover what will help your manifestation come to fruition. How can you define what you really want next? Monte Farber and his wife Amy have been spiritual practitioners for decades. They have written a multitude of books about spirituality and manifestation. Monte explains this concept wonderfully in his book *Quantum Affirmations*: "Of course, the word *want* has two meanings. 'To desire' is the one that springs

18. Christopher N. Cascio, et al, "Self-Affirmation Activates Brain Systems Associated with Self-Related Processing and Reward and Is Reinforced by Future Orientation," *Social Cognitive and Affective Neuroscience* 11, no. 4 (2016): 621–29. doi.org/10.1093/scan/nsv136.

to mind, but want can also mean 'to lack, be without, have need of.'"[19] Use this quote as a guideline to help you define your want as something you fully desire and not something you want out of lack.

Affirmations are different from intentions in that they are even more based around the future self. For example, an affirmation could be, "I am ready to pick up my new car," whereas an intention may be, "I will find a reliable car for a good price that's fun to drive." So, while the differences are slight, using affirmations and intentions together lets you touch on all points of your manifesting energy centers for the greatest benefit.

EXERCISE: AFFIRMATION CREATION STATION

This exercise will teach you how to create and incorporate an affirmation into your daily life. The Affirmation Creation Station method is easy and will help you design an effective list of affirmations for your manifesting.

What you need:

Your journal and pen

A quiet space, your moon altar

What to do:

Begin by bringing your manifestation goal to mind.

Write a positive sentence regarding your manifestation. Next, break the sentence down into a small phrase that makes you feel like it its already happening. Infuse your affirmation into your life. For example, your affirmation could be a screensaver on your phone or computer.

Write your affirmation on pieces of paper and set them around your house. Set a phone alarm for every few hours and have your affirmation pop up on the screen.

19. Monte Farber, *Quantum Affirmations: The New Energy Science of Conscious Manifestation* (Schiffer Publishing, 2012), 31.

EXERCISE: IS THIS WHAT I REALLY WANT? CHECKLIST

In many of this book's exercises, you will be asked to decide your intention. Whether you create your own or use the suggested ones, run through this quick exercise to make sure you are fully aligned with your intention so that you may create powerful affirmations for ultimate success.

What you need:

Your journal and pen
A quiet place away from distraction

What to do:

Settle yourself in your space and take a few minutes to breathe. Once you feel connected and centered, open your notebook and write your first affirmation. Go through the checklist below and adjust your affirmation as needed.

When writing your thoughts and feelings about your affirmations, do so from a place of nonjudgment. All your thoughts and feelings are valid whether you feel they are aligned or not; they are part of your moon manifesting evolution, and you can find hidden gems of insight in answers you might feel are not "right." Give yourself some grace when doing these exercises. Notice how the key letter in each step spells out MANIFEST. You are doing this to align with this immensely powerful word and subconsciously integrate this new reality into your moon manifestation practice.

EXERCISE: AFFIRMATION CHECKLIST

By using the letters from the word *manifest*, you will create specifically tailored affirmations to use during your manifesting moon cycles.

What you need:

Your journal and pen
A quiet space

What to do:

Using the prompts below, write about these questions as truthfully as possible. By adding your true thoughts and feelings, you will be able to create more effective affirmations.

M—Mindful: How does it feel to read your affirmation aloud? Where are you feeling this energy in your body? Write these feelings down.

A—Acknowledge: Think about exactly why this is important to you. Decide if the "want" comes from a place of lack or fulfillment. Write these thoughts down.

N—Not Attached: Making sure you are not so attached to the outcome is vital to bringing your manifestation to life. You do not want your attachment to lean toward desperation. Bringing in an energy like desperation will block you and deflect the flow of your energy another way. If you do decide your affirmation is something you are too attached to, what can you do to shift that energy?

I—Integrate: Repeat your affirmation aloud one more time. Can you see the energy of the affirmation infusing into your everyday life? Can you envision the scenario of your affirmation? Doing so is essential in working this affirmation into your manifesting flow.

F—Fun: Your affirmation creation does not have to be serious and intense. When you envision your full intention, you are creating these affirmations for your new self, so look at all angles of your new reality. What part of this manifestation will bring you more fun and happiness? Work this lighter energy into your affirmations to remind yourself that you are doing this to bring more joy into your life.

E—Excitement: Playing off the last prompt, look to create an affirmation that excites you. Tap into that childlike excitement and infuse exciting words into your affirmations.

S—Say Them: The best way for affirmations to ignite in your subconscious is to say them. Say them as often as you can and saying them aloud is even better. Make this practice a part of everything you do. By repeating your now exciting and fulfilling affirmations, you are training your brain to accept that it is not only possible for these manifestations to become reality, but that the more you say them the easier they are to achieve.

T—Test it out: Do not be discouraged if you add an affirmation to your daily practice and the energy is not where you would like it to be. When creating new affirmations, the first few days are comparable to a trial period. Notice how these words feel for you and see if you can easily step into the excited energy they may offer. If your new affirmation falls flat, that is okay. Come back to this checklist and tweak it or stash it for later and create a whole new one. Remember, you want to come from a place of nonjudgment and always be open to adjustments. You never know what the ideas, thoughts, and feelings you work through while creating these affirmations may open for you.

The more you repeat your affirmations, the quicker these words embed into your subconscious, and that is when your thoughts begin to form your reality. When you take the time to do what seems like small, unimportant steps, you set your magic's foundation and create a new reality for yourself.

Preparation is an essential step in any magical practice, and manifesting with the moon is no different. Your lunar mind is now prepped, ready, and focused on creating the best intentions for the moon cycle you are working with. You have reframed your thoughts to bring in what is best for you. By taking the time to learn and understand why preparation is necessary, you will be able to fully step into the practice quickly. You will also have a great starting point for looking back to see how far you have come, even after manifesting with just a few moon cycles. The magic is all within you; learning how to harness the power of your lunar mind will benefit you and your loved ones because your newfound awareness can bring clarity to almost any situation.

CHAPTER FOUR
YOUR LUNAR BODY

Bringing your magical practice into your everyday world helps fully integrate your energy and creates a physical pathway for your magical work to manifest into reality. The practice of creating sacred spaces and altars for your moon manifesting work brings your intentions for the moon cycle into the physical realm. By including these physical activities in your moon manifesting practice, you are incorporating your lunar body with your lunar mind, creating your own system of magic. Special spaces like altars provide an area where you can focus your magical energy and create a focused space for your manifestation workings.

Your Moon Manifesting Altar

An altar is a sacred space that is usually separate from the rest of your home. The purpose of this space is to perform rituals and magical workings, make offerings, and be a quiet place to focus on your magic. You do not need to choose a large area or move furniture to make space for an altar unless you want to. It can be small or be put on a shelf already in your home. Creating a moon altar specifically for your manifesting practice will give you somewhere to focus your energy when working through the moon manifesting cycle.

You can even put your altar outside. Walk around and ask aloud where the best space for your altar would be. You may be pleasantly surprised by how quickly you are drawn to a specific area. An outdoor altar gives you extra space to work with and can be easier to create than an indoor altar. Store your items in a small box, or if you are able, drape a cloth over your altar and tether it down. Big rocks work great for this. Use items from outside to customize your sacred magical space.

If you are tight on space, use a shoebox or dedicate a drawer to your sacred area. Whatever you choose needs to feel right to you and make you feel your most magical. The specifics of where and how should only serve that purpose, so focus more on that and less on the logistics of building your altar.

As you grow in your practice and moon manifesting, your altar space will grow and change too. I started out using a shoebox. My altar has changed locations quite a few times as I grew my moon practice and moved into a home of my own. One of my favorite altars is my bathroom altar. I had four young boys and did not want them getting into my things, so I cleared a shelf in my bathroom cabinet. My bathroom moon altar was a special sacred space to me, and I used it for a long time. Thankfully, the boys believed it was full of boring towels, not my most magical possessions.

Types of Altars

When creating any type of altar, you want to have a set intention for it, whether it is for general divination or a place to use your magical tools or moon manifesting. Decide the use of your altar before you start planning it out. I have a general altar that is bigger than my dedicated altars that I use for my daily devotions and quick spell work. How many altars you have and what size they are will depend on your space, needs, and living situation regarding children and pets.

Here are a few examples of several types of altars:

Working Altars

Working altars are set up for a specific purpose. Your main moon altar falls under this category. Working altars are used frequently, if not daily. You will be working with and changing up your moon manifesting altar often.

When creating space for this altar, I suggest you place it somewhere you spend a lot of time so it will be easier to access. Your moon altar will also serve as a physical reminder of your moon manifesting.

Ancestral Altars

An ancestral altar is used to honor passed loved ones or to honor and connect with those who have come before you. These ancestors can be blood relatives as well as those with whom you want to work and create a relationship. Your ancestral altar should be maintained regularly, but you usually do not perform your daily magical work there. Place pictures or items that remind you of your deceased loved ones or ancestors on this altar. Since the moon corresponds to memory and emotion, you can always call the moon to your ancestral altar to connect with this energy for guidance and support.

Temporary Ritual Altars

Some witches and magical folk like to have an altar specifically for the seasons or sabbats. The sabbats are eight annual festivals that are honored by many pagans and witches. These seasonal celebrations are derived from western European traditions and together make up the Wheel of the Year. Decorating this altar for the current season helps build a connection to nature and celebrate the magic of the seasons. If you are celebrating a sabbat or another moon event, you might use a seasonal altar to focus the energy you want from the event. For example, if you feel very connected to the Flower Moon in May and its call for growth, creating an altar specifically for this moon can help boost your intention and focus for success.

Altar Advice

I know it seems like you can have a ton of altars always going, and some do indeed practice that way. But when just starting out and working on a moon-based practice, focus on your moon altar and branch out when and if you are ready or feel called to. Having many altars is a preference, not a necessity. Using one space and creating a temporary altar that suits your needs is just as magically effective as having multiple sacred spaces.

I would not want you to become so overwhelmed and concerned about everything being perfect that you do not take the necessary steps to have a successful and abundant moon manifesting cycle. Start your practice with a basic altar and items, then add more as your practice grows. Being open to learning is more important than perfection. Perfect does not exist anyway; creating and defining your practice over time is one of the reward of having a magical practice.

TIPS FOR ALTAR CREATION

- Set up your altar somewhere you will see it.
- If it must be in your bedroom, set it away from your bed. If that is not possible, place a sheet or cloth over the altar when you are not actively working near it. Make sure all flames are out, and your flammable items are not warm to the touch before doing this.
- Keep your altar area clean. Remove old candles, ashes, flowers, or offerings when done working in this area.
- Make sure you have space to work on your altar so there is room for divining or spell work.
- I suggest always keeping a special journal or Book of Shadows specifically for your altar and a pen in this space.
- Have matches, a lighter, and a backup handy just in case.
- If you are traveling during your moon manifestation, think about creating a small portable altar to bring with you. I like to use small tin boxes; they are easily purchased at any craft store.

Creating a sacred space/altar for your magical practice is such a personal and powerful experience. As your altar and your practice grow, you will notice how this outward expression of your magic expresses itself. Your altar space is an incredibly special part of you.

EXERCISE: CREATING AN ALTAR FOR MOON MANIFESTATION

Here you will start to design and create your own moon manifestation altar. Note that you can create your altar at any time. Please do not feel the need to spend a lot of money on all these things. Use what you have around and slowly build your altar.

What you need:

A chosen sacred space

A plain white cloth to cover your working area

Objects to represent the elements: air, water, fire, earth (Examples for representations of the elements: a small dish of dirt from outside for the earth element, feathers or a bell for the air element, a small glass of water or seashells for water, and for fire use a red candle or a small bowl of cinnamon)

Your representations of the moon phases (e.g., a picture of the phase, an object that reminds you of it, or the name of the phase written on a piece of paper)

Something to represent the deities you will work with (if appropriate)

4-inch taper candles for future use, candle holder, matches, and snuffer

Optional:

Crystals of your choosing (Refer to the crystal suggestion included in each phase chapter if you like)

Small vase with flower offerings

Anything else meaningful to you that represents your moon manifestation

What to do:

Choose your space, preferably somewhere you will be close to often. Cleanse the space with smoke, sound, or wiping down with lemon water. Use your chosen cloth to cover your working area.

Place your elemental objects first toward the back of the altar so you have room for everything. As you place the other items on your altar, ask them for their assistance and let these objects know the job they will have on your altar. Do not overthink the placement—let your intuition guide you and your hands place these objects where they want to. You can always move stuff around later.

Now you can perform the altar activation exercise.

EXERCISE: MOON ALTAR ACTIVATION

This simple yet powerful altar activation will connect your energy to your altar and set your magical tools into service. You can also do this to refresh the energy when you move through the moon phases. You will be activating not only your altar but your lunar body as well.

What you need:

4-inch white taper candle, medium firesafe plate or candle holder, matches, and snuffer

Something to etch the candle with (a metal nail works great)

What to do:

Have your altar set up to your liking. Gather your items and sit in front of it for a few minutes and mindfully look at each object, thinking of its role on your altar.

Pick up your candle and your etching tool. On the candle, write "you are activated." Hold the candle to your third eye (between your eyebrows), take a few deep breaths, and imagine a soft violet light coming from your third eye and infusing with the candle. See this energy highlight your words on the candle. Now bring your candle down and touch each object on your altar and say, "You are activated to serve this purpose on my altar (state purpose)," then say, "it is done."

Once you have done this to each object, hold the candle to your heart and say, "I am activated and attuned to my sacred moon altar." Place the candle in the candle holder or warm the bottom of the candle and place on the plate. Put your candle in the middle of your altar. Light the candle and say, "All has been activated to guide me to manifest for my highest good. And so it is."

When the candle burns down, your altar is fully activated. You can snuff out the candle when you cannot be with it and relight until it is burned down. Do not leave your lit candle unattended.

EXERCISE: CREATING A TRAVEL MOON ALTAR

Life happens; there are times you cannot be near your moon altar to perform your daily workings. Creating a travel altar is a low-effort way to extend your altar's energy when you are not home.

What you need:

A small tin (breath mint tins work great)
A moonstone (represents the moon no matter its phase)
Incense cone or small bottle of essential oil such as peppermint or sage
Tea light candle and matches
Four small pieces of paper with the element symbols drawn on them
Symbol of deity you are working with (if applicable)

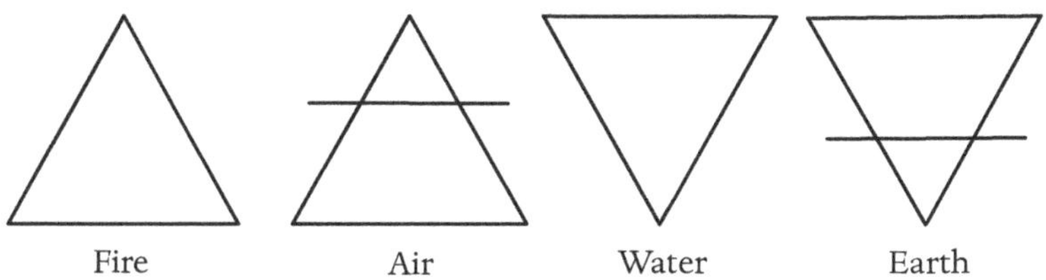

Elemental Symbols

What to do:

Add all the items to your tin. If possible, do your altar dedication exercise and adjust it as needed. Now you can take your moon altar with you. When you use it, set it up in the tin or on a table. Cleanse the space with the incense if you can or use a small amount of your oil on a wet paper towel to wipe down the area.

Spell Work

A spell uses your own magic to change and create change on a physical or vibrational level. You are simply creating a pathway to the vibration of where you want to be and using your magical tools to represent this change of frequency. Using spell work during your moon manifesting journey is an effective way to harness the lunar body aspect of your new mind, body, and spirit practice because you now have the physical work of creating spells at your altar to set that manifesting vibration exactly where you want it to go.

Even if you think you have not formally done any spell work, you may have already done some of which you were not aware. Blowing out birthday candles, pulling petals from flowers to ask if they "love you or love you not," and even celebrating New Year's Eve and wishing everyone a wonderful year ahead are all spell work. Hannah Hawthorn, practicing Pagan witch, talks about why Pagans historically blew out birthday candles in her book *The Magic of Birthdays.* One reason was to honor a spirit they believed was assigned to someone at birth to guide and protect them, as well as ward off evil spirits that may visit on their birthday. In ancient Greek culture, cakes with lit candles on top were made to honor the goddess Artemis.[20]

It is fine if you do not have the proper ingredients for a spell. There are always ways to substitute items if necessary, and most of these substitutions can be found in your home. For example, if you need a blue spell candle but do not have one on hand, check to see if you have a blue birthday candle or even a tea light hanging out in your candle holders. You can also use a white candle to stand in for any color, but only do this as a last resort.

You do not need to purchase any fancy ingredients either; I believe using what is easily accessible to you is best because then you will create the spell you intended rather than worry about sourcing the actual items. The dollar store is a wonderful and cost-effective resource for magical items. As your practice grows, so will your witchy toolbox. There is no rush to have that rare herb or candles in every color. Enjoy the process of creating your spells and try not to get too wrapped up in buying things.

20. Hannah Hawthorn, *The Magic of Birthdays: Rituals, Spells, and Recipes for Honoring Your Solar Return* (Witchy Books, 2021), 18.

The most important aspect of spell work is picturing your intention as if it has already happened—seeing the result of your manifestation just as you want it to look. When first doing spells and talking aloud to the altar, you may feel a bit silly, which is normal. With practice, you will be able to call up a spell without a second thought. You will look back on these beginning spells with amusement, knowing you moved past the whisperings of your ego.

There are so many ways to incorporate spells into your everyday life. Stirring your coffee in the morning and intentionally thinking your day will be fantastic is a quick and effective spell and adds no extra time to your daily routine. Here are a few tips for starting your spell work:

- Do not expect any outcome of your spell to be immediate. Release expectations before performing your spell.
- Make sure you have what you need—and any substitutions if necessary—before beginning.
- Know exactly why you are doing the spell and envision the outcome as if it is already in process. Creating a future vision is different from an expectation because you are calling it in instead of just hoping for it.
- Choose your items with intention and purpose regarding what you are working on. For example, cinnamon is great for money and abundance spells. Incorporating cinnamon will give your spell the right boost it needs.
- Try to do your spell work when you will not be disturbed and can focus.
- When you are done, try not to overthink how your spell went or if it will work. Just let the universe do its thing. You have created the energy flow, and now it is time to release it and let it flow back to you when the time is right.

Here are two spells for you to warm up your spell working abilities. They will give you a feel for the spells you will do during the moon cycle.

Be gracious to yourself when trying out these spells, especially if you are just beginning your magical journey. Do not strive for perfection; just dive in and let your intuition take over. The more you practice performing spells, the more you will notice your own flow develop and even take over.

EXERCISE: OPEN ALL POSSIBILITIES SPELL

This spell is beneficial when you are about to create your moon manifesting intention or are preparing for the next moon phase. It can also be helpful if you are feeling stuck or overwhelmed. Use this spell to open yourself to possibility and clear anything that will hinder you on your path to what you want.

What you need:

4-inch taper candles: one black, one white, plus a firesafe dish or candle holder and matches or a lighter
A pinch dried sandalwood herb or powdered incense
3 drops lemongrass oil or lemon oil

What to do:

Place all your items in your sacred space. Take a minute to ground and center yourself in your space. Now take a deep cleansing breath. Hold the white candle in your hands close to your heart center. Say, "I am open to divine guidance for my highest and greatest good. Thank you."

Place a few drops of oil on your hands and rub onto the candle, going up from the bottom to the wick, but do not get oil on the wick. If you are sensitive to essential oils, you may drip it directly on the candle or use gloves. Adding a few drops of carrier oil like olive oil is also an option. Remember that you only need a small amount—essential oils are powerful and the candles are small.

Warm the bottom of the white candle with the matches or lighter and place on the dish. Hold until it stays. Pick up the black candle and hold it to your third eye, at your forehead and right between your eyes. Say, "I release all thoughts of doubt and those thoughts that were given to me that are not mine. Thank you." Next, place a few drops of oil into your hands and, starting at the top of the candle near the wick (do not get oil on the wick itself), rub the oil on the candle going down. Warm the bottom of the black candle with your lighter and press firmly onto the plate until it stays.

Place the sandalwood at the base of the candles. Now say, "I now light these candles to create a balanced energetic field for me to manifest with a clear heart and head. Thank you. And so it is."

Light each candle and sit for a few minutes, seeing in your mind's eye the aura of energy around you ripple and start to become clearer.

Take a few deep breaths and let the candles burn out. If you cannot be close to them, do not leave them to burn unattended. Snuff them out and relight when you are at your sacred space again.

EXERCISE: SPELL JAR FOR A LUCKY ENERGY BOOST

A little bit of lucky energy is always welcomed. When you are busy working through your action steps during the moon manifesting cycle, this spell jar is beneficial to have in case you need a little boost of high-working vibration to get you moving.

What you need:

A small glass jar (baby food jars or ones of a similar size)
Incense and a lighter/matches
1 tsp rosemary (for cleansing)
1 tsp oregano (for luck)
1 tsp cinnamon (quick abundance)
Small piece of quartz
Small handful of dried flowers
3 T sugar
Small dish

What to do:

Gather your items. Light the incense with the intention of good luck in your mind.

Wave the incense around the items and inside the spell jar.

Place the spell jar on the altar, opened.

Pick up the rosemary and say, "With this I cleanse any negativity that's keeping luck from me." Place in the jar. Pick up the oregano and say, "This will call in any luck that has been near me but not close enough." Place in jar. Pick up the cinnamon and say, "With swiftness and ease good luck is headed my way." Place in jar.

Hold up the quartz and say, "May this quartz help keep me grounded in my abundance." Place in jar. Hold up the dried flowers and say, "May this energy come to me softly and lovingly." Place in jar. Take the sugar (you only need a bit depending on the size of your jar) and fill just so the bottom of the jar is covered. As you pour it in, say, "May good luck stick with me, and I can share my luck with others." Close the jar.

Hold the sealed jar to your throat and say, "May I be able to communicate my wants and needs freely to call luck to me. And so it is."

You can keep this on your altar or carry it with you and shake it when you are feeling lucky.

When you feel the spell is done, return the items to the earth and cleanse and reuse the jar. I like to reuse my items if I can, especially when they are made of glass.

Ritual

There is evidence of ritual being practiced even before written language, as far back as Paleolithic times. Archeologists have found cave art depicting rituals around the seasons and evidence of burial rituals that were performed before written history.[21] It is vital to add ritual to your moon manifesting, as it helps to embody your magic in a way words cannot. By adding rituals to your magical practice you are fully embodying your craft and setting your vibrational energy higher. Doing this will help bring you to the most energetic and self-empowering space to help you rework any part of your life you want. With all that you desire already, you are opening more magical space for these things to become reality by creating rituals.

21. Brian Hayden, *The Power of Ritual in Prehistory: Secret Societies and Origins of Social Complexity* (Cambridge University Press, 2018), 369.

Creating and performing ritual is not as complicated as it may seem. To break it down to its bones, ritual is a set of actions done in a certain order for a certain result. Not so bad now, right? Ritual also creates a space for you to connect to something bigger than yourself and to be an active part of that process. Practicing ritual regularly helps build confidence in yourself and create more profound transformative moments. Rituals can be practiced by yourself and with others. There is something to be said about the collective-focused energy of a group ritual. If you decide to moon manifest along with a friend, this can be a great practice to add to your moon cycle. Even if you only do it once or twice, you both will benefit from working together in this way.

Basic Ritual Structure

If you have never prepared a ritual, here is a basic guide to the structure and actions in order.

To start, prepare your ritual space and make sure you have all the items you will need. There is no faster way to break your concentration than having to move from your space to grab a forgotten item. Complete any research you may need to do before the ritual if you can. Before you even start, for example, find out what the goddess you are working with prefers for offerings. Say you are working with Selene—her preferred offerings are milk and honey, whereas Hecate prefers eggs and incense. If you do forget something, just keep going with the ritual.

Make your rituals as simple or formal as you like. It is okay to keep things simple because what's most important here is your concentration and intention. You can always add steps as you become more comfortable with ritual work.

Once you are ready and settled into your ritual space, cleanse the space using sound, smoke, or crystals.

Speak your intention and call for the ritual energy space to be open. Something like this will do: "My intention for this ritual is to call upon the goddess Hekate and this circle is now open." By stating your intention aloud, you are letting your subconscious know you are working at a higher vibration, as well as alerting the energy of the deity or spiritual team you may be collaborating with that you are ready to receive their guidance.

If you decide to work with the elements and ask for their guidance, have items in your ritual space that represent earth, fire, water, and air, and ask them for their guidance one by one. For example: "I ask you, element of air, to guide me during this ritual to see and speak clearly as I call upon the Divine. Thank you." Adjust your address to each element and what it can assist you with. If you need to, write your lines down and recite aloud or read until you are accustomed to this practice.

If you are collaborating with a goddess, now is the time to ask them for assistance, guidance, or to be present however you would like. Place an offering to them on your altar then ask for their help. Release expectation. Most goddesses will stay silent if you approach your ritual expecting certain things to happen. Know they are there when you call upon them even if you do not think they are. Stay silent and open all your senses.

Light your candles, do your spell work if your ritual includes any, or simply sit silently to receive. Take time to notice how this magical space feels for you and keep note of all sensations, messages, and even smells or tastes you receive.

When you feel things are complete, take a few deep breaths, thank whomever you are working with, and leave an offering—food, money, flowers, or herbs are the most common. As well, thank each element for their time and guidance.

To close the ritual, I state my intention, thank all involved one last time, and say, "This ritual has now concluded, and the circle is closed. Thank you." I like to walk around my space three times counterclockwise to reestablish the room's energy.

After a ritual or any magical working, grounding is an important final action. Grounding not only brings us back to the physical plane but also helps us integrate the experience and get the most out of it. Hydrating after any magical work is also especially important.

Here are a few ways to ground that are quick and easy:

- Sit in a quiet room and just breathe slowly for a few minutes letting any random thoughts fall away. Inhale through your nose for a count of four, hold for a count of four and exhale through your mouth for a count of four.
- Go outside (barefoot if possible) and take a few minutes to focus on what's going on around you. Notice the sounds, smells, and the temperature around you, and steady your breath and be mindful of what's going on for a few minutes.
- Identify five things you can see, four things you can touch, three things you can smell, two things you can hear, and one thing you can taste.

Ritual is an important part of magical practice. Any magical work you do will have elements of ritual, which physically bring forth your energy and intentions to create change. It's important to remember as you embark on your moon magic journey that your practice is your own, and it can be as in-depth as you like or even reflect your current feelings. You now hold the power of the moon within you and with that comes the ebb and flow of your innate magic. Let this soothing but powerful energy be your guide to manifest what your heart truly desires.

Drawing Down the Moon

Drawing down the moon is a special ritual to harness the moon's energy. In this powerful ritual, you ask the goddess moon energy to become a part of you. For a brief time, you ask the moon goddess to enter your sacred energetic field, and when she does, you are gifted with messages, healing, and the power to move through the lunar phases and achieve your goals confidently.

A coven priestess usually performs a drawing down the moon ritual. She goes into a trance-like state to have the moon goddess speak through her to the coven. Wiccan high priestess and author Margot Adler discusses this in detail in her classic book titled *Drawing Down the Moon.* Another favorite book of mine that discusses this ritual is author, activist, and practicing Wiccan Starhawk's classic *Spiral Dance*.

Most books explain ritual in a coven setting, so I've created the guide here to outline ritual for the solitary practitioner because not everyone has access to a coven. What follows is a simplified version. A solitary practitioner can offer themselves as conduits for this energy and keep a journal nearby in case they receive messages. The ritual can be performed alone and is just as successful, if not more heartfelt, when it is just you and the Goddess. With a little preparation, this ritual can be life-changing for you and your magical practice. I suggest doing this exercise on the new, quarter, and full moons.

EXERCISE: DRAWING DOWN THE MOON

Connecting and receiving energy on the new, quarter, and full moons is a wonderful way to replenish your magical mojo and ground your craft to your current intention. Think of this exercise as an extra moon magic boost. I suggest practicing this exercise on these specific moons because the energy of these phases is more intense.

What you need:

Notebook and pen

Optional:

Tarot cards

What to do:

Decide on your intention for the spell or for what you will use this moon energy. Find a comfortable space outside if possible. If you cannot be outside, go near a window where you can see the moon or its light. If it is cloudy, imagine the moon in its current phase.

Ground and center yourself. Stand up. Keep your eyes closed and take a few slow breaths. Say your intention for this ritual in your head three times. Take another breath and let it out in a whoosh. Now open your eyes and look directly at the moon or its light or direct all your energy toward visualizing it. Steady your gaze on it.

Say, "Mother Moon, I am here tonight to call on you for your energy and replenishment. I would like to thank you for your assistance and am grateful for your unwavering presence."

Take a breath and let it out slowly. Raise your arms in a V over your head, angled to the moon. Stand in this position if you can, breathing steadily. Receive the energy and light from the moon; see it fill you up and push away any dark spaces. When you feel things are complete, slowly lower your arms and relax in this space for a few minutes. Sway, hum, sing, or slowly move your arms around as you integrate this energy.

Look up at the moon again and say, "Thank you for your time and energy, I will go forth illuminated and practice gratitude in honor of your magic. Thank you, thank you, thank you. And so it is."

Journal on this experience and how you feel for the next few days. You may receive some intuitive insight or messages.

EXERCISE: BLESSING YOUR MOON TRINKET RITUAL

Sometimes we use rituals to bless an item or piece of jewelry to harness the moon's energy and always have it with us. Doing a ritual like this can benefit your moon manifesting because you will have a blessed moon energy object on you wherever you go and will be able to draw from it whenever you want.

I like to wear moon jewelry, such as a crystal bracelet or necklace with a moon on it. You can use whatever you want, but be sure it represents the moon cycle you are working with right now. I once had a student wear a car charm on a necklace because her manifestation for that lunar cycle was buying a new car. Be creative, and once you find your trinket, perform this ritual.

What you need:

A trinket that represents this moon cycle for you

A firesafe vessel, charcoal disk, and matches/a lighter

A small dish of water (moon water is great)
A small dish of dirt (around ½ C is enough)
A 4-inch white candle in a holder or affixed to the firesafe plate with dripped wax
1 tsp rosemary (dried or fresh)

What to do:

Bring your items to your moon altar or sacred space if your moon altar is not set up yet. Take a few minutes to center yourself and think about why you are blessing this trinket for your moon workings. Place all the elemental items in a semicircle on your space, leaving enough room in the middle for your trinket, dish, and charcoal disk. Include the water, dirt, candle, and rosemary in the semicircle.

Place your trinket and firesafe dish with charcoal in the middle of the semicircle of elemental offerings. Hold the dirt and say, "Element of earth, please bless this trinket for my moon workings and offer grounding support. Thank you."

Next, hold the water and say, "Element of water, please bless this trinket for my moon workings and offer emotional support. Thank you."

Hold the rosemary and say, "Element of air, please bless this trinket for my moon workings and offer clarity when needed. Thank you."

Hold the candle and say, "Element of fire, please bless this trinket for my moon workings and offer support to create effective action steps. Thank you."

Light the candle once you've set it in place. Light the charcoal disk and wait until it turns white. At that point, you will know it is ready to use.

Pick up your trinket. Hold it to your heart. Say, "I ask you to guide and support me during this lunar cycle and remind me of my intention and why I chose it. And so it is."

Take a few deep breaths, and on the last breath, blow on your trinket to infuse it with your energy.

Now add the rosemary to the heated charcoal disk. When it starts to smoke, wave your trinket over it and say, "This trinket is now blessed by the element of air, and so it is."

Next place a small amount of water on your trinket and say, "This trinket is now blessed by the water element, and so it is."

Place a small amount of dirt on the trinket or briefly set it in the bowl and say, "This trinket is now blessed by the earth element, and so it is."

Lastly, wave the trinket over the top of the flame at a safe distance and say, "This trinket is now blessed by the fire element, and so it is."

Place the trinket on your body or in your pocket. Your lunar trinket is now blessed and ready to wear. After the candle has cooled, blow it out and dispose of the charcoal disk safely. Return the other elements to the earth, and feel free to reuse the candle as needed.

Sigil Work

Sigils are magical symbols powered by intention. We can create sigils for most anything we want to send energy to. They have been used for thousands of years—in fact, prehistoric symbols have been found in many caves around the world.[22] What you'll find here is just one technique among many to create a sigil. And as with all magical tools in this book, what's most important is having a solid, realistic intention. You want to be confident in your intention when sending this powerful magic to it.

To make sigils, all you need is a pen, paper, and your intention. It is good practice to create them in your sacred space, where its magical charge will enhance your workings. Be sure to give yourself plenty of time to do this, otherwise you can come back to it later if necessary. The first couple of sigils may seem a bit clunky to you, but that's just a part of the process. Remember that this is about intention. After a while, you will find your own style and flow. Believe me, I am no artist—my first couple of sigils were like stick figures. Remember that what's at work here is your focused

22. Genevieve Von Petzinger, *The First Signs: Unlocking the Mysteries of the World's Oldest Symbols* (Atria Books, 2016), 23.

magic; no matter how the results look, what you make is still immensely powerful.

The sigil working I use is an adaptation of author and artist Laura Tempest Zakroff's method. You can dive deeper into sigil work with her book *Sigil Witchery: A Witch's Guide to Crafting Magical Symbols.*

EXERCISE: CREATE A SIGIL FOR MOON WORK

I will include a sigil working in each moon phase chapter to add to your moon manifesting. But first you will learn the basics of creating a sigil in this exercise.

What you need:

Notebook and pen or pencils
4-inch taper candle (any color), candle holder, source of fire

What to do:

Get comfortable in your sacred space and light the candle on your altar. Pick up your paper and pen.

Write your new moon intention at the top of the paper. What you write should not be much longer than a sentence. If it is, shorten it to a sentence. Once you have done this, go through and cross out all the vowels and letters that appear more than once. Here is an example:

"I have found a new apartment that is affordable and has great energy."

After crossing out vowels and double letters:

I have found a new apartment that is affordable and has great energy

The letters left are V, W, P, M, B, L.

From these letters we will now craft a symbol.

Start with whichever letter calls to you first and intertwine all of them until you have your sigil. Choose a letter and write it down, then add the other letters left and connect them until you get a single image that uses every letter with all of them touching. Do not over-scrutinize this process; just go with the flow of your intuition and see what you create.

This is what I crafted from the previous letters:

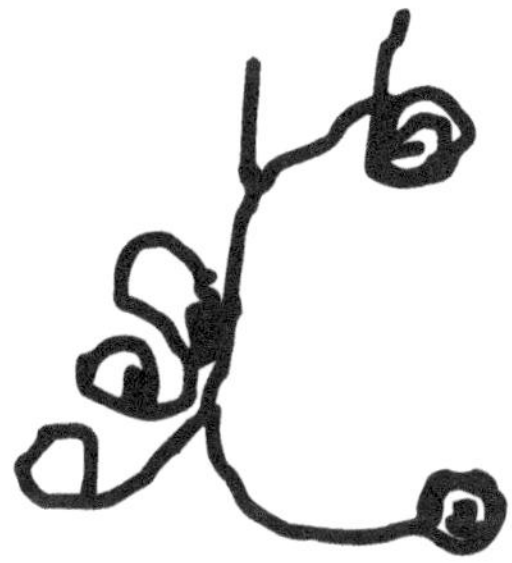

Sigil

I am not an artist, but all the letters are there. I wanted this one to be basic, but you can also make the letters loopy and add your own flair to them.

Now it is time to activate your sigil. Draw three clockwise circles around the whole sigil. As you do this, say your full intention aloud three times. When finished, say, "This sigil has been activated, And so it is."

Now you can leave your sigil on your altar or take a picture of it and keep it on your phone. Carrying it around with you is also an effective way to harness the sigil's power. When I am at my altar, I also like to trace my finger over the sigil a few times. You can create a sigil for any magical workings you are doing. You may use this one for the whole cycle or create new ones for each phase. I like to use these because they are so unique and easy to use.

When you bring your practice to the physical realm, you integrate magic into your life and everyday spaces. At the same time, you are bringing in your new reality; physically seeing, hearing, and feeling this part of your practice incorporates the lunar mind and body, allowing for successful manifestation. This part of your practice also helps keep your intention fresh and gives you an active role as you send out the signal to the universe you are ready for what you are actively calling in.

CHAPTER FIVE

DEITY

Collaborating with goddesses during the moon phases can be powerful and rewarding. There is always an advantage to having extra magical guidance when doing moon magic. Usually, you will work with the moon goddess who gives you a needed nudge when your ego loudly tells you that whatever you are trying to achieve is impossible. Doubt can creep in when you are doing big work; it is completely normal for it to show up at some point. In these moments, a divine moon council will be exactly the support you need to push through that negativity.

Establishing this connection and relationship with a divine being can help you to trust your intuition and learn about the deeper magic inside you. These deities call you to step into your power and make the changes necessary to live your best life. Deity will encourage you to tap into parts of yourself that you've either kept hidden or did not know about. There is magic in devotion to the goddesses, and many rewards as well. For example, a consistent deity practice will keep you on track during the moon cycle, so you are successful. It is like having a higher-magic accountability partner. At the end of this chapter are some suggestions on different goddesses to work with during the moon phases.

One way to ease into this practice is to choose a single goddess to work with throughout the entire moon cycle, which helps you attune to that goddess and see how doing devotional work fits into your magical practice. When researching your chosen deity, be sure that you have sourced the information from reputable people who are known for their goddess work or following. Do not be afraid to reach out to these people to ask questions.

It's important to journal about your experiences as you collaborate with deity for the first time so you can reflect on how it felt. What you record will help you strategize in the future on how to incorporate this profound practice into your moon manifesting magic for success.

A note about living traditions: I have included some goddesses that are a part of living traditions. For example, Lakshmi is from the Hindu tradition, so being respectful of this tradition is very important. Yemaya is from the Yoruba tradition, which is a closed practice. However, with respect, study, and initiation from reputable members of this practice, this goddess may be included in your moon work. Always do your research and wherever possible, speak with someone who practices these traditions to see if honoring their energy is acceptable.[23]

Dark and Light

For reference and consideration, I have included a *light* goddess and *dark* goddess for each phase based on their attributes and guidance specialty. What's included are suggestions; if you feel another goddess resonates with you, then by all means follow your intuition. As for the terms *light* and *dark,* here is how I define the terms. A dark goddess is considered dark because she gained or discovered her power through tragedy, whether it was some event that happened to her or as a result of treatment by her loved ones or peers. She found her power in the darkness and decided to step into and own her magic, however it looked. These goddesses are usually very straightforward and do not make (or accept) excuses. Tapping into the power of a dark goddess can be healing and motivating when you want to get serious about your goals and accomplish them. These goddesses tend to be more direct in their advice and not as gentle as the light goddesses.

23. Amber C. Snider, "Learning to Surrender: The Sacred Lessons of Yemayá," Atmos, June 21, 2022, https://atmos.earth/ocean-conservation-santeria-yemaya-lessons/.

However, dark goddesses are *not* cruel or out to hurt you by any means. They believe lessons are best learned with a loving but firm approach, and all they want is for you to accept the healing they offer and stand in your truth. Sometimes standing in the shadowy parts of ourselves brings realizations about what we really want changed or created in our lives. If you are seeking something expansive and transformative, I suggest collaborating with these goddesses.

Light goddesses work from their divine feminine power and the power within. These goddesses do not necessarily draw from tragedy but rather a more internal magic. Light goddesses present themselves from a divine source with the purpose of working with light energy for transformation. Light energy can be in the form of the sun or created from a place of love. Collaborating with this goddess energy is more nurturing and gentler than the directness of the dark goddesses.

The light goddesses are great to work with when beginning your deity practice. A light goddess's approach and advice are gentle, and their messages are delivered in ways that let you integrate on your own time. You can accomplish a good amount of inner work with these goddesses, but it is a slow process. That may be exactly what you need if you are called to collaborate with them, especially when first getting started. Healing and collaborating with these goddesses can be profound, and the insight and possibilities that open and expand your vibrations can be life changing. When you can move fully from an experience after accepting this light energy, you will have opened so many new opportunities regarding your moon manifesting and magical workings.

Starting Your Goddess Collaboration

There are many ways to work with and incorporate these goddesses into your manifesting moon work. Decide which goddess you want to work with before your next manifesting moon cycle. Do research and look at pictures to see if you are being called to collaborate and further build a relationship.

Incorporating your goddess into your moon manifesting altar is a practical way to begin collaborating with them. Place a picture of the goddess on your moon altar. I like to use a tarot or oracle card that depicts the goddess I chose if I have one, but any printed picture will do. Once you have your photo, take some time to read up on and familiarize yourself with the goddess's stories and symbols as well as items that represent them. Doing this research helps you know what to offer them and will remind you of their guidance when you see things that represent them in daily life.

For example, the ancient Greek goddess of the hunt, Artemis, is known for her bow and arrow; if you decide to work with her energy, having these objects or a picture of them on your altar will help you connect with her. If you see a bow and arrow online or even on a billboard while driving, you will know she is with you. When you see these symbols in the world, that's an ideal time to repeat the intention you are manifesting and send some gratitude her way.

Once you have your picture and item to represent the goddess, you can perform the following simple ritual to infuse their energy into your altar. If time is not on your side and a ritual is too much for you, another option is to sit in front of your altar and ask the goddess of your choosing if they would help guide you on your manifesting journey. Be specific, especially if you are collaborating with different goddesses through the moon phases. Practicing in this way will help you as much as it will help them know the task at hand. Place your items on your altar along with an offering of flowers if you feel called to, and say thank you.

EXERCISE: WELCOMING A GODDESS TO YOUR MOON ALTAR RITUAL

Once you've selected a goddess to work with, this exercise will prepare the items for goddess work as you welcome in your chosen deity.

What you need:

A picture of your goddes of choice
Item to represent the goddess you chose

Silver or gold 4-inch taper candle (white is fine to substitute if you don't have these colors)

What to do:

Bring your items to your altar and take a few moments to ground and center. An easy way to ground and center is to close your eyes, take a few slow deep breaths, and bring your awareness to the present moment. Next, bring the image of the goddess you are working with to your mind's eye.

Intuitively place your items on your altar. Pick up your candle and hold it in front of the goddess picture. Ask her aloud for her guidance; wait to feel your plea has been answered. When you feel your chosen goddess has agreed, ask if she has any messages for you. Close your eyes to see if any thoughts, feelings, colors, or messages come through at that time. If you do not receive any, that is okay too.

Now pick up the goddess offering and state you are sharing this as a gift for her guidance. Thank her for her time. Leave her items on your altar for as long as you decide to collaborate with her. Communicate with your chosen goddess often. If leaving a food or floral offering, refresh every day or two.

When you and your chosen goddess are finished working together, remove her items and store them safely until she calls for you to collaborate with her again. If you feel called to leave an item on the altar, that is also a completely acceptable thing to do. This is your sacred space, so making sure it feels calming and special to you is most important. If you decide to always keep a goddess altar, I recommend having a special separate area to honor them. No one likes to be cramped, and the goddesses are no exception.

EXERCISE: CREATE A GODDESS PLAYLIST

There are lots of effortless ways to bring your chosen goddess's energy into your everyday routines. One way to do this is to create a playlist that you can use when you do not have time to get to your moon altar.

What you need:

A music source

Optional:

Your journal and something to write with

What to do:

Choose a song that reminds you of the goddess you are currently working with. Research songs or choose one that plays in your head when you think of them. If the melody is unfamiliar, record yourself singing or humming it. You can download this song or record it to a device. I use my phone so that my playlist is always at my fingertips.

Play this song once a day or more if you feel inclined and bring the goddess to your mind. Let this image or feeling dance around until the song ends. If you like, write down any thoughts, feelings, or messages you may have received. Music is a wonderful way to receive magical messages if you focus on your intention.

Repeat this daily and change the song when you decide to collaborate with another goddess. Before you know it, you will have a mystically curated goddess playlist.

Deity Dreamwork

Deity often communicates to us through our dreams because we're in a completely relaxed state and can easily receive their messages. I like to ask for messages in my dreams, as I get clear images this way. Although these messages do not always make sense right away, I stay consistent and write down everything. Only later is the message easier for me to piece together, and the "aha" moments show up. Be consistent and document everything—it helps so much. Dreams are a wonderful way to receive guidance and signs from goddesses.

EXERCISE: MOON GODDESS DREAM WEAVER

Working and communicating with deity through dreams is a great way to establish a strong relationship with them and communicate in a straightforward way.

What you need:

Moon journal and pen by your bed

Optional:

A source of music

What to do:

Before you head to bed, set an intention you would like to receive a message about. As you lay down to sleep, ask to connect with your chosen goddess for advice. Ask nicely and thank them frequently. Now picture your question or whatever it is you're seeking advice about in your head as you drift off to sleep. If you like, you can also play your goddess song nearby at a low volume.

When you wake up in the morning, grab a notebook and free-write for about two minutes. Write anything that comes to mind, even if it does not make sense. Sometimes I start drawing symbols or repeating patterns of numbers and letters.

Set your notebook aside and come back to it later (I get the best insight that way). Try out a few diverse ways and see what works best for you. If you wish, this exercise can be repeated every night.

Deity Suggestions for the Moon Phases

Here is a list of suggested deities to help you along as you start your moon manifesting work. The goddesses are listed by phase, beginning with the new moon. For each phase are two goddesses, light and a dark. When you are ready, give them a call.

Selene

Phase: New moon
Origin: Greek
Light goddess

Selene is one of the more well-known moon goddesses. I chose her because of her intense passion for her goals no matter the odds. When you are starting on your moon manifesting journey, her ambition is exactly what you need to assist you in creating the best manifestation. She decides what she wants and makes it happen by creating specific actions. When she saw anything she wanted, she wasted no time, and nothing was going to get in her way. As the lover archetype, she is helpful in finding what you are enthusiastic about and igniting the passion needed to go after your goals.

Ixchel

Phase: New moon
Origin: Mayan
Dark goddess

Ixchel is the Mayan goddess of the moon. She is also known as the Jaguar goddess and referred to as Lady Rainbow. This dark goddess is incredibly determined and knows what she will and will not tolerate, especially after taking the sun as her lover. He turned out to be jealous and treated her unfairly. She decided to start doing what was best for her at once. When you need to dig deep and gather determination during the new moon, maybe because you are setting a big life intention that cycle, this goddess will help you to stay focused on your goals.

Yemaya

Phase: Waxing crescent
Origin: Yoruba
Light goddess

Yemaya is a powerful Yoruba goddess of the sea. Her emblem is a star with a waxing crescent moon. She embodies women's power to grow and be who they are meant to be. Her energy is wonderful for this growing phase of the moon. We know the moon affects the gravitational pull of the ocean, and when you are ready to grow your intention, connecting with water could be helpful. There may be times during the waxing crescent when you need the extra support only a strong female figure can provide. Yemaya will be a symbol to keep moving forward.

Cerridwen

Phase: Waxing crescent
Origin: Welsh
Dark Goddess

Being the goddess of transformation and rebirth, Cerridwen is here to help us grow in our creativity in facets of ourselves we may not have considered before. Stepping into this new manifesting energy can bring up a lot of thoughts and feelings we did not know we had. Cerridwen asks us to see what these thoughts and feelings are and how we can use that energy to grow our intentions. As these deep thoughts and soon-to-be transformations present themselves during this phase, Cerridwen will ease you into your new way of being while allowing you to process those intense feelings.

Mnemosyne

Phase: First quarter
Origin: Greek
Light goddess

The goddess Mnemosyne is the mother of the nine muses and is said to have created or at least invoked memory. In the first quarter phase when we take our aligned actions and go a bit bigger, we want to remember why we are doing what we are doing and envision the end manifestation. This goddess can help guide you to memories that may inspire big action. Mnemosyne wants you to remember who you were so you can become better than ever as you take steps during this moon phase.

Circe

Phase: First quarter
Origin: Greek
Dark goddess

Circe is fiercely independent and does not let others' opinions sway her. This phase is all about taking big, aligned action, so her energy will complement your endeavors. She also lets you be aware that you do not need everyone else to help you along. The power is within you, so use it. When you want to fully harness your power, having Circe by your side with her fiery independence and drive will help you light up your action steps and intention this moon phase.

Demeter

Phase: Waxing crescent
Origin: Greek
Light goddess

Demeter is most famous for being Persephone's mother, but this goddess holds many titles. Some consider Demeter the corn goddess, an embodiment of nurturing energy and creation. This goddess is helpful when stepping into the growing waxing crescent energy as you make bigger actions and start to see the moonlit path to your full manifestation become illuminated. Following her lead and taking time to nurture your intention, will also help you create effective ways to move your manifestation toward success in this moon phase.

Inanna

Phase: Waxing crescent
Origin: Sumerian
Dark goddess

The ancient Sumerian goddess Inanna knows of betrayal and heartache, but she is loyal and nurtures those who stand with her, like her priestess Ninshubar. Knowing who is aligned with your energy as you do your manifesting work will help you immensely. This goddess focuses on the energy to guide you through this phase, when you may realize that not everyone around you is aligned with your outlook. Inanna's loyalty to herself is something she can share with you during this phase, and she may help you create some boundaries.

Themis

Phase: Full moon
Origin: Greek
Light goddess

Themis oversaw Zeus's meetings, so she is an excellent choice for our full moonlight goddess. She is the goddess of justice and can aid you in creating the balance you need at the time of the full moon. She sees both light and dark in humanity and embraces both equally. Call on her to bring in an outside perspective on how you need to move forward to bring balance to your moon phase intention. Right now, your intention, hopes, and emotions are fully illuminated under the moon. Themis sees this and wants to give you the advice you need to accept things the way they are. She also reminds you to always strive for bigger and better.

Sekhmet

Phase: Full moon
Origin: Egyptian
Dark goddess

Sekhmet seeks justice and balance at all costs. Her fiery energy will not let others stand in her way. This energy is good to work with when you want to feel supercharged about your moon cycle manifestation and need that extra boost to keep your successes going. She knows what she wants and how to get it, so asking for her guidance will help your success become more easily reached. She shows you where you may be at a standstill in your intention and share knowledge to guide you to create effective steps for action. Sekhmet will be with you on this bright full moon to maintain balance when your intention is starting to unfold, keep a steady hand on your goal, and remind you to focus on your heart.

Lakshmi

Phase: Waning gibbous
Origin: Hindu
Light goddess

This goddess embodies all that is abundant. As we move into the waning phases of the moon cycle, she will help reignite your *how* and *why* for your intentions. Honoring her is said to bring happiness, wealth, and fortune. As you start your final steps in your moon cycle, she will guide you to enjoy the process. When you want to feel abundant in your everyday activities, call upon her and use that beautiful energy to create bigger, more effective action steps. Even though the moon is starting to wane, Lakshmi wants to remind you to keep your ambitions high as you create effective actions.

Lilith

Phase: Waning gibbous
Origin: Sumerian/Jewish
Dark goddess

Lilith knows in her heart that she does not need anyone to help her accomplish her goals. She will hold her stance even if everyone opposes her. This energy can be welcome in the waning crescent phase, giving you that last push of confidence to start tying up loose ends related to your moon manifestations. If you are easily discouraged, the waning phases may make those whispers from your ego a bit louder. Lilith knows this and waits to give you the push you need to remember why you are manifesting this cycle and why it is important you continue.

Clementina

Phase: Third quarter
Origin: Roman
Light goddess

This goddess embodies forgiveness, and during the third quarter moon she asks you to let go and forgive yourself for what you may have not accomplished yet. With her help, you can release what did not work out, which will help you refocus on your successes. Clementina wants you to be fair with yourself as you choose what to let go of for later and notice how far you have come. During the third quarter phase, she wants you to harness forgiveness with grace.

Persephone

Phase: Third quarter
Origin: Greek
Dark goddess

Persephone is one of my favorite goddesses; despite all she has endured, she is vibrant and strong. Was she a kidnapped maiden or a woman who decided to steer her own fate? Whatever her story, she is no stranger to high emotions and knows how to listen and let go. She does things of her own accord with a mindfulness of what is best for her. Her guidance in this phase will help you realize that sometimes what you want and what you need are two different things, and that is okay. When you know it is time to let go of something and it becomes a part of your lunar intention, Persephone will show you the true power you hold inside.

Idun

Phase: Balsamic / dark moon
Origin: Norse
Light goddess

Idun is the goddess of rejuvenation. As we settle into the dark moon phase, she can assist you in ensuring you are taking care of your heart and mind as you rest and reflect on the now-completed moon cycle. Sometimes letting yourself rest after a powerful moon manifestation cycle can be difficult. Idun sees this in you, and will lead you to the type of rest you need most at this time with her gentle wisdom. With rejuvenation comes balance, and she will help you accomplish this in a refreshing and revitalizing way when you collaborate with her at the dark moon.

Hekate

Phase: Waning gibbous / dark moon
Origin: Greek
Dark goddess

Hekate favors crossroads, as they mark the beginning and end of different paths. Her deep fondness of earth manifests as a comforting and enveloping energy while you are in this resting phase of the cycle. She asks you to reflect on how this cycle felt for you and to connect to your higher self through quiet meditation or dream work. She helps bring clarity to the overall situation. Working with Hekate at this moon phase will lead you to a deep understanding of yourself and why things happened the way they did this cycle.

Be Sure to Listen

As you start this work, you will notice that at various times in the moon cycle, your chosen goddess will call you if she has advice or extra guidance on a particular action step you are taking. It is so important to take time to honor and build a relationship with your goddess. We don't like when someone only talks to us when they want something, and the same is true for the goddesses. Be open to new experiences and take steps toward something you normally would not do. Let these deities guide you. Trust them and the universe.

If you are not sure what the goddess you are working with wants you to do or have questions for them, ask—it is really that simple. Be mindful of all sensations, pictures, colors, words that just seem to pop into your head, or synchronicities that come up for you immediately after you ask. Those nudges are your answers, so make sure to write them down.

Working with these magical beings can also open new ways of receiving messages. I have had clients who started goddess work and now receive messages in ways they never thought they could. For example, one client never had dreams, saying they were exceedingly rare for her. But when she started on her goddess journey, she began to have intense dreams that offered her a lot of information and insight. She had never permitted herself to dream and had some work to do around this. Now having collaborated with her chosen goddess, dreaming has become one of her main ways to receive messages. It was so exciting to see her and her magic flourish. Had she never decided to collaborate with goddesses, she may have never been able to dream in this way or reach that higher vibrational energy to enhance her magic and help her start her moon manifesting.

There is something to be said about having consistent devotional practice—as you give attention and adoration to a higher being, you give yourself that same attention. We are all connected, and you are a part of the goddess you choose to work with. It may be a personality trait you have in common or the symbols she stands for are ones to which you have always gravitated. When you create and stay consistent with this beautiful practice, you also create a wonderful devotion to yourself, which can only raise your vibration, allowing you to attain your moon manifestations and make them more meaningful.

CHAPTER SIX
CRYSTALS IN MOON MAGIC

Crystals as part of your moon manifestation work can help you and assist the energy of the phase you use them with. Bringing crystals into your moon manifestation practice will help to kick up your manifesting vibration and is another wonderful tool for strengthening your practice.

The ancient Sumerians were one of the first recorded civilizations to use crystals in healing and as a part of worship. Some of their favorites at this time were lapis lazuli and serpentine. The Egyptians believed crystals would guide their dead to the afterlife and protect them, lapis lazuli considered the one to master all consciousness. For them, this stone was more precious than even gold. Jade was and is one of the most valued crystals in Chinese culture, considered "the stone of heaven." Jade symbolizes prosperity, success, and luck. It also had historical connections to royalty and divinity, so it was also considered a symbol of renewal, longevity, and even immortality. For the Mayans, jade represented life and death. Many diverse types of crystals were vital to many cultures and were used in their rituals and sacred jewelry. It is always fascinating to me to see that though these cultures could not communicate with each other easily, they used crystals similarly.[24]

Crystals can help amplify your intentions at any moon phase. My first "working" magic crystal was a small piece of quartz. It was the first crystal I got to know and assigned tasks to. After a while, it became easier for me

24. Judy Hall, *The Crystal Bible: A Definitive Guide to Crystals* (Krause Publications, 2003), 161.

to communicate with crystals and ask them for guidance. Be patient and be open to working with crystals, as the process of sensing their energy can take time.

Choosing Your Crystals

When you visit a crystal shop or metaphysical store, the sheer number of crystals in one place can be overwhelming. There are so many to choose from, and the space itself has a lot of energy. Most times you will be drawn to a section of the store where your next shiny friend may be winking at you. Start there, close your eyes for a moment, take a deep breath, and let the crystal guide you to itself. If you find a certain color more appealing than others at that moment, head to that section of crystals.

After choosing a crystal to work with (or after it chooses you), take a moment to sit with it and get familiar with its energy. After you feel this crystal's energy, you will know how your new sparkly ally will best assist you. Now it is time to set an intention. Once you give the crystal a job, that will become its focus until you ask it to do something else.

I must admit I love using crystals for any magical work I do. What is great about working with these high-frequency items is that you can program them and carry them with you. A crystal is like your own portable magic source. The more I studied to be a crystal healing practitioner and really connected with the crystal realms, the clearer it became to me that crystals are here to help us. Using them during your moon manifesting helps you create your magical container of manifestation.

Because we are all at different energetic levels, crystals will affect each of us differently. I have suggested crystals to use throughout the moon phases, but you may find that not all will resonate with you energetically. Once you start working with crystal energy, you will soon figure out which ones really draw you in. If a different crystal calls to you during the phase that isn't one of the ones suggested, always go with your intuition.

What's great about working with crystals is that one day a crystal you never thought you would work with will call you and show up everywhere—I love it when that happens! It is the universe letting you know you are ready for that crystal's energy and that it is time to supercharge your own frequency.

Asking a crystal to focus its energy on a task is especially effective with moldavite. I use this beautiful crystal in the full moon section because it has a wonderful energy to help you work on balance. When you tell your crystal what you would like help with and thank it for its help, you will be setting an energetic boundary for the crystal to guide you in the way you need at that time.

At the end of this chapter is a list of suggested crystals you may work with.

Cleansing Your Crystals

When including crystals in your moon practice, it is always ideal to cleanse them before and after collaborating with them. If you ever feel your crystal's energy is dull or the crystal does not feel the same as when you first began working with it, that's also a wonderful time to cleanse them. You can cleanse your crystals whenever you decide they need to be refreshed, even if they are part of a long-term spell. Cleaning your crystals during a spell is fine, just be sure to restate their job in your spell and the crystal will pick up where it left off.

Here are some suggestions for how to cleanse your crystals:

- Smoke cleanse with incense or smoke sticks. I use rosemary for this purpose. Place your crystals on a table and let the smoke lightly settle on them. A pass or two is fine.
- Sound cleansing, singing bowls, clapping, singing, and music for at least a minute will clear the energy.
- Put your crystals out under the full moon for a full moon cleanse. You can put them outside, on a table by a window, or even on the windowsill. If it's overcast or raining, place your crystals by a window to charge; the moon's cleansing energy knows where to go.

- Remember that some crystals should not get wet; if there is a chance of rain, always charge them indoors. Certain crystals will get damaged when wet; keep this in mind and do your research if you want to use water for cleansing. The most common examples are: calcite, kyanite, moonstone, malachite, selenite, opal, and topaz.[25] Also keep in mind that some crystals can make drinking water unsafe.

Basic Crystal Tips and Tricks

Always be aware of the properties of your chosen crystals before doing anything with them. When purchasing crystals, research the seller or seek referrals from people you trust. There are a lot of unethical sellers and fakes out there. The cheapest option is not always the best one.

If your crystal breaks, you can still use it if that feels right for you. If not, thank it for its help and bury it or repurpose it. I suggest trying a few different methods to see which feels best for you.

If you do not know what stone to use, try selenite. Although I recommend this stone for the new moon, it is an all-purpose crystal that cleanses other crystals and is also self-cleaning. It is handy to have for any crystal work.

If a crystal is not vibing with you anymore, sit with it a while and ask it where it would like to go next. It will usually let you know, and I have found it is usually to someone I know.

Crystal bracelets are also great for moon manifesting work because then your crystals are right there on your wrist, and they will remind you throughout the day of your intention and the current phase you are working with. (It's also easy and fun to make your own bracelets; instructions appear on the next few pages.)

Consider buying only the crystals you need for the magic you are using right now. Purchasing only a few crystals at a time will help you not become overwhelmed and lets you build a relationship with each crystal.

25. Karen Frazier, *Crystals for Beginners: The Guide to Get Started with the Healing Power of Crystals* (Althea Press, 2017), 33.

Before you know it, you will have a beautiful collection and an intentional bond with each piece you bought.

Remember when making crystal water infusions to place crystals outside the water, not in. You will receive the same benefit without having to be concerned about safety and sanitation.

EXERCISE: MOON CRYSTAL BRACELET

Crafting is a fantastic way to connect with your moon manifesting intention and focus your magical energy. By creating a wearable spell bracelet, you will have a constant reminder of your focus for the moon cycle with you.

What you need:

20 to 30 crystal beads of your choosing (For moon work, I recommend moonstone, selenite, quartz, amethyst, and black tourmaline) plus a bowl to hold them in

3-inch piece of tape (clear or masking tape are best)

Elastic bracelet string about 10 to 12 inches long and 1 mm thick

Scissors

What to do:

Find a workspace that has plenty of room. Place your beads in a bowl to keep them all in one spot. Next, tape your elastic string to your work surface. Decide what your pattern of beads will be or just create your moon bracelet intuitively.

Start stringing your beads. As you add each bead, speak affirmations to them. For example, "I will listen to my intuition to create the best life for myself," or "The moon guides me and always has my highest good in mind."

When you near the end of the elastic string, leave about a half inch free with no beading on it. Carefully peel the taped end off your surface and wrap the tape around the elastic to keep the beads on.

Place it on your wrist and decide the best fit; leave a bit of room for stretching. Place the bracelet on your work surface once again and tie it in multiple knots.

Cut off excess elastic string and, if you feel called to, charge the bracelet under the moon.

EXERCISE: MEDITATION FOR CRYSTAL CONNECTION

This exercise will guide you to connect with your new sparkly partner in your moon manifesting work.

What you need:

Your crystal of choice
A quiet place to focus
Moon journal and pen

What to do:

Get comfortable with your crystal in hand and your journal nearby. Close your eyes and take a few deep breaths, allowing yourself to relax. When you feel present in your body, bring your attention to the crystal in your hands.

Feel its surface and notice its weight and texture. As you hold the crystal, visualize a radiant energy emanating from it.

Take a breath as you imagine this energy flowing into your body and filling you with warmth and peace. Feel it cleansing away any tension or negativity, leaving you refreshed. As you sit with the crystal's energy, allow yourself to be open to its wisdom and guidance. Listen to your intuition's whispers as you connect to your crystal.

Take a moment to reflect on the qualities of the crystal—its unique colors, patterns, and vibrations. Consider how these qualities resonate with aspects of yourself and your moon manifesting journey. With gratitude, thank the crystal for its presence and the insights it has shared. You can return to this connection whenever you need support, clarity, or healing.

Slowly and gently open your eyes and bring your awareness back to the present moment. Take a deep cleansing breath and write your thoughts, feelings, and any messages the crystal had for you in your moon journal.

EXERCISE: CONJURING MOON WATER WITH CRYSTAL ENERGY

Create your own magical moon water to use in your moon workings. These are the basic directions that can be used for any moon phase or intention. Refer to it as needed when you go through your moon work.

What you need:

Your chosen crystals
Large dish to fit your water container and crystals
Water
Your intention
Blank address labels to note the moon phase

What to do:

Choose the moon phase you would like to work with and crystals from the list below, or your favorites for the current phase. Fill your container with water and place the crystals around it. Once you have your crystal moon phase water in place (a table near a window is fine), leave it overnight and place in the refrigerator in the morning.

Your crystal moon water will still collect energy even on cloudy or rainy days, so do not worry about whether it's light is visible. Try different crystal combinations for the phases and see what resonates with you most. And be sure to note what went into every magical concoction you make so you can make them again.

This exercise can be done when working with any phase of the moon. Full moon water in particular is great for use during all phases, and setting an effective intention along with it will help it be as powerful as possible.

Crystal Suggestions for the Moon Phases

There are so many wonderful crystals to choose for your moon manifestation work each cycle. Here are some suggestions and my brief explanation on what intentions they are helpful for supporting.

New Moon

Selenite is said to be named after Selene, the Greek goddess of the moon. This crystal is excellent for clearing and rebalancing energies, making it perfect for starting a new adventure. This crystal can be brittle or fragile, so be mindful when collaborating with it.

Himalayan salt is an ancient crystal that relates to the earth and sea and is known for its healing properties. Himalayan salt is an excellent crystal to work with to cleanse and raise your vibration as you call in your new intentions.

Citrine is one of my favorite crystals to work with. This crystal is all about abundance and positivity—the exact vibe you want to harness as you move into your supercharged manifesting moon cycle.

Waxing Crescent Moon

Green jade has the abundant energy of good luck, prosperity, and protection of your heart to aid you during the waxing crescent moon phase.

Carnelian is all about grounding you to help accept change and thrive, making it an ideal choice as the crescent moonlight propels you forward.

Apatite increases motivation, inspiration, and creativity. It is a great crystal for taking bigger action steps to your intention.

First Quarter Moon

Red jasper is known for putting a confident spring in your step.

Calcite is a powerful energy amplifier that clears negative energy to keep you focused on your goals.

Red chalcedony helps ensure perseverance and strength when working on accomplishing important things. This crystal is perfect for the first quarter push of action.

Waxing Gibbous Moon

Tiger's eye aids you in seeing unique perspectives on your situation, which is helpful when close to the full moon phase, related to creating balance.

Diamond is a stone that resets your aura, giving you the nudge to take big action.

Kyanite is a powerful crystal that helps you tune in to your intuition and express yourself clearly and concisely.

Full Moon

Moonstone is one of my personal favorites. It can be used in any phase, but I've included it under the full moon because of this phase's focus on balance. This crystal can aid you in finding the right way to use your physical and psychic energy.

Moldavite is from a meteorite that hit Earth fifteen million years ago. It has become popular only recently, but this stone can help you transform and give you the push you need to fulfill your manifestation goals.

Topaz guides you to balance your energy and directs energy where it is most needed. This is great for giving you that needed energetic boost to make progress with your goals.

Waning Gibbous Moon

Rose quartz is a crystal that gently nudges you to practice self-care. As you are working so hard to reach your goals, it is important to make sure you are taking care of your physical body as well.

Okenite's energy is comparable to a teddy bear; it is that big hug you need to finish what you are doing this moon cycle. It also gently helps you face and deal with any obstacles coming up for you right now.

Stilbite helps ground your energy and turn your thoughts into actions. With this crystal, you will quickly move forward with your manifestation in this cycle.

Third Quarter Moon

Zoisite is a healing crystal that helps you remember your end goal and reminds you not to be influenced by others. When you are at this stage in the moon cycle, this crystal will help redirect your thoughts and create last-minute actions needed to complete it.

Botswana agate is all about being able to look at the bigger picture. Looking at the bigger picture is especially important when manifesting. Botswana agate helps you not dwell on what has not worked for you this phase. The ability to let go of small inconveniences helps you stay focused.

Lepidolite removes room for negativity and will dispel any in its vicinity. Using this crystal at the third quarter moon will help you remove any doubts you have about how this moon cycle went for you and transmute them positively and productively.

Waning Crescent Moon

Tourmaline quartz is a wonderful stone for this phase as you wind down and regroup. This crystal helps turn negative thoughts into positive ones as you gently revisit the phase and practice some self-care.

Black tourmaline presents itself directly and brings along an emotional blanket of comfort. Black tourmaline will help wrap you in your cocoon, gently clear what is no longer needed, and keep your thoughts focused on what you need.

Smoky quartz brings emotional calm to anyone who holds it, and after all the wonderful transformative work done during this cycle, it is a welcome addition. Smoky quartz also brings acceptance. You have done what was needed, and now it is time to rejuvenate and think of what you want to create in the next cycle.

Crystal Grids

Crystal grids are intentionally placed groups of crystals to amplify a goal or manifestation.[26] Incorporating sacred geometry shapes into your moon manifesting grids adds another layer of energy to your moon cycle magic and is something you can customize each phase. You can find sacred geometry templates and tons of books about diverse ways to set up crystal grids and place the crystals to enhance your manifestation workings. Combining

26. Frazier, *Crystals for Healing:*, 26.

the energy of different crystals in a focused way can create a powerful conduit for working with the moon.

As you get to know your crystals and how they best fit into your moon work, the possibilities are endless when you add these crystals to manifesting grids each phase. Author and crystal teacher of more than twenty years, Nicholas Pearson states in his book, *Crystal Basics*, if the crystals you are using, especially quartz, have points, use those points in your grids to direct that energy to you. Placing the points to the center would be a fantastic way to direct manifesting energy when using grids for your moon magic.[27]

Crystal Grid

You can get creative and have fun when creating crystal grids. See making them as a creative outlet and let your intuition guide you. It is inspiring to see a completed crystal grid, and you will soon discover how powerful they can

27. Nicholas Pearson, *Crystal Basics: The Energetic, Healing, and Spiritual Properties of 100 Gemstones* (Healing Arts Press, 2015), 10.

be. By creating crystal grids, you also work your intuition, build a relationship with your crystals, and learn which crystals work best together.

EXERCISE: CREATING A CRYSTAL GRID

Grab your crystals and try this basic exercise to create your own grid. Before starting, do some research to see if you want to incorporate sacred geometry into your design. If you do, modify the exercise to accommodate the chosen pattern. Sacred geometry gives us specific shapes and patterns that can be used to make crystal grids to amplify intentions. A few examples of sacred geometry grids are the Flower of Life with its focus on creation; Metatron's Cube, which is used to connect with your higher self; and the merkaba, which helps activate intentions.[28] Use these images as inspiration.

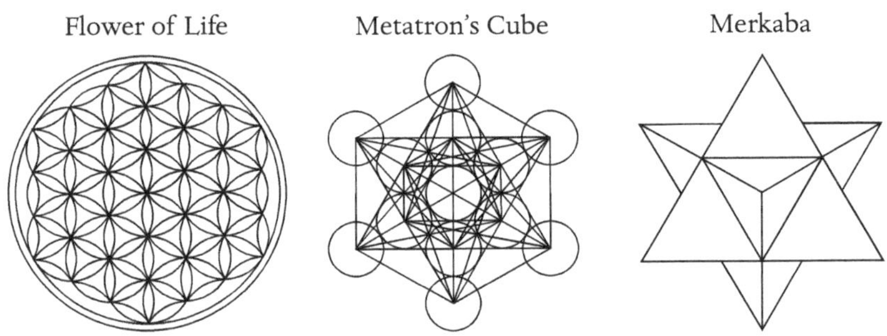

Sacred Geometry

What you need:

Crystals of your choosing that reflect your intention
A center stone (clear quartz is an excellent choice)
Flowers, sticks, or items to represent the moon phase to add to your grid for an individualized touch
Smoke (your favorite incense), sound (sound bowl, singing, clapping, et cetera), or your favorite way to cleanse the space (or Reiki if you are attuned)

28. Pamela Chen, *Enchanted Crystal Magic: Spells, Grids & Potions to Manifest Your Desires* (Llewellyn Publications, 2021), 211–13.

Your moon journal and a pen
Optional:
A wand (your finger or a stick work just fine)

What to do:

Decide your intention for the grid and choose your crystals to support this intention. For example, if you intend to practice extra self-love during the waning crescent phase, rose quartz would be an excellent choice.

Find an area where the crystal grid will not be disturbed. If using a preprinted grid, tape the paper down to the flat surface you are using or draw your grid directly on a piece of cardboard. You will be placing your crystals and other elements on top of the paper or board.

Next, cleanse the area with smoke, sound, or Reiki if you are attuned. Gather your items and crystals.

Place your central crystal first to help amplify your intention. Then place the crystal you are drawn to next near the central crystal. I like to use smaller ones of the same kind. For example, if I choose amethyst, I will place them around the central crystal however they need to go. Then add your next layer of crystals and repeat until you feel the grid is good energetically. If you have other elements to add such as flowers, pictures, or special items, now is the time to place them. Write your intention for the crystal grid on a small paper and place it under the central crystal.

It is now time to activate your crystal grid. Say your intention three times. Use a crystal wand if you have one; otherwise, your hand is fine. Now wave your hand or the wand clockwise around the entire grid three times. Touch the central stone and each crystal in the grid to incorporate the energies. Once complete, the grid is activated.

When your crystal grid intention comes to fruition or has moved your moon intention to the point where you feel it has done its job, you can disassemble the grid. Wave your hand or wand counterclockwise three times, and your grid is ready to be dismantled. As you remove each crystal, thank it for its assistance. Afterward, cleanse your crystals so they will be ready for your next grid.

You can try working with crystals at any time—do what feels right to you. I suggest keeping a crystal log in your moon journal to record the crystals you work with, the energy you receive from them, and whatever else comes up as you get to know them. When you work with the crystals again in the future, you'll be able to see how the energy has either changed or stayed the same. I often dig up some of my older journals to see what worked best for a particular manifestation and if that crystal would like to assist me with a similar one.

CHAPTER SEVEN

HERBS, OILS, AND INCENSES

As you build your magical practice and start doing spell work, you will soon realize you have started quite the collection of herbs. Do not feel as though you must go out and buy them all at once. Like working with crystals, only buy what you need as needed and you will gradually establish a well-stocked magical pantry.

Getting to know your little plant friends one at a time is vital to cultivating your magical practice. Many of these herbs are already in your kitchen, and those work perfectly. Essential oils are a good substitute or addition to any magical workings. I will also discuss incense and its use in moon work.

The suggested herbs can be used in your spell work during the phases or added to the other workings if a plant energy calls to you. Be sure to keep track of whatever herbs you use in your moon journal and note how they worked for you. The notes you make now will be a great reference as you advance in your magical practice.

If you can't or haven't yet acquired herbs, there are many tarot or oracle decks related to plants and herbs. These herbal cards can be easily placed on your altar. I like working with a new plant energy each new moon, making an herbal deck an easier and less expensive way to include the plants' energies.

Herb Suggestions for Moon Phases

In this section are suggestions to get you started with using herbs in your moon manifestation workings. Herbs can be used in many ways: dried, fresh, incense, oil, or tea and can be sprinkled, consumed, and burned. (Remember to use caution if you intend to ingest any herb.) Following is a general list of herbs that correspond with the different phases of the moon.

New Moon Herbs

Ginger (*Zingiber officinale*): Stimulating and calls you to action
Milky oats (Avena sativa): Comforting energy, prosperity, and abundance
Peppermint (*Mentha × piperita*): Purifying and raises vibrations in the space it is used in
Rosemary (*Salvia Rosmarinus*): Protection, cleansing, and increase mental powers
Yarrow (*Achillea millefolium*): Stops fear and grants courage

Waxing Crescent Herbs

Bergamot (*Citrus bergamia*): Success and money attraction
Laurel (*Laurus nobilis*): Success and talisman against poverty
Lavender (*Lavandula angustifolia*): Promotes love, happiness, and inner peace
Nettle (*Urtica dioica*): Offers support and healing
Raspberry leaf (*Rubus idaeus*): Offers support during transformation to a higher-level self

First Quarter Moon Herbs

Carnation (*Dianthus caryophyllus*): Strong action and healing
Masterwort (*Astrantia major*): Grants courage and repels negative energy
Oregano (*Origanum vulgare*): Long-lasting happiness and courage
Oak (*Quercus* spp.): Luck, money, increased potency in whatever it is directed toward
Star anise (*Illicium verum*): Psychic powers and heightened dreaming ability

Waxing Gibbous Herbs

Apple (*Malus* spp.): Self-love and wisdom
Basil (*Ocimum basilicum*): Attraction and wealth
Marjoram (*Origanum majorana*): Happiness and strength of mind and body
Pennyroyal (*Mentha pulegium*): Peace and strength
Vervain (*Verbena officinalis*): Energetically level up and fulfil wishes

Full Moon Herbs

Chamomile (*Matricaria chamomilla*): Balance and grounding
Clove (*Syzygium aromaticum*): Aura purification and increase in positive vibrations
Lemon balm (*Melissa officinalis*): Reduce stress and encourage renewal
Mugwort (*Artemisia vulgaris*): Strength and psychic powers
Lotus (*Nelumbo nucifera*): Opening new energetic portals and blessing

Waning Gibbous Moon Herbs

Caraway (*Carum carvi*): Revitalize memory and encourages you to stay on course
Cinnamon (*Cinnamomum verum*): Enhance spirituality and ignite passion
Balm of Gilead (*Populus balsamifera*): Manifestation and healing
Dill (*Anethum graveolens*): Money and repels those with ill thoughts of you
Vanilla (*Vanilla planifolia*): Loving vibration and improve energy

Third Quarter Moon Herbs

Eucalyptus (*Eucalyptus obliqua*): Protection and healing
Morning glory (*Ipomoea* spp.): Happiness and peace
Rue (*Ruta graveolens*): Clears the head of unneeded thoughts and negativity
Skullcap (*Scutellaria lateriflora*): Relaxation and commitment
Sunflower (*Helianthus annuus*): Wishes and wisdom

Waning Crescent Moon Herbs

Allspice (*Pimenta dioica*): Luck and healing
Copal (*Protium copal*): Love and purification
Rowan (*Sorbus aucuparia*): Power and success
Thyme (*Thymus vulgaris*): Courage and health
Violet (*Viola odorata*): Calms tempers and induces sleep

EXERCISE: NEW PLANT BFF VISUALIZATION

This is a fantastic way to connect with any plant. Taking a few moments to connect to its energy is a very grounding experience, and the plants may let you know exactly how they can assist you during the moon cycle you are working with.

What you need:

A pinch of the herb or plant you want to connect with or receive messages from (see the provided lists in this chapter)
Small bowl
Moon journal and pen

What to do:

Find a comfortable spot; your moon altar is ideal. Place the herb you want to connect with in a small bowl. Take a few minutes to clear your mind and come fully into the moment.

Now pick up the bowl with the herb in it. Look at it—examine the herb's color, texture, and overall appearance. Smell it and touch it with your fingers. When you are done, hold the bowl and close your eyes. Try to sense the vibrations of the herb. You may even see a pattern in your mind's eye. Sit with this vibration for a few minutes. When you feel ready, ask the herb if it would like to be allies with you. Note any feelings, thoughts, or sensations that come up at this moment. If the herb agrees, you can ask whatever it is you want help with and if it would assist you. Ask the herb for any advice about collaborating with it. After receiving your message, thank it for its help. Take a few deep breaths and open your eyes. Write down anything you received from this visualization in your moon journal.

EXERCISE: CREATING A MAGICAL SACHET

Magical sachets are a versatile and easy-to-carry way to strengthen your magical intentions. Adding crystals is helpful; you can use whichever crystal will amplify your intention for this moon phase. Small mesh pouches work best for me, and I save them for this purpose. You can get some cheap ones online or in any craft store easily. Small containers or tins are good options, and if you have any around that are no longer needed, baby socks can also be used. Refer to the suggestions in the crystal chapter and the herbal suggestions in this chapter to make your choices for your sachet.

What you need:

Small bag
4-inch taper candle (any color) plus lighter or matches
Small piece of paper and pen
1 tsp chosen herb (up to three different ones) for your intention
A small crystal to support your intention
6-inch piece of yarn or string

What to do:

After deciding which bag you will use, gather your supplies and head to your moon altar space. Once there, light the candle. Take a moment to be present with a few even breaths. After you feel centered and ready, pick up your pen and paper and write your intention for this sachet. Read it aloud three times and fold it toward you. When you are finished, place in your bag.

Now hold the herb you have chosen. Ask it to guide you on this intention, say thank you, and place some into your bag. If you chose more than one herb, repeat this process for each herb. Next, hold your crystal to your heart center. Ask it to help you, and assign it a task regarding this intention for this sachet. When you are finished, place the crystal in the bag.

Hold the string and say your sachet intention aloud. Then tie a knot and say, "And so it is." Repeat this three times total. Place the string around the opening of the bag to close it. Once it's sufficiently shut tight, knot the string again three times. Your sachet is complete.

Be sure to shake it daily to keep the energy flowing. When you feel it has served its purpose, return items that are biodegradable and nature-friendly back to the earth. Cleanse and reuse the crystal and bag/container if you wish or dispose of it properly.

Working with Incense and the Moon

Incense is a terrific way to get to know your herbs or connect with the energies of plants. By connecting with air energy, you can stay grounded and clear on your moon intention as you work through each phase. Incense burning can be a way to indicate you are starting your moon practice during ritual, cleanse any magical objects used during your moon manifestation cycle, or help focus you during your goddess work at your moon altar. Loose incense is particularly wonderful because you can get a lot of use out of a small pinch, though stick or cone incense is an easier option when starting out because you can just light it and begin your magical workings.

Using charcoal disks is the easiest way to burn loose herbs. It is important to have a firesafe vessel and never leave loose herbs unattended just as you would not leave a candle burning. You can also place the charcoal disk in a bowl filled with salt or sand. Some herbs light up quickly, so you need to be nearby whenever working with loose incense.

There are a few types of charcoal disks. Some are self-starting but give off a bit of an odor when lit. Lighting these disks uses the same principle as using charcoal on the barbeque: light the disk and let it heat up a bit. It will start turning grayish-white when it is ready, at which point you can add your incense. I usually take only a pinch of whatever herbs I want to use. Keep in mind that most dried herbs, even sweet-smelling ones, do smell different when burned. It's best to use a small amount in case the smell of whatever you're burning doesn't appeal to you. You can always add more if necessary.

If you are sensitive to smoke or smells, burning incense indoors may not be the best option. If possible, try it outside first. I add herbs to outdoor fires when I want to add some plant energy to whatever I am doing, and the smell is not as strong as it is indoors.

Smoke bundles are another wonderful way to work with herbs in magic. My personal favorite is a rosemary smoke bundle. I like adding roses to them but only a few because they smell quite different when burned—a very earthy smell that's nothing like the sweet scent we are familiar with. My family likes the smell of rosemary better than other herbs, which is another deciding factor when choosing what to burn. You can purchase these bundles online, but if you have the actual plant stems or leaves of the herb you are working with, try making one. They are easy to make but just take a bit of patience. I like to make my own when I can and usually will do so in batches. Once you figure out your way of making them, it can be a very calming and grounding experience. Now you can make one with the next exercise.

Incense Suggestions for the Moon Phases

Incense is a quick way to cleanse your space and tools or attune yourself to the moon phase you are working with. When you light incense, you know it's time to focus your energy and bring yourself into the present moment. If you are sensitive to smoke, there is usually a spray substitute that is just as effective. Otherwise try diffusing essential oils instead.

New Moon: Sandalwood or myrrh are great for this phase because they open your intuitive centers and help you tap into your subconscious energy to project your intention into the universe.

Crescent Moon: Orange or floral incense are both great to harness the growing energy of your intention in this phase.

First Quarter: Patchouli or blends with geranium will help you focus and give you an extra boost of confidence.

Waxing Gibbous Moon: Lavender or rose blends are great to help you nurture yourself and your intention.

Full Moon: Ylang-ylang and rosemary incense are great for balance at this phase, especially when used together.

Waning Gibbous Moon: Cinnamon is great to help reignite excitement for your almost-complete intention, and vanilla relaxes you, helping you to reflect in an effective way as you prepare for your last push before the cycle ends.

Third Quarter Moon: Lemongrass and sage work wonderfully to help your emotional release and encourage you to be more open to forgiveness during this phase.

Waning Crescent/Dark Moon: Chamomile and nag champa are helpful in relaxation and clearing the mind as you rest during the dark moon.

EXERCISE: HOW TO MAKE A SMOKE BUNDLE

When you make your own smoke bundle, it is easier to work with fresh plants and let them dry on their own. This method creates less mess, and you will not break them when bundling and wrapping the dried plants with twine. This exercise takes you through the steps to make my personal favorite, a rosemary smoke bundle.

What you need:

A large working space
A big handful of fresh rosemary sprigs
A small spool of thin jute twine
Scissors

What to do:

In a decently-sized space for crafting, gather your items. Take a handful of the plants you intend to use and trim them so they are the same size. I like to cut mine so they are about four inches long.

Set the cut bundle of herbs down and cut a piece of twine about twelve inches or so. Lay it down horizontally on your workspace. Pick up the plant bundle and place vertically in the middle of the twine and tie it together with a few knots. Carefully pick up the bundle and start to wrap the ends of the twine around it tightly. Remember that as the plants dry, they will shrink, so we want to accommodate this. You don't want to end up with a loose bundle that falls out of the twine. Tie the ends together when you are finished.

Leave in a cool, dry area to dry out completely, and remember to turn the bundles every few days to make sure they are completely dried. It can take anywhere from one week to three for things to dry and be ready to use depending on your location, temperature, and humidity.

Essential Oils and Moon Work

Essential oils are another way to work with herbs. These plants have been specially treated and heated to extract the purest concentrated oil for the most benefit. When deciding to use essential oils, do your research and ensure they are pure and sourced ethically. Keep in mind that many essential oils in stores are not pure and have harmful additives. Using essential oils is a great option for anyone with smoke sensitivity.

How to tell if an essential oil is pure:

- The label reads: 100% pure
- Research the company; they should list their ingredients and sources on their website
- Most high-quality oils list the botanical name on the bottle.
- The oil should have a strong smell because it is concentrated. If the smell is faint, the oil may be diluted.
- Check for GC-MS testing on the website. Suppliers will batch test the oils using this method to evaluate the purity of the oil.[29]

29. "Gas Chromatography-Mass Spectrometry (GC-MS)," EAG Laboratories, accessed November 25, 2024, https://www.eag.com/techniques/mass-spec/gas-chromatography-mass-spectrometry-gc-ms/.

Oils are also beneficial to have around if you run out of physical herbs during your spell work. I have done this on many occasions and use essential oils in spell jars and ritual baths. Adding them to a diffuser is especially useful when working at your moon altar. The diffuser is like your own little magic cauldron, and many types are available. Even moon-shaped ones! I like to create different blends because the oils have the same magical properties as their physical counterparts. Essential oils can also be helpful when you are not home because you can easily take them with you and be reminded of your intentions in moments when you need a quick energetic boost.

When applying oils to your skin, I would suggest using a carrier oil like olive or almond oil. If you are allergic to a certain oil or sensitive to essential oils in general, you can skip using them or place pictures of your oils on your moon altar. You can also write the names of the oils on a card and draw a picture of the herbs. Be creative and you will still be able to harness the energy of the oils you would like to incorporate in your moon manifestation workings.

EXERCISE: MOON PHASE DIFFUSER BLENDS

There are so many varieties of oils that can be used with a diffuser, and it's fun to create your blends using your intuition—in fact, I have found some of my best ones this way. Remember that some diffused oils are not safe for pets, so do your research before using if you have animals.

In a way, diffusers are like mini cauldrons that are perfect for holding the many blends you'll make for any intention or moon phase. Be sure to wipe down your diffuser after you finish diffusing a blend, and always wear gloves to avoid getting oils—hot or otherwise—on your skin.

What you need:

Diffuser

Essential oils related to the phase you are working with

½ C water or less depending on the size of the diffuser

What to do:

Fill diffuser with water. Add your essential oils. Turn the diffuser on when you begin your moon workings or when you want to connect quickly to the moon phase you are working with. Clean diffuser when you are done.

NEW MOON BLEND

3 drops orange
2 drops lemon
2 drops frankincense

This blend helps you to open your senses fully and tap into your intuition as you start to create your moon manifesting intention.

WAXING CRESCENT BLEND

4 drops vanilla
3 drops lavender
2 drops clove

Diffusing this blend will help to create a comforting environment for your new intention to expand.

FIRST QUARTER BLEND

4 drops lemon
2 drops peppermint
1 drop patchouli

Take your intention to the next level to guide you to focused actions with this blend.

WAXING GIBBOUS BLEND

3 drops juniper
2 drops cedarwood
1 drop pine

This grounding blend helps you assess your progress in a gentle way.

FULL MOON BLEND

4 drops frankincense
1 drop myrrh
2 drops orange

Here we look to bring balance, and this blend will bring balance to both mind and body.

WANING GIBBOUS BLEND

3 drops cinnamon
4 drops peppermint

This simple blend will help reignite your excitement for your moon manifesting and inspire you to start that last action push before the cycle ends.

THIRD QUARTER BLEND

4 drops cedarwood
3 drops black spruce
2 drops bergamot

These oils bring you to a mental space of forgiveness and grace.

WANING CRESCENT BLEND

3 drops ylang-ylang
2 drops vetiver
2 drops marjoram

A soothing and relaxing blend for rest and integration.

Developing relationships with your herbs is a wonderful way to connect with the earth's energy. Before you know it, you may even start to grow them yourself. That is what happened to me, and I love being able to grow my herbs. You start to connect with them quickly; unbelievably, they all have unique personalities. I encourage you to try it even if you do not consider yourself a "plant person." The right herbs always find you at the best times and the hardiest ones will call to you initially so you can try your hand at growing them without worry. What you need is usually easily found, making work with plants an option for everyone, green thumb or not.

CHAPTER EIGHT

TAROT

Tarot is a form of divination that heightens intuition and provides much-needed guidance when we don't know what our next steps are in life. When you are unsure about what to do next in your moon manifestations, tarot can help you pinpoint exactly the steps needed to move on to the next phase of the moon and decide the best course of action during each phase.

Incorporating tarot into your moon manifesting cycle can provide profound insight and is an effective way to bring your focus into the physical realm. Taking time to pull cards and use the moon phase tarot spreads will also help you create a clear path of action to bring your intention to life.

When you set up your moon altar and start working with the moon goddesses, tarot is a reliable source of communication as you perfect your intuition and confidence working throughout the cycle. Asking your specific moon goddess for advice through tarot will help to build this relationship and assure you these deities are willing and ready to assist you.

Tarot Basics

Tarot consists of seventy-eight cards, divided into two sections, the major arcana and the minor arcana. Most decks are based on the Rider-Waite-Smith (RWS) deck first published in 1909, however there are a few other tarot systems, like the Thoth. The tarot systems covered in this book are based on the RWS deck.

The major arcana cards are numbered from 0 (the Fool) to 21 (the World). The majors represent significant life events, such as momentous changes in life, love, major personal transformation, and death. These are things that, when they develop, create whole-life shifts. *Arcana* means "secrets" in Latin, and with these cards you will unlock your life secrets and navigate through them to create the life you most want. Those same big shifts will happen when you create a moon manifesting practice. When the major arcana show up during the moon phases, they can point you in the right direction or to where attention is needed at that time.

The minor arcana consists of the remaining fifty-six cards in the deck. They are divided into four suits: wands, cups, pentacles, and swords. They are further divided into court cards: king, queen, knight, and page of their respective suits. The court cards usually represent people in everyday life or a particular energy a person can have. The other cards are called pips or numbers, ace through ten in each suit. These cards correspond to the everyday situations we all deal with, such as our careers, happiness, home life, health, and love. Although you may expect the major arcana to be more helpful in creating action steps during your moon manifesting cycle, it is actually the minors that make the best helpers. These cards guide you to creating detailed actions and let you know which actions can wait. I do a lot of action step creation with tarot, and it has really helped me make decisions and encouraged me to try things I had not considered.

A minor card's nuances can change depending on the cards surrounding it. Always trust your first intuitive thoughts, even if they do not align with the suggested keywords. When you do tarot readings or spreads, you are creating a story, so using a story framework allows you to tweak and rewrite what happens as needed to fit your intention and action steps. Write down the thoughts and feelings you pick up from the first card and then see what common thread runs through the meanings you divined.

One last note about the minor arcana: the suits are directly related to the four classical elements, and each suit corresponds with a particular aspect of our lives. Wands relate to fire; cups signify water; pentacles are related to earth; and swords correspond with air. As with other magical components and correspondences, these can be interwoven into your work.

The Major Arcana

The major arcana are the cards most people who have not delved into the world of tarot are familiar with. We see them referenced often in movies and other media outlets these days. These first twenty-two cards tell the story of an archetypal story called "the Fool's Journey." As you go through the numbers, you'll see the progression of the Fool (card zero) as they go through life, including all the difficulties, life lessons, and "aha" moments they'll experience along the way. The major arcana ends with the World card, a message that the current cycle is complete and the Fool will soon start on another life journey.

Major arcana cards in a reading may indicate there will be bigger changes on the way, or you need to focus on whichever energy that card embodies right now. Making these big life changes can be exciting, and the major arcana can guide you on the energy to harness on a given moon manifesting cycle. When major cards show up in your readings or spreads, see where your attention needs to be directed regarding the moon phase you are in. You may have to confront a part of your life that needs change, or a message may show up when you are on the right path and encourage you to keep going.

The Major Arcana Key Words

0 *The Fool:* New beginnings, trust in the universe, optimism

1 *The Magician:* Creativity, manifesting, action

2 *The High Priestess:* Spiritual mentorship, intuition, insight, mystical energy

3 *The Empress:* Nurturing energy, fertility, abundance, passion

4 *The Emperor:* Structure, rules, power

5 *The Hierophant:* Tradition, rules of society, spiritual blessings

The Major Arcana Key Words

6 *The Lovers:* Relationships, love, choices

7 *The Chariot:* Power, success, will

8 *Strength:* Emotional openness, personal strength, transforming negative to positive

9 *The Hermit:* Wisdom from within, maturity, contemplation

10 *Wheel of Fortune*: Karma, fate, luck

11 *Justice:* Fair outcomes, truth, self-honesty

12 *The Hanged Man:* Attachment, overthinking, a unique perspective

13 *Death:* Change, endings

14 *Temperance:* Balance, calm, patience

15 *The Devil:* Obsessions, unhealthy habits, sexual energy

16 *The Tower:* Release, sudden change, revelation

17 *The Star:* Hope, peace, optimism

18 *The Moon:* Instinct, emotion, mystery

19 *The Sun:* Happiness, freedom, clarity

20 *Judgement:* Profound change, reunited relationships, truth

21 *The World:* Completion, success, fulfillment

Deep Dive into the Moon Card

I feel it is important to highlight this card in the tarot deck because of its obvious association with the moon. The Moon card highlights what is felt but not seen, much like the moon signs in astrology. The Moon card steps into the area of things hidden, whether that be emotions, truths, lies, or revelations. Tarot expert and author Mary Greer explains the Moon card in her very popular *Tarot for Your Self*. One quote that stood out to me regarding moon manifestation was that practitioners "need to explore unknown territory and working with the realm of unconscious along with having a sense of being guided or pulled," which plays out when you start to connect your lunar spirit, mind, and body as you continue with your manifestation work.[30] Another piece of wisdom from *Tarot for Your Self* that applies to moon manifestations is what she calls "acting instinctively. Doing something automatically, as a well-known skill you no longer need to think about."[31] By using the tools in this book and harnessing your lunar magic you will be doing exactly that: manifesting automatically. It will become a part of who you are and a part of your magical practice.

Moon Tarot Card

The Court Cards

Court cards are helpful when you want to step into a certain energy for your moon manifesting but are not sure exactly how. Sit with these cards and ask them for advice. Journaling what you see in the card and how it relates to your situation is another way to tap into the court card energy. When they show up in a reading, consider how the characters of the court card can help or hinder the reading and situation.

The court cards are commonly used to represent the energy of a certain age group or people in your life. Each court card is assigned certain personality traits; when these cards come up in your readings, they'll help

30. Mary K. Greer, *Tarot for Your Self: A Workbook for Personal Transformation,* 2nd ed. (Weiser Books, 2002), 175.

31. Greer, *Tarot for Your Self,* 196.

you to determine how to approach your action steps or the personality type to embody to create effective actions. These cards may also show up in a reading as a personality type you can embody as you create action steps to push you toward your moon intention.

The Court Card Keywords

Kings: Fatherly, leadership, authoritative, older or mature male figure energy
Queens: Motherly, nurturing, older or mature female energy
Knights: Young adult, moving, quick thinking, impulsive
Pages: Teenage energy, ambitious, enthusiastic, sees wonder in everything

Suits

To go a bit further, here are some attributes of the suits:
Wands: Actions
Swords: Thoughts/ideas
Cups: Emotions/relationships
Pentacles: Related to everyday tasks

The Minors or Pips

The rest of the cards, called pips or minors, correspond with everyday situations and topics we all deal with: career, happiness, home life, health, and love. For example, even though love is listed in the majors, there are various kinds and degrees of love, which the minors represent here. When these cards come up in your moon tarot spreads or for creating action steps, these are the actions or everyday considerations to bring into your moon practice.

Because the minors deal with our day-to-day lives, they are important to consider when creating action steps during your moon manifesting. This is especially true when you need to make a choice. Tarot can be helpful when both options seem like the best option but there can only be one. When pulling cards for your moon practice, the simple yet effective answers you will find from the minor arcana can determine what your next step right now will be.

The minors' nuances can change depending on other cards pulled during a reading as well as where these other cards are placed. For example, if you pulled the Two of Wands and directly to the right is the Three of Pentacles, the suggestion may be basing your next action step on finding help from someone to make it successful. Perhaps there is an action step you need to take for your intention during this moon phase but you aren't sure how to make it happen. The cards suggest here that seeking advice from someone with experience will be most helpful.

Pip or Minor Card Keywords

WANDS

Ace of Wands: New beginnings, creativity, innovative ideas
Two of Wands: Choice, balance, contemplation
Three of Wands: Reward for your efforts, committing to something new
Four of Wands: Structure, home, celebration
Five of Wands: Competition, struggle, disagreements
Six of Wands: Celebration of success, achievement, unequal relationship
Seven of Wands: Action needed, defensive, aggression
Eight of Wands: Movement, quick manifestation, swift action
Nine of Wands: Feeling intense, courage, defensiveness
Ten of Wands: Burdens, excess responsibility, feeling oppressed

SWORDS

Ace of Swords: Fresh start, sudden gift or opportunity, clarity on an idea
Two of Swords: Choice, balance, a need to decide
Three of Swords: Sorrow, heartbreak, accepting something is over
Four of Swords: Rest, meditation, retreat
Five of Swords: Walking away from something, quarrels, hostility
Six of Swords: Leaving, accepting help, secrets
Seven of Swords: Trickery, dishonesty, thinking you got away with something
Eight of Swords: Feeling lost, confused, overthinking causing you to be stuck

Nine of Swords: Self sabotage, sorrow, focusing too much on the past
Ten of Swords: Extreme situations, defeat in a big way, exaggerated fears

CUPS

Ace of Cups: Emotional fulfillment, joy, healing
Two of Cups: Balanced relationship, commitment, compatibility
Three of Cups: Celebration, family, deep bonds
Four of Cups: Detachment, missing opportunities because of attitude, boredom
Five of Cups: Regret, dwelling on the negative, loss
Six of Cups: Nostalgia, kindness, someone taking care of you
Seven of Cups: Indecision, unrealistic expectations, fantasy
Eight of Cups: Time to leave something behind, moving on, change within yourself
Nine of Cups: Wishes granted, indulgence, satisfaction
Ten of Cups: Happiness, fulfillment, spiritual happiness over material possessions

PENTACLES

Ace of Pentacles: Abundance of money or work, goals, clarity of life purpose
Two of Pentacles: Multitasking, balance, juggling life
Three of Pentacles: Mastery, finding spirituality within your work, artistry
Four of Pentacles: Hoarding, greed, being emotionally closed off
Five of Pentacles: Outsiders, money troubles, over-identifying with health issues
Six of Pentacles: Charity, giving and accepting help
Seven of Pentacles: Waiting for results after completing work, patience
Eight of Pentacles: Slow and steady progress, excellent work ethic, focused effort

Nine of Pentacles: Financial and material comfort, completion of a project, achievement

Ten of Pentacles: Wealth, security, strong business relationships

Choosing and Preparing Your Deck

An old wife's tale out in the tarot world suggests you cannot buy your own tarot deck, but it is very outdated and does not apply anymore. You can and should purchase your own deck because what you've chosen will be a deck you fully resonate with. If I did not buy my deck, I would not be where I am today. Renowned tarot reader Rachel Pollack writes in her foundational book on tarot reading, *Seventy-Eight Degrees of Wisdom* that the right deck can find you if you let it.[32]

As mentioned earlier, most tarot decks are based on the RWS deck, so it is much easier to choose than when I started reading. Once you feel comfortable using this deck, you can confidently try exploring other style decks.

While it can be visually helpful to have a moon themed deck, having one isn't necessary. The messages you receive from any deck you choose will give you the answers you need. I believe it is more important to have a tarot deck you fully resonate with rather than one that is moon themed. I like to use one tarot deck dedicated to the moon manifesting cycle I am working with just to keep the flow of the readings in line with my intention as well as to use the cards on my moon manifesting altar if needed.

Using a tarot deck with people in it will make it easier to gain insight when moon manifesting. Abstract symbols and animals can sometimes be confusing, especially if you are a newer reader. When you have some tarot reading hours and a solid basic understanding of the cards, tapping into your intuition will help you easily gain messages from any card.

Another way to try out a potential deck is to download a tarot app on your phone if available. Most apps are only a dollar or two, and some are free. Download a few, see how well you connect with their images, and

32. Rachel Pollack, *Seventy-Eight Degrees of Wisdom: A Tarot Journey to Self-Awareness*, 2nd ed. (Thorsons, 1997), 23.

then choose from them. Tarot phone apps are well worth having on your phone ready whenever you are.

It is always a good idea to cleanse a new deck. There are many ways to do this: knock on it three times to clear it of old energy, smoke cleansing, putting a selenite crystal on top, or leaving it in full moonlight. Additionally, you could use sound or Reiki energy if you are attuned. After your deck is cleansed, it is time to get to know one another. You can turn your deck with the card images facing you. Look at each card briefly and let the image imprint into your mind. Feel each card's energy and allow the images to merge with your energy. This is a great way to get close to these cards as you manifest through the moon phases.

When you finish your readings, you can store the cards in the box you received or a tarot bag. There are many options online, or you can make your own. Some tarot decks have flimsy boxes that fall apart easily, so I store those decks in makeup bags, labelling the front so I know which deck is nestled inside. I have also purchased beautiful silk bags for some of my decks. It is all up to personal preference and practicality when you use your decks often, but at the very least they should be stored in a place free from moisture and out of direct sunlight.

How to Read the Cards

If you are a tarot newbie, do not let that stop you from grabbing a deck. Start using it when you begin your moon manifesting. The guidebook that comes with it can give you insight on the cards if needed, but I recommend tapping into your intuition for moon manifesting and using the answers that come to you as you go through the tarot spreads. You can go back and look up the keywords afterward.

When you draw cards for the phases, pay attention to the little symbols, colors, and pictures your eye is first drawn to. Write down these clues and any thoughts you have even if they seem nonsensical or silly. These first insights are your initial intuitive thoughts and even in the smallest note you make there can be great insight, especially if you notice a pattern. Patterns indicate something to pay extra attention to and may be helpful when creating your action steps for the moon phase you are currently in. The best way to learn tarot is to use it consistently and take out your deck for everyday questions and guidance. The more you use it, the easier your intuition will flow.

EXERCISE: QUICK DRAW TO GET TO KNOW THE CARDS

Try this exercise to quickly assess if a deck will fit your energy for the moon cycle you are working with.

What you need:

Tarot cards plus their guidebook
Pen and paper

What to do:

Shuffle the tarot deck. Flip a card over and write down the name of the card and your first intuitive thoughts immediately. Do this with all the cards or as many as you feel like. When you are done, take out the guidebook and compare your answers. Write notes on each one and read it over a few times. Remember, your intuitive answers are correct. What you're doing now is meant to exercise your intuition and help you notice the smaller details in the cards.

Practice this often and try it out with a friend. It is a wonderful way for quick practice.

EXERCISE: VIBE OF THE DAY READING

Try this exercise out to gauge the energy of the day.

What you need:

Tarot deck

What to do:

You can do this at the start or end of your day. Try both ways and see which you like better. For the start of your day, take out your cards and shuffle them. As you do, think of what energy you should focus on that day. Pull a card. If you decide on the end of the day, take out your cards and shuffle them. As you do, consider how the energy of the pulled card related to your day and any insights you may have.

Tarot Moon Spreads

I have included a tarot spread for each moon phase and some extra ones in the bonus chapter. These spreads will help you stay on task with your current moon phase and harness the energy of the action steps you should be working on. Tarot spreads—cards with predetermined questions—keep you from pulling many cards, which can happen to newer and seasoned readers alike. In those cases, it's most often because your ego tries to take a front seat when you pull cards that may be tasking you to do a little extra inner work that keeps you pulling. It is okay; we have all been there and know it happens easily.

Tarot spreads are questions in particular positions, with specific questions regarding a subject. For example, a very well-known tarot spread calls for three cards for the past, present, and future. This spread can be used to ask about the timing on a situation you may have a question about or for general guidance on where to focus your energy. For example, for a past, present, and future spread, I pull the Ace of Cups for past, Queen of Swords for the present, and Seven of Swords for future. Right away, I decide some past emotions from a situation may be coming up for me and I need to communicate my thoughts and feelings clearly, or I will be left unhappy and burdened by them. If I use this spread during the waning gibbous phase, I may need to work through these emotions by straightforwardly chatting with someone who might have caused the upset. Even though taking this action may be hard to do, I have cleared that energy and made more room for my intention to solidify as I reach the end of my moon manifesting cycle.

While reading tarot cards isn't necessary, the practice can be helpful when manifesting and deciding on action steps through the moon phases. Sometimes it can be hard to read for ourselves because if we do not love the card pulled ... well, we pull another, and before you know it you have a mess of cards on the table and no answers. Another great benefit of tarot spreads is how it focuses energy. The tarot map for your moon intention or workings is all laid out in front of you. Pull a card for each question; unless instructed otherwise, you can pull one more for extra clarity. The tarot spreads in each moon phase chapter are tailored to that phase and can help you stay in the flow. They are optional, so feel free to use your own if you want to.

When learning to read tarot, it is important to read all the tarot books you can get your hands on. Reading different perspectives will give you a rich tapestry of knowledge to pull from when you do your tarot readings and spreads. Practicing with close friends and family is also a good option. It is a bit nerve-wracking initially, but the best way to get started is to go for it, especially because these close people will not mind if you need to stop and reference the guidebook a few times. Reference the book as needed but really try to form your intuitive thoughts first and *then* peek. It may also help to watch readers on social media to see how they conduct their readings. Even if their readings do not resonate with you, that is okay. What you're looking for is what does and does not work and, in the meantime, you will see unique styles of readings. When watching others read tarot, make sure not to fall into the comparison game. We all read from a unique perspective, and no two people read the same way. This is what makes the tarot community rich and diverse, just how we like it! Carrying your cards with you and practicing will boost your intuition and confidence as a new reader.

If you have not used tarot before, beginning with your new moon manifestation practice is the perfect time to start. If you do, you'll be building your magical and divination practices alongside each other. You will look back at your first moon manifesting cycle and fondly remember taking the initiative to learn and practice to build a uniquely you moon manifesting blueprint.

EXERCISE: NEW TAROT DECK INTERVIEW SPREAD

When you find the deck you want to use for your moon manifestation work, doing an interview tarot spread is an insightful way to connect to your new moon magic helper.

What you need:

Your tarot deck of choice

What to do:

Shuffle your cards. Lay them out in the following spread:

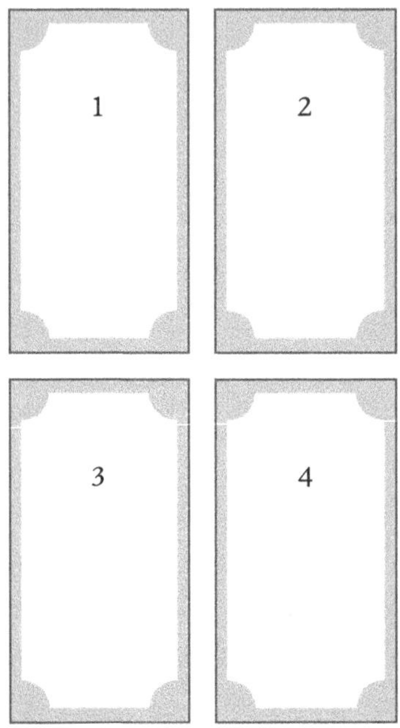

Card 1: What energy best describes your personality?
Card 2: How will we work best together?
Card 3: How can we effectively communicate with each other?
Card 4: Are you the deck I should work with for moon manifesting?

EXERCISE: THIS OR THAT TAROT SPREAD

Do you need to make a quick decision? If you are feeling stuck, this tarot spread can help you decide what to work on during the next moon cycle.

What you need:

Tarot deck

What to do:

Shuffle your cards and randomly choose two cards, placing them face up. Now, quickly flip the top card in the pile and place it above one of the cards in front of you. Do the same for the second card, placing it above the one on the table. Remember—do this quickly; do not overthink it! The card you added to is the intention you should go with, and the second card is why you should pursue it.

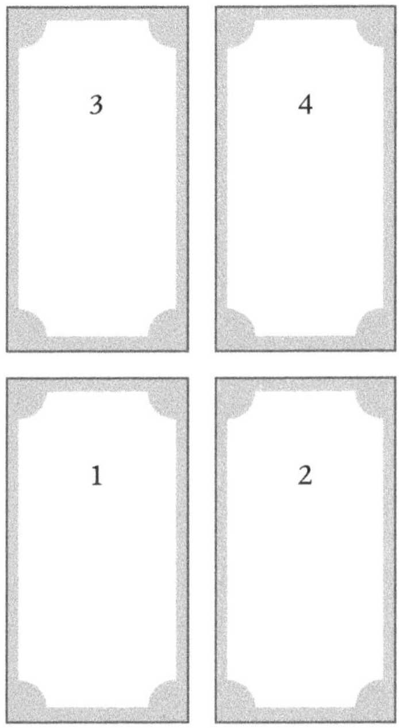

Do not be afraid to experiment with the cards to see what works for you. There is no rush to learn all the meaning and symbolism of tarot right away; take your time with your new deck. The most important aspect of learning tarot is to use the cards as much as you can. When manifesting, using tarot during each moon cycle will give you broader insight and practice working your intuitive muscles.

PART TWO
THE WORK

Now that you have prepared and practiced using your magical tools, it is time to start your moon manifestation work. The journey begins. You are ready to embark on your first moon cycle of manifesting. Each chapter in this part deals with a single moon phase, starting with the new moon and working your way through until the waning crescent phase. Each phase chapter lays out everything needed to do for that phase. I am excited for you to start your new leveled-up magical manifesting moon practice. Happy manifesting!

CHAPTER NINE

NEW MOON

Your lunar manifesting journey begins with the new moon. This lunar phase is about starting new things, creating fresh ideas, and trusting the universe and the new opportunities waiting for you right around the corner. Encompassing this energy means going on a journey defined by your soul, and then, through creating your intentions, shaping how you want this cycle to play out and sculpt your reality. Whether you want to work toward the house of your dreams or the job that makes your heart sing, you are the one who gets to make the choice.

When you step outside on a night where the stars twinkle above you, the moon may be hidden from your vision, but she is there. During the new moon, you will feel most open to new and exciting possibilities. Like the moon in darkness, your new ambitions are like seedlings: they are starting to stir underground and getting ready to grow and move toward the sky. The new moon phase also connects to the energy of your inner child and taps into the excitement of childlike energy when you feel ready to leap into something new and exciting. You need only what you already have.

Stepping into your full magical self can be exciting, if a bit scary. When that fear of change and newness presents itself, you know you are on the right path and ready to transform. Like a child standing on a diving board the jump may seem so high and scary, but you still take the plunge. Bravery is feeling a little scared but jumping anyway.

In this phase, the moon is preparing for the new cycle and ensuring you have fertile and viable energetic ground to flourish. At this point in the cycle, the new moon calls you to look inside yourself with no interference from her light. Here you decide what you want; whatever you choose will bring your special magic forth. Do not be afraid to think big; just know that sometimes it is the small steps that lead you to success.

Right now, the how of your manifestation is not as important as being mentally prepared and creating magical-focused energy to set you on the course designed just for you and what you most want. Being aware of your feelings during each new moon and journaling on them is helpful in planning your intentions as you learn to integrate the moon manifesting method into your life. Most of what you do magically involves intention and mindfulness of your thoughts. Like the moon, your feelings also ebb and flow from one phase to the next. Embrace that energy of change and use it to catapult your intention for this cycle.

The new moon shows you the potential lies within. She will also show you what you need to move energetically and what to clear to continue your desired path. As you fully combine your three lunar selves within the lunar anima, you will see that your outer world will follow suit—this is how you tap into your magic.

Moon Moment

The new moon is considered the first phase of the moon cycle. It is invisible in the sky because the sun, moon, and Earth are in complete alignment, blocking the sun's light and preventing us from us seeing the moon. The moon is in between the sun and the earth and leaves the earth's side dark because sunlight only shines from one direction from our perspective. The only time we can only see a new moon lit up is during a lunar eclipse. The new moon occurs every 29.5 days, and the energy lasts about three days.[33]

33. Arnold L. Lieber, *The Lunar Effect: Biological Tides and Human Emotions* (Anchor Press, 1978), 62–63.

New Moon

Lunar Spirit

As you prepare to start this moon cycle, it's most helpful to connect with your lunar spirit and tap into your intuitive sense to help create a focused magical mindset as you start to create your intention as well as actions that support that intention.

EXERCISE: NEW MOON MEDITATION

This meditation will help ground you as you start your moon manifesting journey.

What you need:

A quiet space
Moon journal and pen

What to do:

Sit in a chair or on the ground with your spine upright. Take a few breaths to bring yourself to this space. When you feel ready, say aloud: "New moon, I ask you to guide me in choosing the best intention for me or to embrace the intention I have chosen fully."

Now quiet your mind and become aware of your breath. Start sending each inhale deep into your core. As you do, begin making your inhales and exhales longer. Visualize soft white comforting light from the new moon surrounding your body. Imagine that this white comforting energy gently clears anything that no longer serves you.

Continue to focus on your breath and imagine the comforting energy cleansing your outer energy body that surrounds you. When you feel your energy has been balanced, thank the new moon. Say aloud: "New moon, please share any guidance with me about what I should focus on in this moon manifesting cycle."

Continue to focus on your breath. Be open and receptive to any guidance that may come up for you. Trust any intuitive vibrations and messages you receive. Continue to focus on your breath, inhaling and exhaling slowly. Stay in this space for as long as you would like and thank the moon for any information shared with you. Afterward, open your eyes, connect with your body, and write down any messages you received.

New Moon Lunar Spirit Focus

The new moon and the excitement of creating a new reality fit right in with inner child energy. Here you can harness the energy and wonder of your inner child to give you that little push into the enthusiasm for newness and assurance that the universe has your back. Through this powerful combination, you are creating a solid start to successfully manifesting with the moon cycle ahead. You can use this sparkly enthusiasm to help you create the action steps in this chapter by harnessing that inner child energy to dig deep into what you would like to manifest.

As a child, you may have had a favorite item and used it as your trusty companion to guide and comfort you. When you start manifesting with the moon, your trusty companion is the moon. Your uninhibited wonder also brings a sense of adventure and excitement to your intentions. Holding on to the eagerness of this youthful energy throughout the lunar cycle will help make those action steps easy and increase your success in manifesting your desired intention. If you stay in the excitement of your childlike vibration, creating action steps and achieving them can be met with that same excitement. Your trusting inner child encourages you to go all in because they know you have the support of the new moon.

We all have busy lives, but carefree and intentional focus will make it easier to bring your moon manifestations to life. Your inner child knows that your best advice comes from within, where your true wants and needs reside. Why give attention to things, people, and events that don't support or help you manifest your most beautiful life?

What about your inner child can help you manifest with the new moon? Let us explore your inner child now and see how this part of your subconscious can help your moon magic be successful. Your inner child has been collecting and receiving messages before you could consciously know or recall them. According to Carl Jung, your inner child can dictate many of your emotions in your daily life, even if you are not aware of it. When you lose conscious awareness of your inner child, you lose awareness of a part of yourself.[34] Bringing forth and being aware of your inner child creates a container of safety and success for you to embark on your new moon intention.

With this activation, you can tap into your true beliefs and change them when you feel they are not benefiting your manifesting goals. All emotions and memories are thoughts you have picked up along the way or things you have been told. You can change these and reroute those pathways in your brain to live a happier, healthier life.

EXERCISE: INNER CHILD RITUAL ACTIVATION

Here are some suggestions for activating your inner child to reconnect with them, so they can be fully present when you create your new moon intention. Stepping into this childlike energy can spark your imagination and reignite your creativity. Letting your inner child come out to play also helps you to remember the core of who you are, to help you remember who you were before the realities of adulthood took over. Children have an innate nature to trust that everything will work out. We need to embody this way of thinking as we create our intention for the new moon.

What you need:

An open imagination

What to do:

Choose one of the suggestions below and give it a try.

34. Margareta Sjöblom et al, "Health Throughout the Lifespan: The Phenomenon of the Inner Child Reflected in Events During Childhood Experienced by Older Persons," *International Journal of Qualitative Studies on Health and Well-being* 11, 1 (2016): 31486. doi .org/10.3402/qhw.v11.31486.

Do activities you enjoyed as a child. Did you like roaming outside, pretending you were in a fantasy world? Was coloring for hours something that made you happy? Revisit these small activities and see how your body and mind remember and quickly refocus on that joy.

Spend time with children and bring your inner child front and center to connect with them. Sit down and have a tea party or build some Legos with a little one. Remove yourself from the adult world for a while and see through their eyes. Just being present in that moment can help you relax and open your creative centers.

Practice mindful self-care. Simple tasks that comfort you are great for connecting to your inner child. Did you like wrapping yourself up in blankets like a burrito and tuning in to your favorite show? Splurge a bit on your favorite snacks from when you were younger. Go ahead and do something that brings you comfort.

Connect with your inner child and send love to them in quiet moments. When you have extra stress in your life or know substantial changes are ahead, it can cause you to retract from everything going on or bring up memories of when you felt this way in the past. Taking time to send your inner child some reassurance and love will help you process those feelings, making it easier for you now to face these challenges. Stand firm in the knowledge that you can support and comfort yourself—adult and inner child alike.

Consider these questions:

What excited you most as a child? What can you do to harness this energy to focus on your intention? When you have found or rediscovered that excited childlike energy, how can you use it? Weave the excitement into every action step and know you can revisit these feelings whenever you need inspiration.

EXERCISE: NEW MOON DEVOTIONAL

Curate this energy by connecting with the new moon with this devotional.

What you need:

The outdoors (if possible)

Moon journal and pen

What to do:

Step outside at night for this first phase moon devotional and sit in the darkness.

How does this feel for you? Clear your mind and stay in the present moment as long as possible.

Pay attention to the sounds, smells, and the feel of the darkness around you.

Imagine yourself soaking up the energy of the darkness and think about how this comforting energy will stay with you as you move through the upcoming phases.

Hold your hands to your heart and thank the moon for her comfort.

Journal or record any experience you may have had for future reference.

Lunar Mind

The new moon is a beautiful time to get your writing muscles working. This beginning phase of the moon cycle is about creating and manifesting the intentions you want. At times, some past thoughts, beliefs, and feelings can creep in as you focus forward on all the newness and creation. These thoughts are part of the process, and that is a good thing. When these thoughts and feelings appear, you are ready to let go and bring in improved things. Drawing or writing down your thoughts and feelings will help you focus on your intention and the action steps to get you there.

In this section, you'll use your creative energy to plant and sow your seeds of intention. This is where you fertilize your ideas and sprinkle them with positive thoughts while weeding out and letting go of limiting beliefs as they arise. Doing this work in the new moon phase helps you clear any stray thoughts and prepares you for the next phase you will be working with.

You may notice that you have become more attuned to fears or concerns that arise for you and that you are able to see more clearly what needs to be addressed first as part of the clearing-out process. Nonjudgmentally address those "weeds" of fears, doubts, and concerns. As you allow this process to flow, you will see doubts fall away, and your new thoughts will blossom because they have room to grow. You may also notice you can easily identify repetitive triggers and limiting beliefs. Identifying these limiting beliefs as soon as you see their pattern and proactively creating action steps to disengage from these behaviors will set you on the right path for a bountiful moon cycle.

Use these new moon prompts to help shape your intentions and solidify your thought processes related to them.

- What three actions can I take to move my intention forward?
- How do I feel about making recent changes?
- Who do I want to be at the end of this cycle?
- What boundaries do I need to set for my intentions to flourish?
- What am I grateful for right now?

Gratitude Suggestions

Write at least ten things you are grateful for during this moon phase, no matter how big or small. Establishing an attitude of gratitude is vital to your moon manifesting practice. For example:

- I am grateful for the opportunity to gain experience in abundance.
- I am grateful for being able to adjust my time to help make space to create my practice.
- I am thankful for my inspiring morning cup of coffee.

Affirmations

Following are several affirmations to try during this phase.

- I am worthy of living the life of my dreams.
- I release any storylines that do not serve me.
- I welcome abundance into my life.
- I am open to new possibilities.
- I embrace fresh starts and new beginnings.

Lunar Body

In this section you will start to incorporate the physical objects and practices to bring your moon practice together.

EXERCISE: NEW MOON ALTAR

Now it is time to personalize the altar you created for moon manifestation work for the new moon phase.

What you need:

New moon picture

Crystal (from listed suggestions on page 161 or one that is special to you)

4-inch white taper candle, candle holder, matches/lighter, and candle snuffer

What to do:

Place the picture or card that represents the new moon on your altar. Choose a new moon crystal from the list or find one that is extra sparkly when you think of what you want to manifest. Use your intuition to place the items where you feel they need or want to go.

Now light your white candle and say your intention three times. Focus on the cycle you are working on at this moment. When you are done, snuff the candle out—do not blow it out because we will continue to work on this intention.

Relight your candle whenever you come to this sacred space to journal or create action steps.

EXERCISE: NEW MOON ACTIONS

The new moon phase is where you start bringing in what you want and building your moon base of success. After working through the previous exercises, it is time to create your intention. You have a few days to tweak and mold this intention, so it is perfect for this cycle. When you decide on your intention for the moon cycle, write it down and leave it for a few hours. When you come back to it how does it make you feel? Do you need to change it at all?

Asking these questions as I create my new moon intention helps me make sure it is aligned with my energy and that I'll be ready to take on every action step needed to make it happen.

What you need:

Your moon altar
Moon journal and pen
Piece of paper

What to do:

Make a list of what you would like to bring in this lunar phase. Use your intuition to select one intention. Once you have it, write it down on a piece of paper or make it the background image on your phone/computer. Place it on your new moon altar and keep a copy of it somewhere you will see it throughout the moon cycle. Repeat the new intention a few times and really let it settle into your mind and feel good for you. When you are doing any of your moon manifesting work from now on during this cycle, be sure to repeat your intention or write it on whatever you work on.

Remember to write your intention as if it has already happened. For example, "I am excited I will be going on a vacation and can't wait to relax with friends" instead of "I want to go on vacation." You will be saying this intention a lot and using it throughout your moon manifesting cycle and magical work. Let it become a part of you for the next month. Step into this intention fully to ensure a successful cycle.

Tarot: The Fool

The Fool is the first card of the major arcana, numbered zero. This card starts the journey of self-realization and to me also represents a clean slate—the number zero is not attached to anything, so it is open to all possibilities. Now is the time to give yourself the expansion of newness and create your own shiny new reality.

On the Fool card, we see a figure standing precariously close to a cliff, but they do not seem too concerned about it. Their furry little friend is letting them know they are too close to the edge, but the Fool is not paying attention; they are focused only on their goals and the opinions of others do not sway them. The Fool also carries a small satchel with them, inside of which is said to be only the Fool's most prized possessions. See how even the Fool taps into their inner child, bringing along all they care about? They trust the universe will take care of the rest. We collaborate with the Fool in the new moon phase because this energy is like our inner child's energy and is a useful way to see this phase's possibilities. Let yourself embody the vibe of the Fool during the new moon phase, and you'll create openness, possibilities, and opportunities you may not have even considered before.

The activities included in this book are an effective way to focus your desires on the current moon cycle. Moon phase tarot spreads are designed to help you work through the moon phase energy and gain deeper insight to integrate your lunar spirit, mind, and body to create a magical confidence that will lead you to succeed with this method.

EXERCISE: YOU ARE NO FOOL TAROT WORKING

Try this Fool tarot exercise and spread for greater clarity when creating your intention and action steps for the new moon.

What you need:

Tarot deck

Moon journal and pen

What to do:

Find a surface you will be able to spread out cards on.

Take out the deck that has your favorite Fool in it, one in which you can see yourself as most aligned with your intention. Look at the card for a moment. As you bring your intention to the front of your mind, see yourself starting this new adventure. How do you feel about envisioning this? What thoughts come up for you? Write them down. Remember, the new moon and the Fool are here to guide you on your new endeavor. Now place your Fool card at the top of your reading area.

Give your cards a shuffle and pull two cards from the top of the deck. Place them below the Fool. Follow the spread diagram below to interpret what the cards mean.

EXERCISE: YOU ARE NO FOOL TAROT SPREAD

Tap into the energy of the Fool card in this exercise for insight on creating your intention.

What you need:

Tarot deck

Moon journal and pen

What to do:

Lay out the cards face down in a diamond shape as follows:

Card 1 is at the top of the diamond, card 2 to its right, card 3 at the bottom of the diamond, and card 4 to the left. Set the rest of the deck down and start with card 1. Flip it over. Answer the question for card 1, and write your insights in your moon journal. Do the same for the other three cards.

Card 1: What part of the Fool's energy is best for me to focus on for the new moon cycle?

Card 2: Where must I adjust to add my new action steps into my everyday life?

Card 3: How can I best support this intention?

Card 4: What should I release to make room for this new intention?

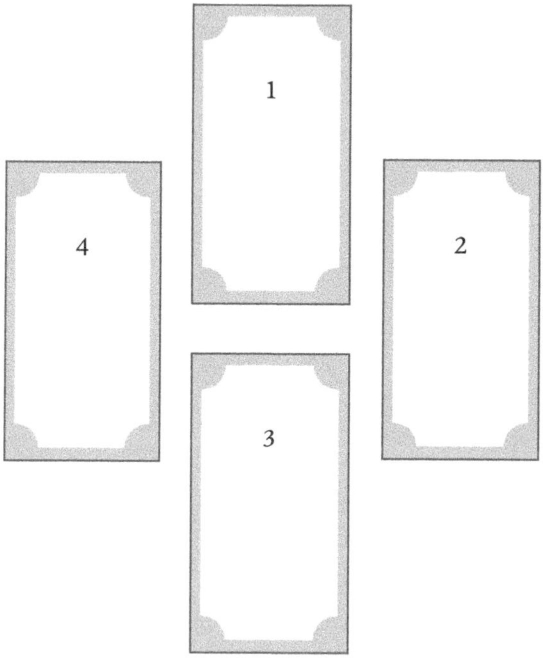

From the detailed answers of your tarot spread and Fool exercise, create at least three realistic steps to take during the new moon phase that involve a bit more effort than usual. Make sure these action steps support your intention and are easy to incorporate into your day.

SIGIL WORKING: NEW MOON

Using your intention, create a powerful sigil to kick off your moon manifestation cycle. For example, "I will buy a new car that is exactly what I need or better."

What you need:

Your sacred space
Notebook plus pen or pencils

What to do:

Get comfortable in your sacred space and pick up your paper and pen. At the top of the page, write your new moon intention. It should not be much longer than a sentence. If it is, shorten to a sentence. Once you have done this, go through and cross out all the vowels and double letters. From these letters we will now craft a symbol.

Start with whichever letter calls to you first and intertwine all of them until you have your sigil. Do not over-scrutinize what you make; just go with the flow of your intuition and see what you create. Leave enough room on the paper to draw three clockwise circles around the whole sigil. As you do this, say your full intention aloud three times. When finished, say, "This sigil has been activated. And so it is." Now you can leave your sigil on your altar or take a picture of it and use it as the background image on your phone or computer.

RECIPE: NEW MOON TEA

Try a refreshing blend of green tea with a hint of mint for a fresh start and to support your new moon practice. You can add a sprig of fresh mint and a wedge of lemon to your tea for revitalizing and inspiring energy.

What you need:

Your favorite green tea (bag or loose) for creativity and inspiration
A quarter slice of lemon for a fresh outlook
A sprig of fresh mint to clear any doubt and spark intuition

What to do:

Add ingredients to a cup of freshly boiled water. As you add the ingredients, think of your intention for this moon phase. Steep for six to eight minutes.

After it has steeped, stir three times clockwise as you say your intention aloud. Enjoy your tea as you envision a successful new moon cycle.

New Moon Closing Thoughts

You are now prepared to initiate the manifestation process. Take a deep breath and feel the excitement build in your mental, physical, and spiritual body. You are starting a new and exciting journey to embrace the moon's manifestation magic fully. You can now move forward, having paved the way for the next phase of creating life-changing action steps with the waxing crescent moon.

New Moon Correspondences

Suggestions that align with your new moon workings.

Deities: Selene, Ixchel

Herbs: Rosemary, yarrow, peppermint, milky oats, ginger

Incense: Sandalwood, myrrh

Crystals: Selenite, Himalayan salt, citrine

Oils: Orange, lemon

Colors: Black, dark blue

Keywords: Beginnings, setting intentions, seeds of potential

CHAPTER TEN

WAXING CRESCENT MOON

In the waxing crescent phase, an intuitive spark of the mind and heart has been lit. You now hold the flame to blaze the trail of your manifestations. Be mindful as you tap into these new thoughts and feelings and visualize your goals. Give some notice to those seeds you sowed on the new moon; how can you nurture them further? How can you ensure the soil is rich and fertile through your action steps? Now is the time to deepen and tailor your actions to your ultimate manifestation of the entire cycle. The crescent phase offers a force of light pushing forward within you and another element to help your new seedlings flourish. Follow her lead and step into this light to start illuminating your magical self.

With this growth phase, you need to reassure yourself that you will accomplish what's needed to create a successful moon manifesting cycle. Do not try to force action right now. See yourself step into that silvery sliver of moonlight and feel your actions, see them happening in your mind's eye.

By being intentional with your action steps, you will avoid being overwhelmed and step into your creative manifesting flow. Be sure to take breaks and rest when needed. Listen to your body and honor it. You want to keep action steps in the receiving flow and your lunar anima balanced.

Moon Moment

This phase is called the waxing crescent because the lit-up part of the moon is in the shape of a crescent and the word "waxing" means "increasing," referring to the light that will increase as the moon phase progresses. At this point, it is one-fourth lit. This is the moon's first step toward fullness. The waxing crescent moon rises before noon and sets around midnight, and this phase lasts about seven days. As the waxing crescent moves toward the perpendicular position at the first quarter moon, the sun and moon's gravitational pulls on the tides cancel each other out, decreasing the amount of tidal pull on Earth.[35]

Waxing Crescent Moon

Lunar Spirit

As you move into the waxing moon, now is the time to spark your intuitive fire and start creating action steps that are a bit bolder and bigger. Tuning into your lunar spirit at this phase will help you to keep magical focus and start to create a spiritual moon practice.

EXERCISE: WAXING CRESCENT MEDITATION

Connect with the waxing crescent for determined focus during this phase.

What you need:

A quiet space
Moon journal and pen

35. "Phases of the Moon," Kopernik Observatory & Science Center, accessed November 25, 2024, https://www.kopernik.org/visitor-info/science-park/phases-of-the-moon/.

What to do:

Sit in a chair or on the ground with your spine upright. Say aloud: "Waxing moon, I ask you to ignite a fire within me to give me all the passion and wisdom needed to be successful in my moon intention."

Quiet your mind and become aware of your breath. Inhale and exhale slowly. Now start sending each inhale deep into your core as you gradually make your inhales and your exhales longer. Visualize a silver light from the moon connecting with your solar plexus region (between your sternum and belly button). Imagine this light sparking a fire within you. The fire and the silver light grow bigger and brighter with every inhale, filling you with excitement and inspiration. As you breathe, visualize the silver energy flowing throughout your body, infusing all your energetic spaces and filling them with this light where needed.

Take one long inhale and exhale with a whooshing sound. Then allow your breath to return to normal. Say aloud: "Waxing moon, please give me a sign over the next few days to indicate that I am taking the right action." Continue to focus on your breath. Inhale and exhale. Be open to any intuitive information that comes to you. Trust any sensations, feelings, or messages you experience. Continue to focus on your breath. Inhale and exhale. Stay in this receiving space for as long as you would like. To end, thank the moon for its energy and guidance, and take one last inhale and exhale.

Now open your eyes, connect with your body, and write down any information you received.

Waxing Crescent Lunar Focus

Now that you have set your intention in motion for this moon cycle, it is time to really start to feel it happening. Here your action steps need to be aligned with building the base of whatever you want to manifest. This phase is where you start to lean into your intuition to make the best-aligned action steps for your success. Trust in yourself and the universe is key. Focus your energy on this phase of the moon's energy. Using the activation below will help direct the abundance flow toward you; this can be done on the first day of the cycle or daily depending on how you are feeling and how focused you are. Be sure to ground after doing this so you can fully integrate the experience.

EXERCISE: TRUST YOUR INTUITION RITUAL ACTIVATION

Activate your third eye to help with your action step creation.

What you need:

A quiet place
Moon journal and pen

Optional:

Crystal for grounding

What to do:

Take a moment to sit and center yourself, at your moon altar if you can, and take a few deep breaths. Now bring your attention to your third eye, the area between your eyes. Imagine a soft glowing light in your third eye area and see it clearing out any debris. (I see it as gray smoke.) Now place your left pointer finger on the area between your eyes and tap it lightly three times. Say, "My intuitive centers are clear and any messages I receive will be for my highest good."

Next, put your hand on your heart, and in your mind's eye, see your third eye gently absorb the glow. When the glow is gone, take three deep breaths and say, "So it is." Open your eyes.

Be sure to ground yourself. For example, you can run your hands under cool water, stand outside with your bare feet on the ground, or sit with your favorite crystal for a few minutes.

Now you have activated your third eye, and your intuition is ready to guide you into the next phase. Before moving on, however, do not skip taking a few moments to ground; this step is particularly important. It's essential that you stay grounded to create and integrate your actions for a successful manifestation. Grounding also helps to keep you in the manifestation flow by anchoring you to your intention.

EXERCISE: WAXING CRESCENT DEVOTIONAL

Using a specially channeled chant I created for you, harness the waxing crescent moon energy.

What you need:

A piece of paper with this chant: "Blessed be the waxing crescent moon, a symbol of growth and potential. I welcome your energy into my life as I embark on this journey of manifestation and growth."

The same chant written in your moon journal, plus a pen

What to do:

If you are able, sit outside or near a window. Take a few minutes to center yourself and take a few cleansing breaths. Take a few moments to reflect on what action steps will support your intention during the waxing crescent lunar phase.

Gaze up to the moon and feel the powerful light that now shows itself during this phase. Feel the heavy, calm energy as it washes over you, filling you with ambition and confidence. Repeat the chant you wrote down three times, aloud if possible. Hold your hands up in prayer position and thank the moon for her guidance and energy. Sit quietly for as long as you want, and journal or record any experience or messages you may have received afterward.

Lunar Mind

Here we are in your first action phase of the moon cycle. Making sure your intention and how it feels in your body are aligned will be most beneficial for you now. Trusting your intuition is important as you go through all the phases, but here is where the real work begins. Aligning your mind's eye to your desires helps you navigate the moon's energy and your purpose. This phase calls to your inner knowing or that gut feeling deep inside your body to come forth and take the reins of your destiny.

- How am I feeling as I start this journey?
- I am confident in my intention because …

- I believe in my intuition, and it will guide me. I will listen because ...
- How can I be sure I am in abundant flow right now? This looks like ...
- I stand in the sliver of moonlight; how does this make me feel?

Gratitude Suggestions

During this phase look for gratitude in whatever action step you take or create. List ten ways you have tapped into your ambitious moon magic. For example:

- I am grateful for the energy of moving away from the thoughts of my ego.
- I am grateful for the challenges presented to me so I can grow and expand.
- I am grateful for the space of uncertainty to make grounded decisions.

Affirmations

Try these affirmations during the waxing crescent phase.

- I choose this moment to step into abundance.
- My journey is divinely guided.
- I create with focus and flow.
- I am the creator of my reality.
- I trust that I am always supported and have everything I need.

Lunar Body

As you begin to welcome the change of the waxing crescent phase, you will now start to move and change your physical moon manifesting spaces.

EXERCISE: WAXING CRESCENT ALTAR

The waxing crescent phase is the time to refresh our altar and energy. If there are items from the last cycle you want to leave, that is fine—just make sure to rearrange the altar so you can still do your magical workings there comfortably. Start feeling and tap into the expansiveness of this phase as you do your spell work at your altar.

What you need:

Crescent moon picture
Crystal from the correspondences list at the end of this chapter (page 161)
4-inch green taper candle, matches / lighter, candle snuffer

What to do:

Remove the picture of the new moon from the last phase and replace it with one of the crescent moon picture or an item that represents the crescent moon to you. At this time, also replace the crystal and candle with your new ones along with anything else from the previous moon phase on your altar.

Take a moment to connect with your altar and feel the shift in energy. Light your candle and repeat your intention for this moon cycle aloud three times. When you are finished, snuff out the candle. Relight it whenever you are working at your altar during this phase.

EXERCISE: WAXING CRESCENT ACTIONS

Now that you have activated your intuition, it is time to use it. During this phase, let your intuition take the lead regarding the actions needed to support your intentions. The small but mighty sliver of light from the moon is pushing you forward and lighting the way. What can you do to give your actions an extra push? When creating these steps, envision them as already in progress and successful. Do not worry about details; just start moving toward your intention. Creating your action steps is vital to the moon manifesting process and exciting as you move into changing your reality Use this exercise to get started.

What you need:
Moon journal and pen

What to do:
Sit near your moon altar. Make a list of your action steps based on your intuition—just the first few things you think of. The universe wants you to start with these, so trust there is a good reason.

Use the tarot spread included in this chapter (page 159) to help you narrow down two or three actions, depending on how involved they are. You can also use divination to create smaller action steps if needed. Set a date to start or have them done by. Even though you should start these actions as soon as possible, you may need to plan them out; this will help you stay accountable.

Celebrate the start of this process. You are on your way to creating a new way of life for yourself, and that deserves celebration. Give yourself credit for leaving your comfort zone and trying something new.

Tarot: The High Priestess

The High Priestess is associated with the Egyptian goddess Isis. The horns on her headpiece are a symbol of prosperity and fertility. This major arcana card asks you to call upon and listen to your intuition. She reminds you that you are divinely guided and fully ready to harness your intuition. When you look at the High Priestess card, both the crescent moon resting at her feet and the horned shaped headpiece are easy to spot.

The High Priestess also reminds you that you can discover much about yourself and your true feelings in moments of silence. Practice meditation or even sit quietly and clear your mind, and you'll find that your intuitive insight can give you answers you did not even know you were searching for. Sometimes the things you seek in your life are unexplainable, and this card wants you to trust the divine mysteries of the universe and allow them to guide you.

Your intuition was activated as you stepped into this phase. The spark has ignited your heart, mind, and spirit—you have all the magic you need. It is time for you to be still and listen. Dive deeper into your magical self and see what you can bring to light. Your emotions guide you but do not rule you, and the High Priestess wants you to recognize your deeper emotions but not let them envelope you in a way that can keep you from action. What is forming in your mind's eye that will help to propel you forward in your intention for this phase?

You sowed your seeds at the new moon, and now they must be nurtured. It is time to moisten the earth with new insight from your intuition. The first showing of the light in the crescent moon is the universe lighting your path to what you are seeking. Step into this intuitive light and let your higher self guide you down the right path. As you start to open your intuitive centers and rely on this higher energetic self, seeking guidance from the cards can help you hone and develop your intuition. Receiving guidance from the High Priestess can prevent feelings of overwhelm.

EXERCISE: HARNESS HIGH PRIESTESS ENERGY

Harness energy and guidance from the High Priestess for your waxing crescent moon workings.

What you need:

High Priestess tarot card

Waxing crescent picture from moon altar

Moon journal and pen

What to do:

Take your High Priestess tarot card and journal to your moon altar. Ground and center yourself, taking a few deep breaths and releasing them slowly. Pick up the waxing crescent picture from your altar. Sit for a few minutes and look at all the details of the tarot card and moon picture. Note how you feel when you look at the pictures.

Close your eyes and imagine the small sliver of light from the waxing crescent moon creating a path. In your mind's eye, walk down that path until you reach a garden. As you walk into it, you see the high priestess sitting on her throne and looking your way. Introduce yourself and ask how you can further expand your intuition. Listen for any guidance she offers and thank her when she has spoken. As you go to turn back to the path, she stops you and tells you to harness this moon phase and let the moon's light guide you. Thank her again and proceed back down the path. Gradually become aware of your surroundings and slowly open your eyes.

Return the picture to the altar and place the High Priestess card near it for the remainder of this phase. Journal about your experience and any messages shared with you.

EXERCISE: LIGHTING THE INTUITIVE SPARK TAROT SPREAD

Try this tarot spread for guidance from your higher self regarding the waxing crescent phase.

What you need:

Tarot deck

Moon journal and pen

What to do:

Shuffle your tarot deck and think of how you are activating your intuition. Find the High Priestess card and place it on the table. Now take the cards above and below the High Priestess in the deck and place the top one above the High Priestess card and the bottom one below the High Priestess card on the table. Shuffle again. Now draw one card for the right side of the

High Priestess and one for the left side. Place them on the corresponding side of the High Priestess card.

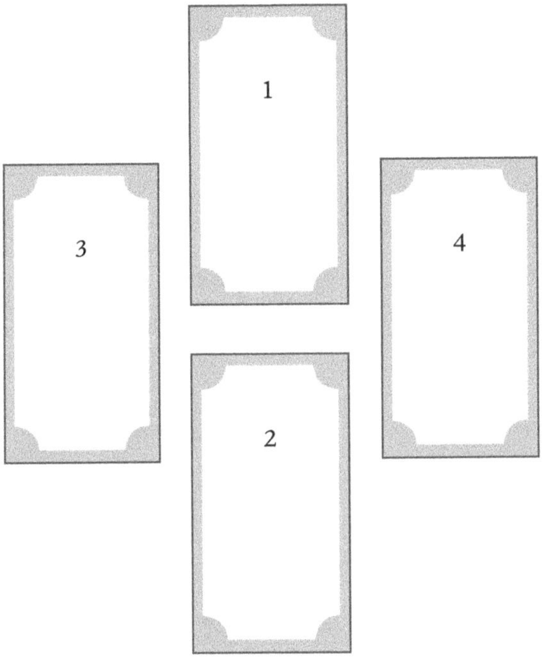

Card 1 (top card): What message does my higher self have for me?

Card 2 (bottom card): How can I best stay grounded as I illuminate my intuition?

Card 3 (left card): This card tells you why you need to trust your intuition.

Card 4 (right card): What is the best way for me to align with my higher self?

From the answers you received, focus on any words, phrases, or feelings that show up when you are ready. These may be important messages. Decide how you will best include working on your intuition throughout the day. As you create your action steps for this phase, use this newly activated insight to guide you. Know that you are being supported by the universe and tap into that energy whenever you need to.

SIGIL WORKING: WAXING CRESCENT

Use this sigil in your waxing crescent moon workings. Use one of your action steps to craft the phrase that will become your sigil for this moon phase, such as, "I will sell any items in my house I don't need."

What you need:

Paper and pen or pencils

What to do:

Get comfortable in your sacred space and pick up your paper and pen. At the top of the page, write your intention. As before, it should not be much longer than a sentence, so shorten it as needed. Once you have done this, go through and cross out all the vowels and repeating letters. From these letters we will now craft a symbol.

Start with whichever letter calls to you first and intertwine all of them until you have your sigil. Do not over-scrutinize this process; just go with the flow of your intuition and see what you create. Leave enough room on the paper to draw three clockwise circles around the whole sigil. As you do this, say your full intention aloud three times. When finished, say, "This sigil has been activated. And so it is." Now you can leave your sigil on your altar or take a picture of it and use it as the background image on your phone or computer.

RECIPE: WAXING CRESCENT TEA

The comforting blends below will guide you to focus on your moon intention during this phase. During this phase, a soothing floral tea can help you focus and prepare for your next big action steps toward your intention. I suggest chamomile tea with a touch of lavender, a perfect blend for calming the mind and focusing your energy for successful moon manifesting.

What you need:

1 C water fresh off the boil
Chamomile tea (loose or bag)
Lavender tea bag or a sprig of English lavender
1 tsp honey

What to do:

Add the ingredients to your cup of freshly boiled water. Let the tea steep for about ten minutes. After, stir the tea clockwise three times while seeing your doubts dissipate in the swirls in the water. As you sip the tea, feel it filling you with a soft purple light and creating a space of calm, focused energy.

Waxing Crescent Closing Thoughts

The waxing crescent phase ignites your "get 'em" energy and starts to point you toward what steps to take. When you start to work with this energy and begin to understand how to use your intuition daily, your moon manifesting process will start to develop in a way that is most effective for you. On to the first quarter moon and diving into your big action for that phase.

Waxing Crescent Correspondences

Consider these choices for the waxing crescent moon for your moon magic.

Deities: Yemaya, Cerridwen

Herbs: Laurel, lavender, nettle, raspberry leaf, bergamot

Incense: Orange, floral

Crystals: Tiger's eye, diamond, kyanite

Oils: Vanilla, lavender, clove

Colors: Yellow, amber

Keywords: Gathering resources, fine tuning, stay focused

CHAPTER ELEVEN

FIRST QUARTER MOON

The first quarter moon phase urges you to step fully into your intention with your first big action. Laser focus on making big moves and envision a positive outcome. The increasing light of this phase offers you the confidence you need to succeed. Here, you start to formulate your stream of action steps in an organized and doable way. Enjoy this process and see the changes in your mindset as you take control of what you want right now. See your light grow as the moon's light grows above you. You and your magic are now working in coordination.

The first quarter moon is shining bright overhead, and you can use its strong energy of success to dig deep and create bigger actions that will move the dial of your intention. The movement in this phase is expansive and creative. Now that you are stepping into action-oriented energy, you must realize the choices you make at this point are changing the trajectory of your reality. Knowing you can direct the outcome based on your intuitive decisions from this point on is an exciting and powerful realization.

Moon Moment

The moon is half-light and half-dark in the second major phase of the moon cycle. This phase occurs in the first quarter of the moon cycle before the full moon. The first quarter moon rises about noon and sets at midnight. You can easily see this phase illuminated high in the evening sky. This phase is called the first quarter because it has completed one quarter of its orbit around Earth and lasts for about three nights. With this phase's extra energy, you may be a bit hungrier or thirstier than usual. Dreams may become more vivid, and you might experience a tendency to overwork.

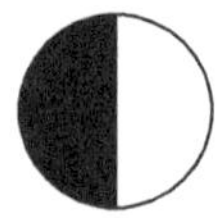

First Quarter Moon

Lunar Spirit

The first quarter phase may challenge what your naysaying ego has to say. Being fully present in your lunar spiritual self can help move past these unneeded whisperings so you may focus on substantial change.

EXERCISE: FIRST QUARTER MEDITATION

This meditation focuses on your throat area to open more space and freedom to say what you want in an effective way.

What you need:

A quiet space
Moon journal and pen

What to do:

Sit in a chair or on the ground with your spine upright. Visualize in your mind's eye that you are sitting outside under the night sky, and the first quarter moon is close to you. Feel the warm glow on your skin and see it filling you with confidence and ambition about your intention.

Now quiet your mind and become aware of your breath. Inhale and exhale slowly. Start sending each inhale deep into your core. Gradually make your inhales and your exhales longer. Visualize the glowing moon energy focusing on your throat area. See it clearing any blocks that are keeping you from expressing your wants and needs constructively. As you breathe, visualize the glowing energy flowing throughout your body and infusing all your energetic spaces, filling them with this light where needed.

Take one long inhale and exhale with a whooshing sound. Then allow your breath to return to normal. Say aloud: "First quarter moon, thank you for clearing any communication blocks I had and giving me a boost of motivation to curate action steps for a successful manifestation."

Continue to focus on your breath. Inhale and exhale. Be open to any intuitive information that comes to you. Trust any sensations, feelings, or messages you experience. Continue to focus on your breath. Inhale and exhale. Stay in this receiving space for as long as you like. When you feel you've done enough, thank the moon for its energy and guidance. Take one last inhale and exhale. Open your eyes, connect with your body, and write down any information you received.

First Quarter Lunar Focus

Your voice is important in your moon manifestations. You need to communicate your needs and wants clearly and confidently. Effective communication may also include setting boundaries for those around you as you start to pave your new way of living. Unfortunately, more than ever today, we are encouraged to say yes to situations to keep everyone happy. Saying yes to everyone else's needs can dampen your magic. You may feel you are not being authentic to yourself and what you need at that moment. Adding the activation in the next exercise to your morning routine before you start your day can help you to be mindful of how you use your words and to say no effectively.

EXERCISE: SPEAK MY TRUTH RITUAL ACTIVATION

When creating bigger actions toward your moon intention, it is important to be able to say what you need regardless of what others may believe. Try this activation to give yourself the power of self-truth.

What you need:

Warm beverage of your choice

Spoon

What to do:

After preparing your warm beverage of choice, bring a spoon and the beverage to your moon altar to sit. Take a moment to center yourself by taking a few deep breaths. Pick up your beverage and think about your actions so far regarding this moon cycle's manifestation. Say thank you three times and take a sip of your beverage after you say it each time.

Now think about what you want your bigger action to be. Place your spoon in your beverage and say the action with a strong voice. Stir three times. As you do, say, "I will take aligned actions to serve my manifestations and communicate my needs effectively." Stir again three times. State your full intention for this moon cycle three times loudly. Stir three times. Say, "And so it is" three times. Sip your beverage until you feel your words have fully integrated.

Recenter yourself and place your beverage down. Hold your hands to your heart and feel the warm, grounding, loving energy the next time you sip your drink. Take a deep breath and let it out slowly.

Go about your day. When a situation comes up, remember the warm energy of your ritual activation and express yourself confidently.

EXERCISE: FIRST QUARTER DEVOTIONAL

Connect with the first quarter moon with this devotional.

What you need:

Moon journal and pen or pencil
A quiet place (outside if possible)

What to do:

If you are able, sit outside or near a window. Take a few minutes to center yourself and take a few cleansing breaths. Take a few moments to reflect on what bigger action steps will support your intention during the first quarter lunar phase. As you sit under the light of this first quarter moon, give attention to any doubts or fears these bigger actions may bring up.

Say, "May the growing light of the first quarter moon bless me with determination and courage as I create my new reality. May the doubts and fears I present now be burned away in the strong but loving moonlight."

Cup your hands in front of you and imagine the fears and doubts you brought forward today sitting in your hands. Offer them to the moon and see them dissipate and be transmuted. Sit for as long as you like, letting this lighter, more confident you integrate. Thank the moon for her time and write about your experiences in your journal.

Lunar Mind

As this first quarter phase gifts you with more direct energy, you will start to feel the universe shift around you. You may feel clearer about your intention, and the way is now illuminated. Just as the first quarter moon is half-light and half-dark, you are starting to find your footing. This phase calls to your inner focus.

You see how your goal is attainable, and your inner calling shifts to meet the physical reality. Allow your renewed confidence to flourish. Do not hold back, take the advice of this moon phase energy, and as you align, you will also begin to hyper-focus on what essential steps are next. Try the suggested prompts to guide you and make the most of the first quarter moon energy.

- What expectations are creeping up, and how can I release them?
- How do the recent changes from my actions feel?
- How can I make sure to keep my actions aligned with my intention?
- Is it time for me to re-evaluate my action steps?
- What can I do to stay in the moon's energetic flow?

Gratitude Suggestions

For this big-action moon phase, it is time to make our gratitude practice bigger as well. Create ten big reasons why you are grateful right now. What big accomplishments are you most grateful for? Here are some examples:

- I am excited and grateful for all new possibilities.
- I am in abundant flow and will do what I need to keep it going with a thankful heart.
- I am grateful for this new expansive energy, and I accept it.
- I am thankful for my new magical laser focus.

Affirmations

Here are some affirmations when doing work during this phase.

- I am confident in my actions.
- I release all expectations.
- I trust my perfectly timed flow of abundance.
- My moon manifestation is fully in the flow.
- I am calm and open to receive.

Lunar Body

Incorporating these physical aspects into your first quarter moon practice will move the dial on your intention and refocus what you genuinely want to accomplish during the moon cycle.

During this phase you will feel the big energetic push from the first quarter moon, not only throughout your spirit and mind but also your body. Step into your actions confidently and positively.

EXERCISE: FIRST QUARTER ALTAR

Make your moon altar more colorful this phase, with bigger crystals and candles. Go all out. You want to feel that this altar fully represents all the growth you have done so far and your commitment to absorbing all of it.

What you need:

First quarter moon picture or an item to represent it
Crystal for this phase (see list of suggestions at the end of this chapter or your own)
4-inch blue taper candle, lighter or matches, candle snuffer

Setup Instructions:

Remove the waxing crescent moon picture and replace it with a first quarter moon picture or item representing the first quarter moon for you. Next, choose a crystal that feels the best to you and harnesses that growing energy for the first quarter moon. Place the items on your altar and remove anything placed there for the previous phase. Take a moment to connect with your altar and feel the energy shift.

Now light your candle and repeat your intention for this moon cycle three times. Snuff out the candle when you are finished and light whenever you work at your altar during this phase.

EXERCISE: FIRST QUARTER ACTIONS

Now is the time to make those unseen parts of your lunar intention a physical reality. At this point of the lunar cycle, it's key to focus your energy on what you are manifesting. What's needed in this phase is building on your previous action steps and making them more expansive. Step into these action steps with joy and excitement and remember to engage in that childlike trust for the universe to recognize your actions and guide you forward.

You have all the tools you need to reach your goals, so now it's time to use them confidently. Make bold moves. You may feel like you're jumping off a high dive—you know everything will be fine but still feel scared. Anxiety may try to hold you back, but you have what you need as well as an unclouded vision of your manifestation. The time to expand is now, so let's begin. Remember, you are building on previous action steps with bolder moves. Before beginning, ask yourself: How can you make this even bigger?

What you need:

Moon journal and pen

What to do:

Sit yourself in front of your moon altar. Ask yourself how you can get this intention moving with innovative ideas and steps. Even small adjustments can bring about substantial changes. Write your answers as truthfully as possible.

Keep yourself focused and grounded. Step into this receiving energy and expand, even if it feels a little nerve-wracking. Remind yourself that this is how your intention will become a reality, and trust the process. Do something you have not done before related to your manifestation for this cycle. Step out of your normal mindset and think creatively for new ideas and inspiration.

Tarot: The Magician

You started this journey with the Fool's energy and tapped into your intuition with the High Priestess. Now it is time to start streamlining your manifestation with the Magician. The Magician shows you that you have everything you need internally to manifest your intention for the lunar cycle.

He calls you to step into a clear stream of consciousness as you mold and shape your reality. The Magician harnesses the energy of creation and participates in every aspect of it. He does not try to control or direct this energy; he lets it flow through and around him. The Magician then observes outcomes and keeps mental note of what works and what does not.

The Magician recognizes the polarity of everything around him. He wants you to see the half-light and dark of the first quarter moon to recognize that polarity within yourself. The best way to harness the magic of your light and dark sides is to fully accept your innate magic and create the actions that will move your intention to the finish line at the end of the lunar cycle.

It is time to rededicate yourself to your goals and fully tap into your magic as you move toward the next phase. Now is the time to shift and reorganize your actions, intentions, and mindset. The seedlings of your desires are starting to grow and stretch; it is time to be productive and take action-aligned steps. Start to recognize how your reality has changed since the new moon and is still doing so. Fine-tune your next actions because you are well on your way to bringing your intention for this lunar cycle to life.

The Magician guides you to enjoy the creation process as you move forward, using your newfound abilities and tools to create steps that are uniquely you.

EXERCISE: THE MAGICIAN'S FIRST QUARTER POLARITY WORKING

In this exercise, we see what the Magician has to say and receive guidance through a tarot spread that will guide our first quarter moon action steps.

What you need:

Tarot deck

Moon journal and a pen

What to do:

Go to your moon altar and place the Magician card on it. Take a few moments to look at all the elements of the Magician card and write down what stands out to you. Next, shuffle your deck. Draw four cards and place them near the Magician.

Look at these cards and write about any symbols, colors, or intuitive feelings you receive from them in your moon journal.

The first card on your left (card 1) represents your positive traits regarding taking big actions. Write them down in list form. The second card from your left (card 2) represents your shadow aspects regarding taking big actions. Write those down in list form. The third card from the left (card 3) is the Magician's advice for steeping in your magical actions. Write those in list form. Finally, the last card (card 4) is guidance from the first quarter moon about the direction you must go for success. Write this down in list form.

Now look at your answers in the cards and notice the ebb and flow of your light and dark polarities. Are some similar? Can you transform a shadow quality to supercharge a positive quality? Use this as extra guidance when creating your actions for this moon phase. Integrate the advice of the Magician and the first quarter moon when taking your next big action.

EXERCISE: GATHER YOUR MAGIC TAROT SPREAD

Explore how the power of the elements can guide you and send you messages about your moon journey so far.

What you need:

This tarot spread and tarot cards

Moon journal and a pen

What to do:

Shuffle your cards and place four cards face-up next to each other: these are positions 1 through 4. They represent the elements: water, earth, fire, and air. You will receive a message from each of them here.

Next find the Magician in your deck. Then choose the third card after it and place it above the row of cards you previously pulled. This is card 5.

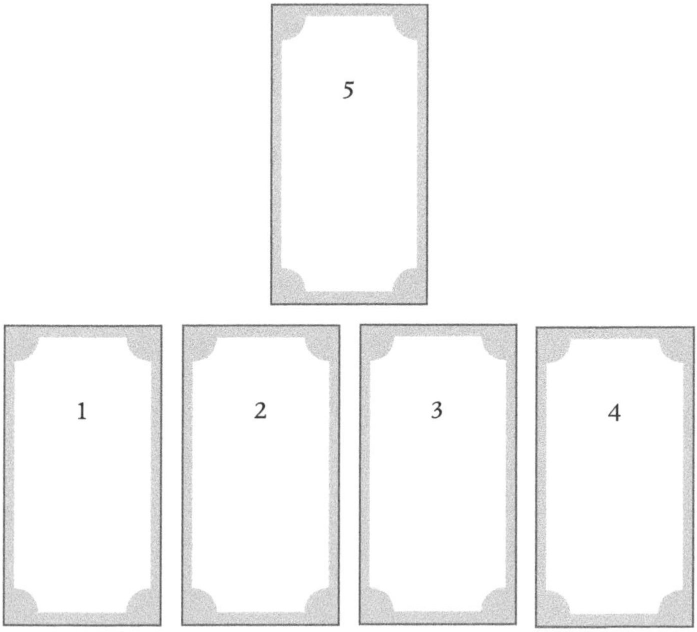

Card 1: Water: What emotion must I work through to move forward?
Card 2: Earth: What everyday habit do I need to shift?
Card 3: Fire: How can I fuel my ambition?
Card 4: Air: What recurring thoughts need to be reframed?
Card 5: (Top): What message does the Magician have for me?

SIGIL WORKING: FIRST QUARTER

Create a powerful sigil for each phase of your moon manifestation cycle. Use your favorite inspiring phrase to craft a sigil for this moon phase. For example, consider this quote, attributed to Thomas Edison: "Genius is one percent inspiration and ninety-nine percent perspiration."[36] Thomas Edison said this, but you do not need to add the creator of the quote to your sigil.

36. Adam Chandler, *99% Perspiration: A New Working History of the American Way of Life* (Pantheon Books, 2025), 14.

What you need:

Paper and pen or pencils

What to do:

Get comfortable in your sacred space. Pick up your paper and pen, and write your favorite inspiring phrase out at the top of the paper. It should not be much longer than a sentence, so shorten it as needed. Once you have done this, go through and cross out all the vowels and repeating letters. From these letters we will now craft a symbol.

Start with whichever letter calls to you first and intertwine all of them until you have your sigil. Do not over-scrutinize what you make; just go with the flow of your intuition and see what you create. Leave enough room on the paper to draw three clockwise circles around the whole sigil. As you do this, say your full intention aloud three times. When finished, say, "This sigil has been activated. And so it is." Now you can leave your sigil on your altar or take a picture of it and use it as the background image on your phone or computer.

RECIPE: FIRST QUARTER TEA

As you are turning up your action steps and entering this powerful first quarter moon phase, use these blends to foster an environment of excitement. Energize yourself with a zesty and invigorating tea for this moon phase that will keep you motivated as you create bigger and bolder action steps. This bold combination of black tea, ginger, and a slice of orange will kick your energy into high gear.

What you need:

1 C hot, freshly boiled water
Black tea for a boost of magical power
Fresh ginger or ginger tea to add a boost of motivation
An orange slice to awaken your senses
Cooling rack
Your mobile phone

What to do:

Add your ingredients to a mug and let steep for three to five minutes. On your phone, pull up a picture of what your intention would look like in reality. For example, if your intention this phase is for a new car, save a picture of the one you want. As you sip your tea, imagine in your mind's eye the biggest and best outcome for what you will bring to fruition this cycle.

When finished, lay your orange slice on a rack to dry out. Once it has dried completely, place it on your altar as a reminder to dream big and take big steps to achieve your desires.

First Quarter Closing Thoughts

This phase was all about big action, and even though it may feel more expansive than you are used to, do not let that stop you from going all in. You are moving through the phases now; big action is how you call in big results. It is up to you to start creating change in your life, and with the energy of the first quarter phase, you can do just that. Next, you'll head into the waxing gibbous phase to nurture the seedlings of your lunar intention.

First Quarter Moon Correspondences

Use this list of correspondences for the first quarter moon phase.

Deities: Mnemosyne, Circe

Herbs: Oregano, masterwort, star anise, carnation, oak

Incense: Geranium, patchouli, amber

Crystals: Red jasper, calcite, red chalcedony

Oils: Lemon, peppermint, patchouli

Colors: Orange, gold

Keywords: Perseverance, taking charge, motivation, doing

CHAPTER TWELVE

WAXING GIBBOUS MOON

The waxing gibbous phase calls you to nurture the action steps already in process and lead with your heart. Decide how this moon manifestation period feels for you both physically and energetically.

Now's the time to embrace the abundance mindset and integrate it into your new action steps. Harness all facets of this manifestation process and use it as an opportunity to learn about yourself and the new, higher-vibrational you. Note how this cycle has changed your intuitive vision and how your awareness of your energy is more powerful than it was even a few weeks before.

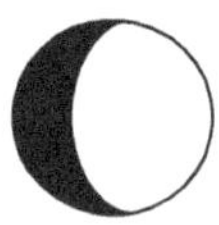

Waxing Gibbous Moon

Moon Moment

The sun is now illuminating more than half of the moon. "Gibbous" means "bulging outward," but a gibbous moon is not full. This phase lasts about a week, and its energy causes the earth's tides to shift with its gravitational pull. Because this is the phase before the full moon, the pull is stronger, and it's possible you may feel it in your body as an extra burst of energy.

This moon is easy to see as it rises during the day and sets after midnight.[37] Fun fact: the line you see where the light and dark areas on the moon's surface meet is called the terminator.

Lunar Spirit

While this phase is about nurturing your intention, it is also a great time to nurture your lunar spirit. Use the suggestions in this section to cultivate your spirit, which in turn helps to create space for your intention to grow.

EXERCISE: WAXING GIBBOUS MEDITATION

Making energetic space is a way to nurture your spirit and push anything that will keep you from moving forward out of the way. Try this meditation to move away from what you no longer need.

What you need:

A quiet space
Moon journal and pen

What to do:

Sit in a chair or on the ground with your spine upright. Quiet your mind and become aware of your breath. As you start to inhale and exhale slowly, send each inhale deep into your core. Gradually make your inhales and your exhales longer.

Now visualize a little book in your hands. As you look through the pages, you realize the pictures inside show the things that are holding you back from your full potential. As you breathe in and out slowly, pause on each page and take note of these barriers. Take one long inhale and exhale with a whooshing sound.

Now see yourself ripping the pages out and tossing them up one by one to the waxing gibbous moon. Say aloud: "May the waxing gibbous moon transmute these barriers into a space for growth and new potential. And so it is."

37. "Waxing Gibbous Moon," EarthSky, January 1, 2023, https://earthsky.org/moon-phases/waxing-gibbous/.

Continue to focus on your breath. Inhale and exhale. Now bring your attention to the book in your hands, where you notice that the pages have been restored but are blank. Hold the book in your hands and imagine all new potential regarding your manifestation filling its pages. As you do so, trust any sensations, feelings, or messages you experience. Feel the excitement of success fill your entire body as you continue to focus on your breath. Inhale and exhale.

Stay in this receiving space for as long as you would like. Thank the moon for its energy and guidance, and take one last inhale and exhale. Open your eyes, connect with your body, and write down any information you received.

Waxing Gibbous Lunar Focus

When new and exciting opportunities present themselves as part of attaining a higher energetic perspective, you can get lost in those exciting intuitive spaces.

Taking a step back and making sure your heart is aligned with these actions is not only an important part of this process but also makes sure you are fully aligned and ready to step into this new energy.

EXERCISE: ACTIVATE YOUR HEART RITUAL

Checking in with your heart space can help create a loving environment perfect for your moon workings.

What you need:

Pen and paper
Your moon altar
Green 4-inch taper candle plus matches/lighter

What to do:

Grab a pen and paper and sit by your moon altar if you can. Take a few deep breaths, light your candle, and become aware of yourself in this space. Now bring your intention for this cycle into your mind. How is it feeling? Write the first thing that comes to mind. What actions are most important right now? Write your answer down. What new action needs to happen? Write down whatever you come up with. Now take a deep breath and put your hand on your heart.

How does your heart feel energetically? See your intention settling into your heart space and the soft pink glow surrounding it.

Now set your writings aside, leaving them at your altar for at least fifteen minutes.

After that time has passed, go back to your space, recenter yourself, and pick up your writings. Read them aloud to yourself and decide if they align with what you are doing so far. If so, great! Create at least one big action step to take now. If not, use your answers to identify areas where things are not going as planned and create at least three smaller action steps to get you back on track. Jot down any intuitive messages you receive and thank your sacred space. Take the paper with you and use this to create your waxing moon phase plan.

EXERCISE: WAXING GIBBOUS DEVOTIONAL

In this activation, you will seek assistance in creating effective action steps.

What you need:

An offering for the moon (water, wine, bread, or something you feel called to offer, preferably biodegradable)

Moon journal and pen

What to do:

Go outside if you can; otherwise sit near a window. Bring your offering with you to the space of your choosing. Take a few moments to center and focus on your moon devotional. As you sit and bring awareness to your present self, check in to see how this phase has affected you. Notice the energy and let your thoughts float away.

Now bring your attention to the moon in the sky. Say your intention for this phase aloud, followed by, "Moon Goddess, as you work your way to fullness, please grant me the energy of this phase to create actions that will bring me to a successful manifestation. Please accept my offering and gratitude for this guidance." (If you are working with a specific goddess, address this to her.)

Hold up your offering and lay it on the ground or the windowsill if you are inside. Close your eyes and feel as you receive the energy, guidance, and insight the moon goddess offers. Once you feel you've gotten everything, write these insights in your moon journal. Say thank you once more and you are finished. If you placed your offering inside, leave it for twenty-four hours and dispose of it as you wish.

Lunar Mind

Remember that your intention was chosen because it is the right time to step into that energy. Do not rush the process; be mindful of it and appreciate the work you have already put in. Show yourself some compassion and be proud of what you have come here to do, no matter the result. Manifesting takes time and patience. Being mindful of patience and its importance will help when resistance comes up. At the same time, remember that resistance is part of this journey—only by facing and understanding it will you open the flow of manifesting energy to your own source of energy. Nurturing this energy flow will assist you in staying on track for the future moon phases. Here are a few prompts to try to see where your energy is at and where your focus needs to be.

- What emotions are you feeling at this moment? Explain them individually.
- How do you feel about your developing magical practice? How can you help support it?
- How can you best nurture new ideas and mindsets?
- What about your work so far do you feel most proud of, and why?
- What self-care act can you focus on to nourish your mind and body? How will you incorporate this into your day?

Gratitude Suggestions

When we actively manifest and change our realities, we also need to nurture our bodies and minds. As you integrate new vibrational energies, you can also feel them physically. What ten things are you grateful for that help you feel nurtured? For example:

- I feel nurtured when I drink water with purpose.
- I am nurturing myself by putting myself first.
- I nurture myself by moving my body mindfully every day.

Affirmations

Try out these affirmations during the Waxing Gibbous Moon.

- I am an abundant creator.
- I am proud of myself.
- I am a dynamic change-maker.
- I know what I want and will do what is necessary in a loving way.
- I believe in myself.

Lunar Body

The practice of changing the items on your moon altar is an example of how a physical act can help to shift your lunar spirit to what is coming next in the moon cycle.

EXERCISE: WAXING GIBBOUS ALTAR

Think of a favorite item from your childhood that makes you feel nurtured and add it to your altar for this phase. Take time to care for your moon altar—it is an extension of your magical moon manifesting. Cleanse it in your favorite way before adding the items for this phase. Call in that warm, fuzzy, comforting feeling when doing your spell work and send it to yourself and the universe as a big hug of energetic gratitude. Use incense or essential oil sprays that are calming and comforting to create a nurturing area in which to do your magical work.

What you need:

Waxing gibbous picture

Crystal (from the suggested list or one of your own)

Red 4-inch taper candle, matches/lighter, candle snuffer

What to do:

Remove the first quarter moon picture and replace it with a waxing gibbous moon picture or item that represents the waxing gibbous moon for you. Next, place your waxing gibbous moon crystal on your altar, one that feels best and harnesses that growing energy. Remove any items placed on your altar for the previous phase, the first quarter moon. When you are done, take a moment to connect with your altar and feel the shift in energy.

Light your candle and repeat your intention for this moon cycle three times. Snuff it out when you are finished and light whenever you work at your altar during this phase.

EXERCISE: WAXING GIBBOUS ACTIONS

Use the waxing gibbous phase to notice any challenges coming up for you and see how you can create some actionable steps to move past them. It is important to happily accept where you are and do what works for you to move past obstacles. We do not want to ignore challenges because those little inconveniences will reappear in later phases if not dealt with now. Take the time to nurture yourself in whichever way you need. This will also keep you in the manifesting flow, ensuring you are on your way to a fruitful moon manifesting cycle.

Notice any challenges that are coming up for you. Give them some space and see how you can divert or fix them.

What you need:

Moon journal and pen

What to do:

Head to your moon altar. Once you are there, create action steps that nurture your intention. Are there any smaller details that need to be addressed? Make sure to take time to assess yourself mentally and physically. Is your intention still aligned with what you really want? If not, what needs to change? Rewrite your moon manifestation plan if necessary to freshen it up as you move to the next cycle.

Tarot: Wheel of Fortune

The waxing gibbous phase can be thought of as the womb of potential. The moon manifesting process is well underway for you; imagine the Wheel of Fortune tarot card turning as you navigate the phases. Now that you have lovingly given your intention care in this phase, the wheel will start to turn and prepare you for the next one.

Your seedlings are poking through the soil and are now vulnerable to the elements; the utmost diligence is needed to help them thrive. This may be the part of the moon cycle where challenges arise, and you must be attentive to all the details of your action steps. What can you quickly solve, and what needs more attention right now?

The Wheel of Fortune reminds us that no matter what we do in our lives, the world keeps moving, flowing, and changing. This card shows up in the waxing gibbous phase to remind us to follow the flow. Change what you can and adjust as needed. Confront what you must; your new reality has the space to evolve. Karma and good luck are in this waxing gibbous space, so take advantage of them. Approaching your intention with love will help steer you in the right direction and help you take the best actions. It is time to spin the wheel of the universe and step into your next manifesting phase. Accepting that everything has its flow and energy will help you to accept the movement of the universe. Keeping the energy flowing and realizing you can nurture it is a part of this grand journey. Releasing expectation is a beneficial way to discover more about yourself and tap into new magical parts that you may not have known existed within you.

Embracing change is as important as initiating it. Sometimes we like where we are and don't want to let changes happen. But as the Wheel of Fortune shows, they'll happen regardless, and learning to accept this part of life is important to your moon manifestation process and understanding how your magic works.

EXERCISE: GO WITH THE FLOW TAROT SPREAD

Use this tarot spread to help reestablish magical focus.

What you need:

Tarot deck

What to do:

Shuffle your cards, choose the tenth card from the top of your pile, and place it on the table. Leave enough space—you will form a loose circle with the cards as you place them down.

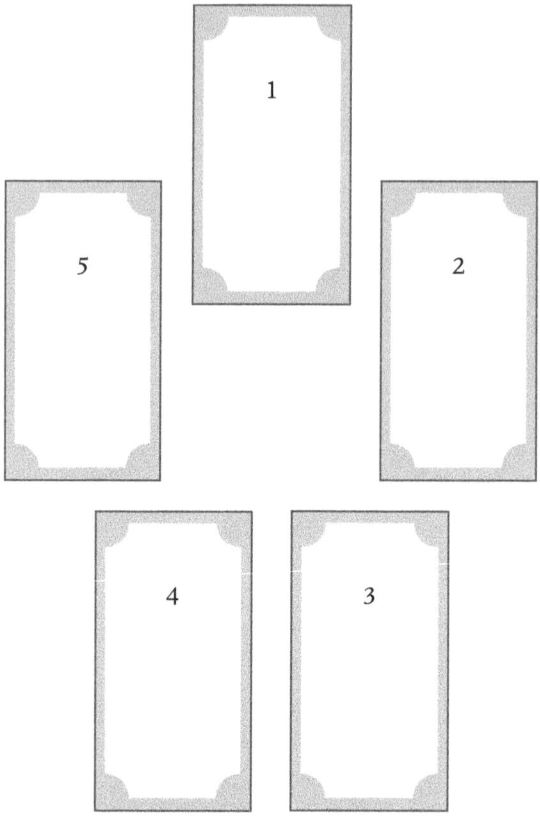

Choose a card from the middle of the deck and place it to the right of the first card.

Shuffle and choose the third card from the top of the deck. Place this at the bottom right of the second card.

Take the top card and place it next to the third at the bottom. Now pull the bottom card from the deck and place it near the top to complete the circle.

Card 1 (top card): How can I best embrace the flow of my desires?

Card 2 (right): Where can I find support when I am overwhelmed?

Card 3 (bottom right): What idea must I release to stay in the flow?

Card 4 (bottom left): Is there anything subconsciously holding me back that I can reframe?

Card 5 (left): How can I best nurture myself through this new manifesting flow?

Sit with what you feel needs to be adjusted, notice how it feels in your body, and tap into your intuition for answers. Reach out for support if you feel overwhelmed or need to talk it out. Make sure to take care of yourself through this process. Know that when you level up to a higher version of yourself, new paths of abundance will appear and it is up to you to take a chance, even if it is something you have not done before.

SIGIL WORKING: WAXING GIBBOUS

Create a powerful sigil to kick off your moon manifestation cycle. Create a single-sentence statement about how you will move past difficulty to craft a sigil for this moon phase. For example, "Giving space to my feelings when I am creating my best life is important."

What you need:

Paper plus pen or pencil

What to do:

Get comfortable in your sacred space. Pick up your paper and pen, and write the sentence you chose at the top of the paper. Now go through and cross out all the vowels and repeating letters. From these letters we will now craft a symbol.

Start with whichever letter calls to you first and intertwine all of them until you have your sigil. Do not over-scrutinize this, just go with the flow of your intuition and see what you create. Leave enough room on the paper to draw three clockwise circles around the whole sigil. As you do this, say your full intention aloud three times. When finished, say, "This sigil has been activated. And so it is." Now you can leave your sigil on your altar or take a picture of it and use it as a background image for your phone or computer.

RECIPE: WAXING GIBBOUS TEA

With these comforting ingredients, you will be able to find the serenity you need to create good feeling action steps in this phase.

For the waxing gibbous phase, indulge in a comforting and aromatic tea that will warm your soul. Spiced chai with cinnamon, cardamom, and cloves can create a cozy and heartwarming experience as you delve into your manifesting work.

What you need:

Small pot of boiling water
2 or 3 cinnamon sticks to ignite passion for your manifestation
Small slice of fresh ginger to clear and freshen your senses
Black tea bag for comfort (Darjeeling works great)
⅛ t cardamom will help strengthen your will
1 whole clove bud for courage
¼ C preferred dairy or dairy alternative beverage
Sugar to taste

Optional:

Moon journal and pen

What to do:

Bring a cup of water to a boil in the small pot. Add cinnamon sticks, ginger, clove, and cardamom. Simmer for ten minutes. Add your tea bag and let sit in the water until the water is a rich amber in color. Remove the tea bag and add milk. Simmer for another five minutes. Pour into mug and sweeten as you like.

Find a cozy spot and slowly sip your tea as you imagine the potential of your manifestations making themselves known. If you receive any ideas or insights that show themselves, be sure to write them down.

Waxing Gibbous Closing Thoughts

As you move through this phase, you will see how approaching change with gratitude and loving energy will help you navigate your new way of life. Regardless of how much has changed, you have been working toward a goal, and that energy alone is creating changes you may not yet realize.

As your confidence grows with the moon, you will be able to decide what you want your future to be like and create new ways of thinking because you know you are in full control of your emotions. Next is the full moon and all she has to offer you in this confident new moment you have been cultivating since the new moon.

Waxing Gibbous Moon Correspondences

Consider these suggestions for your waxing gibbous moon manifesting.

Deities: Demeter, Inanna

Herbs: Pennyroyal, vervain, apple, marjoram, basil

Incense: Lavender, rose

Crystals: Tiger's eye, kyanite

Oils: Juniper, cedarwood, pine

Colors: Amber, yellow

Keywords: Building momentum, growth, expansion

CHAPTER THIRTEEN

FULL MOON

The full moon has arrived, and it is time to gauge how your manifestations are progressing. You can also reassess and release things that are not serving your intention. Take the action of an intentional release so you create a brightly lit full moon path to secure your manifestation for this moon cycle.

The full moon is what you can consider the cosmic sigh of the moon phases. I first saw this phrase used in astrology author and teacher Yasmin Boland's book, *Moonology: Working with the Magic of Lunar Cycles*, which explains that the full moon phase is when you let go of expectations and worries and secure the energetic balance you have worked toward during this cycle.[38]

We have all stepped outside at one time or another to gaze at the full moon and her beauty. While you have the entire illuminated side of the moon facing you and what you may be focusing on, it is important to note that the other side, which is dark to you, is still influencing all that goes on and the energies at this moment during your moon manifestations. Your once-seedlings of intention from your new moon work are now in their fullest bloom. You can allow yourself some grace to reaffirm or adjust your intentions at this time. The full moon represents the light and dark aspects of yourself and is where you not only secure your energetic balance but

38. Yasmin Boland, *Moonology: Working with the Magic of Lunar Cycles* (Hay House, 2016), 15.

embrace it as well. When working in this phase, you must be aware of balance and its importance in your moon manifesting journey.

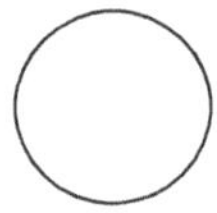

Full Moon

Moon Moment

The full moon is the fifth phase of our moon cycle. The moon is full when it is opposite the sun and appears illuminated fully from Earth. The moon does not produce light, so it depends on the sun to be visible as it moves through the phases. The full moon rises at sunset and sets at sunrise. Tides are stronger during this phase, and your own emotions can be too—after all, you are made of 60 percent water.[39] Having a few restless nights or intense dreams is not unheard of during this time. The balance of the energy in this phase is important, being able to recognize the light and dark of this phase as well as that in yourself will help you to be able to utilize it in a meaningful way.

Lunar Spirit

When the full moon steps in during your moon manifesting, balance is exactly what it is calling for. By stepping into a balanced spirit, you will be able to plan and effectively release anything not pushing your intention along the moon phases.

EXERCISE: FULL MOON MEDITATION

Find the balance you need with this full moon meditation.

What you need:

A quiet space

Moon journal and a pen

39. "Water Science School: The Water in You: Water and the Human Body," U. S. Geological Survey, May 22, 2019 https://www.usgs.gov/special-topics/water-science-school/science/water-you-water-and-human-body.

What to do:

Sit in a chair or on the ground with your spine upright. Say aloud: "Full moon, I ask you to fill me with gratitude and energetic balance as it reveals the magic around me."

Quiet your mind and become aware of your breath. Inhale and exhale slowly. Start sending each inhale deep into your core. Begin making your inhales and your exhales longer. As you do so, visualize the bright, silver light of the full moon enveloping you in its sparkling glow. Bring something to mind that you are grateful for and something you need to release. Allow the sparkly silver light of the full moon to absorb and transmute what is not needed.

Sit in this place of energetic balance for as long as you need to and continue to focus on your breath and the sparkling silver light of the full moon. You can stay in this place of magic for as long as you need. As you do, continue to focus on your breath. Inhale and exhale. Be open and receptive to any guidance you receive, and trust any intuitive nudges you experience.

Keep your focus on your breath, inhaling and exhaling. Stay in this healing space for as long as you would like. Thank the full moon for its guidance, healing, and any clearing you received. Now bring your awareness back to your breath. Inhale and exhale. Open your eyes, connect with your body, and write down any information you received.

Full Moon Lunar Focus

The full moon phase is calling for balance, use these exercises to balance your spirit to achieve your full lunar equilibrium to step into the next moon phase with confidence. Note also that the full moon would be an ideal time to try drawing down the moon (see chapter 4).

EXERCISE: BALANCE YOUR LIGHT AND DARK RITUAL ACTIVATION

You have made it to a vital phase in your moon manifesting cycle, and now you take this cycle's energy to focus on the complete balance of self. Tap into your confidence and make sure the flow of self-assurance is aligned with your magic and your moon intention. When you are confident, you can make decisions quicker and without the extra baggage of all the "what ifs" because you *know* you oversee your destiny and do not feel the need to explain it to anyone.

This activation reignites that confidence as you head into the waning phases to give you a boost of moon energy as you start to wind down this lunar manifesting cycle and see your intention becoming fully realized.

Try this exercise to confidently balance your spirit.

What you need:

Two 4-inch tapers, one yellow, one black; matches or a lighter, and a firesafe dish

Moon journal and a pen

What to do:

Bring your yellow and black candles, firesafe dish, and matches to your moon altar. Next, sit comfortably near it. Ground and center yourself. Pick up the yellow candle and imagine a yellow light in your solar plexus region right at your diaphragm. See this light travel up your chest and into the hand where you hold your candle; this may feel cool, warm, or even tingly. Fill that yellow candle with your fiery energy and do so until you see or feel it glowing in your mind's eye. Now take your matches, candle, and firesafe dish, warm the bottom of the candle, and firmly hold it against the plate until it stays.

Sit down again and take a deep breath. As you do, see that yellow light now receding to your solar plexus right at your diaphragm and slowly fading back into your energy center. Rub your hands together, recenter, and grab the black candle.

As you hold the black candle, recall one aspect of yourself that you try to hide or push away. Feel that energy and ask the candle why this concerns you. Now ask the candle how it can help bring you balance. When you receive an answer or feel a new emotion, warm the candle bottom and place it near the yellow one. Lightly place a hand on each candle and say,

"May the light and dark inside me combine and bring me enlightenment. And so it is." Light each candle in whichever order feels right.

Sit for as long as you can and imagine those energies swirling together, creating a new energy to empower and help you. When you feel you are done, snuff out the candles and thank them. Ground in a way that is comforting to you. After, write down any thoughts, feelings, or messages you received.

EXERCISE: FULL MOON DEVOTIONAL

Try this full moon devotional to harness the light and dark within you with the moon's full energy.

What you need:

2 small glasses of water, around 2 oz. in each
A vessel to hold the water from both glasses
Moon journal and a pen

What to do:

If you can, go outside; otherwise, sit near a window. Have your two glasses with equal amounts of water in each nearby as well as the larger vessel. Get comfortable and relax in this space. Take three cleansing breaths and sit for a few moments as you feel the strong, powerful energy from the full moon. Now hold one of the glasses up and think of the light part of yourself, the parts you are not afraid to show to others. Say, "With the energy of the full moon, I work to balance the light within me." Set the glass down.

Pick up the other glass of water and think of your shadow areas: What do you keep hidden from others? Say, "With the energy of the full moon, I work to balance the dark within me."

Pick up the other glass so you have the light and dark glasses in both hands. Slowly pour them into the bigger vessel while saying, "I now integrate and balance all aspects of myself. I accept all parts of who I am. I am confident and worthy of all I desire."

Leave this vessel on your moon altar for the full moon phase and hold it when you need to rebalance. Thank the full moon and goddess with whom you are working. Journal about any insights, feelings, and messages you received.

Lunar Mind

It is time to dig deeper into our psyche during the full moon. This phase is about creating the magical balance needed to keep your momentum going through the remainder of the cycle and encourage a successful lunar manifestation.

Your intention may have come to fruition already, if so, you can use this phase to release what is no longer useful to you in your life. On the other hand, things may not have happened as planned, and you may need to refocus your mindset to help decide what is next in your manifesting process.

This phase can bring up lots of feelings, thoughts, or memories. Let them flow through you as you do your work, and you'll notice how much lighter you feel afterward. By balancing the light and dark aspects of yourself, you can learn much about how you react to change and how to best work with it.

You may decide this intention is not what you want anymore, and that is okay. When this happens during a manifesting moon cycle, it indicates you have evolved in the past few weeks. You may have had to work through what you thought you wanted to get to what you truly desire.

Embrace the light and dark inside you and fully accept who you are. The sun shines on you, and this is your light side; like your astrological Sun sign, it is the part of yourself that you want the world to see. And in these days when the sun is completely shining on the moon's surface, you may feel exposed or seen. This may be something you need to work through to feel more confident as you take on a bigger role in your own life.

With the full moon illuminated, the emotions you would rather keep hidden may now show themselves to you. There is a reason these aspects show up now, and you should give them space to be recognized. Use these aspects as a tool to manifest by integrating your light and dark to harness the power within yourself.

Try these journal prompts to bring your lunar mind to where you are right now in your journey and gain insights to help you stay on your path and figure out what can be released.

- What balance do you need to focus on in your daily habits?
- What innovative ideas or thoughts have come up since the new moon?
- How are you feeling right now?
- What changes have you felt proud of in the last two weeks?
- How do you feel about releasing what no longer aligns with your intention?

Gratitude Suggestions

Repeat these gratitude suggestions to help connect your lunar mind to your intention. Use the prompts here to intertwine your intuition and gratitude for a successful outcome.

- I am grateful for the lessons I learned from not paying attention to my intuition.
- I am grateful for the people I have let go of and for how they taught me who I do not want to be.
- I give thanks to the past beliefs I was able to identify and let go of so that I could grow.
- I am grateful for being curious as a child and asking questions even when it annoyed the adults around me.

Affirmation Suggestions

Add these affirmations to your full moon workings.

- I am in complete balance.
- I am thankful for my light and dark self.
- I am clear on what I want in my life.

- Change is good for me.
- I incorporate my intuition in my decisions.

Lunar Body

As you move to fully encompass this full moon and decide how you will create balance, it is important to integrate your physical body and create your altar for this phase. As you may have noticed, doing the physical part of magical work helps solidify your intention even more.

EXERCISE: FULL MOON ALTAR

Now it is time to prepare your altar for the full moon energy. Your altar space will center on refocusing and rebalancing. Focus on balancing your physical altar; arrange and rearrange as needed. Remove what you do not resonate with anymore and even sit with a quartz crystal in each hand, sending balanced vibes to yourself and your altar.

What you need:

Sun and Moon tarot cards or a picture or symbol of the full moon
Crystal (from the suggested list or your own)
4-inch taper, white; matches or lighter, plus candle snuffer
Moon journal and pen

What to do:

Place the Sun and Moon tarot cards or your favorite full moon picture on your altar. Choose a full moon crystal from the list at the end of this chapter or one that is extra sparkly and seems to jump out when you think of what you want to manifest. Use your intuition to place the items where you feel they need or want to go.

Now light your white candle and say your intention three times. Think of three things you would like to release during this phase. As you concentrate on the flame, see the things you want to release as tendrils of smoke moving toward the candle flame. Watch these need-to-be-released things be absorbed by the flame. They have now been transmuted and no longer worry you or at least do not feel as important.

When you are done, snuff the candle out with a candle snuffer—do not blow it out because we will continue to work on this intention. Relight your candle whenever you come to this sacred space to journal or create your action steps.

EXERCISE: FULL MOON ACTIONS

Your action step during this phase is to check how you feel emotionally about your intention and readjust it as needed. Connecting with your lunar anima in the right way will help you make a fair judgment of what you need right now.

Take some time to recalibrate your intention and releasing anything that is not beneficial for your moon manifestation work. It is okay if your intention changes. Your previous steps got you to right where you are now. You are exactly where you need to be. Use this exercise to create your full moon action steps.

What you need:

Moon journal and pen

What to do:

Action steps to create balance in your magical moon manifesting are important here. What steps can you take to make sure you are in sync with your intention right now? How are you pushing past areas that may feel a bit resistant? Do you need to adjust your intention? How can you do this in a way that is aligned with your current state? What steps can you take to ensure your intuition and physical self are in sync?

Tarot: The Sun and the Moon

The full moon phase gets two tarot cards. The Sun represents the openness and wisdom of the past moon phases shining outward—the hope and child-like wonder you had as you began creating your best life that you are now taking steps to manifest. Unlike the moon, the sun shines its light on the shadows, so the Sun card therefore can also represent the revealing of truths. But these truths will be revealed gently, even in a childlike way, as we see the child in the card. In the Rider-Waite-Smith deck, we see the sun within the Moon card, further strengthening their partnership. While the sun shines wonderfully and happily on everything, it can also make us feel exposed. The moon brings up feelings from the depths of our emotional selves.

During this phase, it is time to give these feelings the attention they need to transmute into something better. Moon energy may also show up as the level of commitment you have in your magical practice, and you may feel your magic is a bit more pronounced during this phase.

The Moon card focuses more on the shadows that are casted, representations of our emotional selves and the sides we like to keep hidden. You can use both cards' energy and balance your energetic body emotionally and physically so you may manifest in the best way possible. We have many facets to our identities, so to step into our full magic requires integrating all parts of ourselves. The moon also lures us to tap into our psychic self, our deep knowing, and desires we may keep stowed away.

We can discover so much about ourselves if we allow these deep mysteries to surface. You must work on limiting beliefs during moon manifesting work—it is a part of the process. This phase is a time to realize what is not working and let that go to bring balance to your intention, all so you can better decide what needs to be done next. There is a new magic for you in the shadows.

EXERCISE: THE DANCE OF THE FULL MOON AND SUN TAROT WORKING

This tarot spread is a fantastic way to focus your desires on the current moon cycle and decide the best actions to make sure they become known. Try this spread and see how it feels when two tarot cards represent the full moon's energy.

What you need:

Tarot deck
Sun and Moon tarot cards
Moon journal and pen
Space on your moon altar to lay cards

What to do:

Take out your Sun and Moon cards from your tarot deck. In this ritual, we work with the polarity of light and dark, so aligning our cards with this purpose is a good idea. While looking at the cards, consider your intentions. Has there been a balance regarding your intentions in the last few phases?

Ask yourself the following questions as you envision this: How are you feeling? What thoughts come up for you? Write your impressions down. Remember: We must harness both light and dark. The Sun and Moon cards call for balance.

This spread has six total cards. First, place the Sun and Moon cards at the top of your reading area. Give your deck a shuffle and pull two other cards each for both the Sun and Moon, placing these four new cards below the Sun and Moon respectively. Follow the spread diagram to interpret what the cards mean. You will use these to help you create your actions and adjust your intentions. The cards will also help you recognize where balance is necessary so you can move forward to the next phase confidently.

EXERCISE: ENERGETIC BALANCE: FULL MOON AND SUN TAROT SPREAD

Use this spread to remind yourself of the balance you seek to create a successful intention. The cards you pull will help create action steps with the Sun. The cards pulled for the Moon will hint at what you need to release.

What you need:

Tarot deck

Moon journal and a pen

What to do:

Shuffle your cards. When you feel you've shuffled enough, trace with your finger a moon and sun on the top card of the deck. Find the Sun and Moon cards in your tarot deck and place them on the table. Shuffle again and draw two cards for the Moon card and two for the Sun card. Place the cards you drew for the Sun card beneath that card and do the same for the Moon card

Card 1 (Sun card): What parts of my intention is the Sun illuminating that I can consider complete?

Card 2 (Sun card): What must I release regarding my intention to keep moving forward?
Card 3 (Moon card): Where do I need balance in my life to help this intention become reality?
Card 4 (Moon card): What lessons should I focus on moving forward?

From the detailed answers of your full moon exercises, create at least three steps to take during this phase that to you are realistic but still a bit more than you'd usually do. Make sure these action steps support your intention and can be incorporated easily.

SIGIL WORKING: FULL MOON

Add this sigil to your full moon magic. Choose a word or short phrase that you want to let go of this full moon. For example, "I release the need to always say yes."

What you need:

Moon journal and pen or pencil

What to do:

Gather your items and find a comfortable spot near your moon altar. Pick up your moon journal and pen, and write your word or phrase three times on the top of the paper. Put an X through each one and state, "I release this statement and send it away to be transmuted. Thank you." After you have done this, rewrite the phrase or word. Now cross out all the vowels and repeating letters. From these letters we will now craft a symbol.

Start with whichever letter calls to you first and intertwine all of them until you have your sigil. Do not over-scrutinize what you make; just go with the flow of your intuition and see what you create. Remember to leave enough room on the paper to draw three clockwise circles around the whole sigil. When you have done that, say, "This sigil has been activated. And so it is." Now you can leave your sigil on your altar or take a picture of it and use it as a background image for your phone or computer.

RECIPE: FULL MOON TEA

At this point in your moon manifesting journey, balance is key. To bring complete equilibrium to your physical and mental selves, enjoy this elegant and captivating tea that sends balancing energy where needed. This fragrant, uplifting tea is exactly what you need as you start reaping the benefits of your magical work.

What you need:

1 C water, freshly boiled
1 tea bag Jasmine green tea for rejuvenation
Pinch of lemon balm to help clarity of thought
Small sprig of rosemary to clear and remove any energetic blocks
Honey to sweeten your action steps (to taste)
Small dish to cover the mug

What to do:

Add ingredients to a mug of freshly boiled water and cover with a small dish. Let steep for about five minutes, and then slowly turn over the dish. Use your finger to write your moon intention on the condensation on the dish. Dab the water over your third eye (middle of forehead between your eyes) as well as your heart.

As you drink your tea, the intention will settle where it is needed in your body to help give you the boost to see it through to the end of the cycle.

Full Moon Closing Thoughts

The light and dark aspects of the Sun and the Moon tarot cards can bring up many thoughts and feelings. As you balance your magic and intention through tapping into and integrating your lunar spirit, mind, and body, you will start to see exactly what you want and how you want it to begin to come to life. And as you move into the next chapter on the waning gibbous moon, you will learn how to embody your unique flow.

Full Moon Correspondences

Although there are many, here's a selection of figures and items associated with the full moon.

Deities: Themis, Sekhmet

Herbs: Chamomile, clove, lemon balm, mugwort, lotus

Incense: Ylang-ylang, rosemary

Crystals: Moonstone, moldavite, topaz

Oils: Frankincense, myrrh, orange

Colors: Silver, white

Keywords: Abundance, culmination, illumination, balance

CHAPTER FOURTEEN
WANING GIBBOUS MOON

As you step into the moon's waning gibbous phase, you are now leaving behind the waxing phases. Big actions are behind you, and now it is time to notice all the changes that have happened through this moon manifesting cycle. The waning gibbous moon implores you to share your experience of moon magic with others. Sharing your successes and where you plan to adjust in your moon manifesting work helps solidify your intentions and integrate your experience for success in this and other cycles.

This phase reaches out to you, calling you to step into the power of your true self and confidence. You have done so much profound inner work, and the mysteries of the full moon's balance have brought you here with new insight. Talk to those you trust and share your magical journey with them; it is time to make it a true reality for you, and sharing with others is the perfect way to speak your manifesting abilities aloud so they are heard and received by the universe.

As you share your moon manifesting journey, you will reignite your excitement and passion for the intention you created for this moon cycle. Gratitude during the waning gibbous moon phase is imperative—your appreciative energy will show up when you least expect it, causing you to realize that you are a powerful manifester. When you can show appreciation for anything, good *and* bad, you will have leveled up subconsciously and fully integrated your lunar mind, body, and spirit.

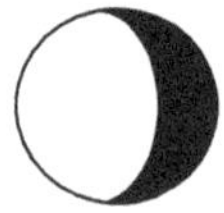

Waning Gibbous Moon

Moon Moment

As we move past the powerful illumination of the full moon phase, there is a subtle shift in energy with the waning gibbous moon. Now the moon wanes as it moves away from the sun and the light starts to decrease. This phase lasts about a week and is the sixth phase of the moon cycle. At this point, the moon, sun, and Earth are almost vertical, and this causes the tides on each side of our planet to cancel each other out.[40] In lunar scientist Arnold Lieber's book, *The Lunar Effect*, he discusses how the tides affect emotions. According to his studies, this phase is calm since the tides are at a low point, giving you a clear headspace to start sharing your journey and communicate effectively.[41]

Lunar Spirit

Your lunar spirit is bountiful, and those intuitive muscles have been working full time. During this phase, share your experience with harnessing your lunar spirit and how it has helped you accomplish all you have this moon cycle.

EXERCISE: WANING GIBBOUS MEDITATION

Clearing out any mental or spiritual clutter is helpful when you are ready to share your moon manifestation journey with others. Try this meditation and start sharing your moon magic experiences.

What you need:

A quiet space

Moon journal and pen

40. "Phases of the Moon," Kopernik Observatory, kopernik.org.

41. Lieber, *Lunar Effect*, 27.

What to do:

Sit in a chair or on the ground with your spine upright. Say aloud: "Waning moon, I ask you to show me what needs to go and what needs to stay, and what lessons I need to listen to most." Quiet your mind and become aware of your breath. Inhale and exhale slowly.

Now start sending each inhale deep into your toes and back up to your head. Begin making your inhales and your exhales longer. Visualize a soft green light coming down from the waning moon and weaving itself into all parts of your physical self. Imagine that this soft green light is sending away any stagnant energy and limiting beliefs that no longer serve you along with any physical pain you may be experiencing. Imagine the moon sending anything it takes from you up into itself to be dispelled and transmuted into helpful energy for someone else. Some things that you wish to go might stay, and that is alright; it may not be time for it to go.

Imagine this green light is now surrounding you like a soft cloud of loving energy. Say aloud: "Waning moon, I ask you to help me love and accept myself where I am right now in my journey."

Continue to focus on your breath. Inhale and exhale. Remain open and accepting of any love or truths you receive, and trust any intuitive feelings and thoughts you may experience. Continue to focus on your breath, inhale and exhale. Stay in this loving space for as long as you would like.

After you feel enough time has passed, thank the moon for the release and love it shared with you. Release any control of your breath. Inhale and exhale. Open your eyes, connect with your body, and write down any information you received.

Waning Gibbous Lunar Focus

You have now worked through the first half of the moon's cycle, but that does not mean it is time to slow down and rest just yet. This phase is where you work to reignite your ambition and intention and take your next steps to complete your manifesting cycle in the best way possible. Tapping into the excitement from when you first started this journey will help drive you to renewed action and harness passion and excitement.

The waning gibbous phase is the time to allow yourself to flow into the dimming light, dig deep, and push through. As you move forward in your journey and start to come close to your full intention whether it changed a bit along the way or is still the same, you will now move through the emotions of showing gratitude for all you've gained during this cycle.

EXERCISE: INNER SELF-REFLECTION RITUAL ACTIVATION

Harnessing joy during deep work is profound and validating. Do this activation to help your inner spirit become vibrant and ensure the flow moves along your moon manifesting.

What you need:

Small piece of paper and pen
Small dish
Orange crystal (orange calcite or one of the crystals at the end of the chapter)
One sprig of dried rosemary

What to do:

Gather the items and sit in front of your moon altar. Ground and center yourself. Pick up the pen and paper as you think about your current manifestation. What about it makes you the most excited? Write this down on the paper and place it in the bowl. Now pick up the orange crystal and repeat what you wrote aloud three times with passion! Place the crystal in the small bowl on the top of the paper.

Sprinkle the rosemary on top and say, "I activate this crystal with excitement and joy so that whenever I hold it, I can be reminded and inspired by it, and so it is." Place the bowl on your moon altar. Afterward, ground and center yourself. Leave the bowl on your altar overnight and do not touch it. The next day or whenever you need to revive your excitement, hold or carry the crystal for as long as you need.

EXERCISE: WANING GIBBOUS DEVOTIONAL

Offer gratitude to the moon as you are coming near the end of the moon cycle.

What you need:

Soothing music
Moon journal and a pen

What to do:

Go outside if possible or sit by a window. Center yourself and feel the calming waning moon energy; let it wash over you and settle around you for a few minutes. Next, turn on your soothing music and listen to it quietly for as long as you feel you need to.

After a few moments, pick up your journal and without thinking about what you write, jot down whatever comes to mind when you think of the last few weeks and how you are feeling in this moment. When you are done, go back to each thought you wrote and write something next to it for which you are grateful.

On each corner of the paper, write: "Thank you waning moon for the space to be grateful and appreciate myself and others who have supported me. I also thank those who have not supported me to teach me important lessons about myself. And so it is." You may write the name of your chosen goddess instead of naming the moon phase. When you are finished, hold the paper up and say, "This is my offering of gratitude for this moon cycle, may all be pleased." Place this paper on your waning gibbous moon altar as a reminder to stay in this mindset of gratitude.

Lunar Mind

As you move into this waning phase, it is important to allow its energy to slow your thoughts and work to organize them. Here you start to reflect on what you have accomplished so far and how it has changed you. Look around and see how your environment has adapted to accommodate your new reality. Even though you slow your thoughts during this phase, that does not mean you slow your actions. Now is the time to let the racing thoughts that an enthusiastic outlook can bring turn into a more controlled, focused energy.

The waning gibbous phase is not for slowing down or rest; slowing your thoughts is more about creating centered, intentional actions to finish out this moon cycle successfully. You want to reflect on your actions in this phase to create new direct actions that will solidify your manifestations. Briefly step back into new moon energy as you do this. Do you recall how you felt at the beginning, that sense of excitement at creating something new? Tap into that exciting nervous energy and bring it forth right now. You want to fully step into an abundant life so you can decide on the direct, focused action you must take to reach that successfully. A whole new dynamic is taking form. When this happens, you have set yourself up to receive from the universe; wonderful shifts are on their way to you. Be open to where you are and how you can always create something better than before. Try the following prompts for deeper insight. Check in with your lunar spirit, mind, and body with these prompts.

- How does your current state of gratitude feel in your body right now?
- Have you been fully open to receiving from the universe?
- What shifts are the most noticeable to you and why?
- Are you feeling any resistance to becoming your true self? How can you shift this?
- What part of your intention are you most excited about? How can you harness this energy again right now?

Gratitude Suggestions

Give yourself some gratitude for all the work you have done with these suggestions. Giving yourself credit is most likely something you don't do often enough, so try these examples to get you started.

- I am grateful for the love I showed myself through this manifesting process.

- I am thankful for those who supported me through this life-changing moon cycle.
- I am grateful for my excitement and ambition to start making changes in my life for my greater good.
- I am grateful to share my story to inspire others.

Affirmations

Remind yourself how powerful you are with these suggested affirmations.

- I am a radiant being.
- I can move mountains.
- My excitement for my new reality radiates from me.
- I feel butterflies in my stomach because I know I will succeed.
- I receive with love, acceptance, and gratitude.

Lunar Body

As you have been making space for gratitude and creating your last batch of action steps through your lunar spirit and mind, make sure your physical self is also taking the time to practice this same gratitude and grace as you move through the last phases of the moon manifestation cycle.

EXERCISE: WANING GIBBOUS ALTAR

Let us spice up this waning phase altar by adding items in deep, rich colors to incite the enthusiastic energy needed to complete this phase.

What you need:

Waning gibbous moon picture or symbol
Crystal from correspondence list at the end of the chapter
4-inch purple taper candle (or color of your choice), matches/lighter, and candle snuffer

What to do:

Remove the full moon picture and replace it with a waning gibbous moon picture or item that represents it to you. After, select the waning gibbous moon crystal that feels best to you. Choose your candle for this phase: I suggest purple but choose what you like best (white always works too). Place the items on your altar and remove anything placed there for the full moon.

Take a moment to connect with your altar and feel the shift in energy. Light your candle and repeat your intention for this moon cycle aloud three times. When you are finished, snuff the candle out; you will relight it when you work at your altar during this phase.

EXERCISE: WANING GIBBOUS ACTIONS

Take time to reflect on how this cycle has been going for you in a kind, loving way. Once you have a positive perspective on how this cycle has been going, you will be able to create the last few actions needed to end the phase how you want. Focusing on what you need to succeed and what you can leave for the time being will give you the clarity necessary to project you forward. How can you create action steps to carry you to the end of the moon cycle with this excited energy?

Journal on these questions to focus on where your energy needs to go right this moment.

What you need:

Moon journal and pen

What to do:

Journal on the following questions. As you do, resist the urge to overthink; write whatever comes to your mind first.

- What smaller action steps can you take to support the bigger steps you made on the first quarter moon?
- Have you gained any insight into the balancing vibration of the full moon cycle that you can use to create enthusiastic action?
- What part of your intention is close to becoming reality? How can you give it a push forward?

Include a self-care action in this phase and create an action step immediately after.

Tarot: The Star

The hope the Star provides is always refreshing after you have dived into your manifesting work and honed your magical practice. The waning gibbous phase is for sharing your hard work during this moon cycle and giving hope to others. Find ways to share your newfound abundance and mindset. It is a wonderful time to use your inspiration to fuel you to keep going and inspire others.

At this point, you have experienced many changes big and small, and the Star is here to show you that with perseverance, anything is possible. You may have begun noticing that your intuition is fully blossoming—with intuition comes confidence. There is also a chance your intention may not have fully come to fruition, but you have come so much closer to it and gained invaluable insight along the way. Honor this new insight.

Walking in this new vision of your true self and shining like the Star is exactly what you need to move through the next couple of phases to complete the cycle. The figure in the Star card has one foot on land and one in water, a position that indicates you know what is needed to keep your energy balanced and can bring that aspect into your moon manifesting practice because your lunar anima is integrated. You can use all parts of yourself for magical work.

Your sprout from the new moon phase is now a full, thriving plant; now you get to show it off to the world. The Star also calls you to shine and be proud of who you are becoming. Shine your light and help others shine too. When you give hope to others, it flows back to you.

With this tarot spread, you are going to tap into positive, hopeful energy to help you define your magic further and step into the Star's bright, hopeful energy.

EXERCISE: YOU ARE A STAR TAROT SPREAD

Harness messages of hope with this tarot spread to give you the last big push needed to finish out your moon manifesting cycle.

What you need:

Tarot deck

Moon journal and pen

What to do:

Divide your tarot deck into two piles and shuffle each separately. Now let your intuition guide you and pick up one of the piles.

Choose three cards in whatever way you feel called to and place them in a row. Quickly pick up the other pile and do the same. Place them on the table right next to the other three.

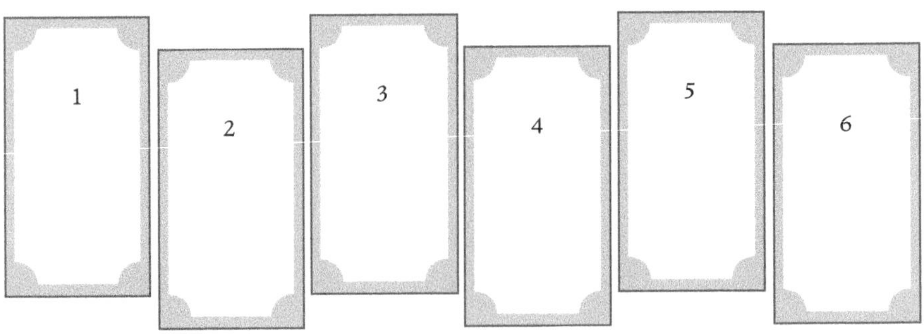

As you read the cards, interpret them from a place of hope and passion. You could even say the word "hope" aloud before you read them.

Card 1 (far left): How can I fully step into my power?

Card 2 (next one): What will help me stay in this state of hope and passion?

Card 3: What should I share about my experiences in this moon cycle?

Card 4: What message does the Star have for me?

Card 5: Where is there hope I might have missed?

Card 6: How can I help someone regain hope?

From the answers you received, plan smaller action steps to support your bigger action steps as the moon cycle ends. Share your experiences with someone who will benefit from it. Make that last push to start rounding out your intention for this cycle. Tie up any loose ends to make last-minute miracles happen.

SIGIL WORKING: WANING GIBBOUS

Create a powerful sigil to kick off this phase in your moon manifestation cycle. Here you will create this sigil to encourage you to share all the hard work you have done to this point and be able to help others by sharing your magic. In this exercise you will use a sentence about how you will share your moon magic to craft a sigil for the phase.

What you need:

Paper and pen or pencils

What to do:

Get comfortable in your sacred space and pick up your paper and pen. Create a sentence about your intention. For example, "I will create a social media post sharing my moon magic." What you end up with should not be much longer than a sentence; if it is, shorten as needed. Write that sentence out at the top of the paper. Now go through and cross out all the vowels and repeating letters. From these letters we will craft a symbol.

Start with whichever letter calls to you first and intertwine all of them until you have your sigil. Do not over-scrutinize what you make; just go with the flow of your intuition and see what you create. Leave enough room on the paper to draw three clockwise circles around the whole sigil. As you do this, say your full intention aloud three times. When finished, say, "This sigil has been activated. And so it is." Now you can leave your sigil on your altar or take a picture of it and use it as the background image on your phone or computer.

RECIPE: WANING GIBBOUS TEA

This tea blend will help you to relax and slow down your energy for reflection as you tie up any loose ends related to your intention for this moon cycle. This particular blend is cooling, refreshing, and detoxing, perfect for helping you feel refreshed and renewed as the moon cycle ends and your manifestations become reality.

What you need:

Mint tea (loose or bagged)
⅛ t fennel seed
1 C freshly boiled water
Fresh cucumber, 1 or 2 slices
Lemon wedge
1 C ice
Teacup for brewing
Tall glass

What to do:

Add mint tea and fennel seed to a cup of hot water. Cover and let steep for ten minutes. As you wait, add the cucumber slices and squeeze a lemon wedge into the cup of ice. After squeezing, add the wedge itself. Pour steeped tea into the glass of ice and give a vigorous stir. At the same time, imagine anything holding you back at this time being transmuted. As you drink your cold tea, imagine it filling any spaces of stagnant energy in your body with fresh, clear purpose.

Waning Gibbous Closing Thoughts

Even though we have come to the waning phases of the moon cycle, do not let it stop you from continuing to take the actions needed to manifest your moon intention. Remember to keep your mindset in a positive receiving space to signal to the universe you are doing the work needed. Continue to create and implement action steps and the universe will respond with a little energetic push toward your goal. Shine bright, share and inspire others as we move forward to the last quarter moon phase.

Correspondence List

A list of waning gibbous focused items for your moon workings.

Deities: Lakshmi, Lilith

Herbs: Cinnamon, caraway, vanilla, balm of Gilead, dill

Incense: Cinnamon, vanilla

Crystals: Rose quartz, okenite, stilbite

Oils: Cinnamon, peppermint

Colors: Lavender, light gray

Keywords: Gratitude, integration, forgiveness

CHAPTER FIFTEEN

LAST QUARTER MOON

The last quarter moon phase is the time to release any expectations that may have crept up these last few days as the moon has been darkening. Look honestly at how your manifestations are shaping up and all you have learned about yourself through this process to give yourself a new outlook and personal understanding. When you look back and decide how to close this moon manifesting cycle, it's important to come from a place of respect for yourself. Be kind, forgive yourself for any hurdles, and decide how to learn from your experiences.

You are divinely guided and have become more in tune with this aspect of your magic through the process of moon manifestation. Everything in this cycle played out the way it did for a reason—the way it needed to. When you take a step back to assess the past few weeks, be sure you can do it in a productive, useful way and, most importantly, without judgment. If you use whatever information you receive for upcoming moon manifesting cycles, you'll have a prepared, documented blueprint for future reference. Regardless of what has happened, you are still closer to your goals and have developed a new magical practice. When you reach this darkening phase and reflect on the ones before it, nourish your physical body and hydrate to cleanse yourself in preparation for the next moon cycle.

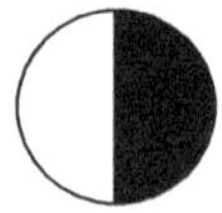

Last Quarter Moon

Moon Moment

At last quarter, we are back to a half-light, half-dark moon, but this time it's on the opposite side of the sky as it has rotated to the other side of Earth. In most areas of the world, this phase rises in the middle of the day. The last quarter phase lasts about a week. The light from the little bit of sun shining on the moon is directed downwards. I compare this to a person looking at where their feet touch the earth, thinking about where they are now. The moon's downward gaze embodies the need to reflect during this phase. Because the tidal activity is so low at this point, it is called a neap tide, meaning the high tides are a little higher and the low tide is higher than it usually is.

Lunar Spirit

During this last quarter phase, your lunar spirit has been doing so much wonderful work. You should be proud of your accomplishments big and small. Right now, it is important to let go of whatever did not work out or shifted regarding your moon cycle intention so you can focus on the needed changes made in your life the last few weeks.

EXERCISE: LAST QUARTER MEDITATION

Spiritual strength reflects on your capacity to forgive yourself and others. Do this meditation to try the act of letting go and forgiving.

What you need:

A quiet space
Moon journal and a pen

What to do:

Sit in a chair or on the ground with your spine upright. Quiet your mind and become aware of your breath. Inhale and exhale slowly. Send each inhale deep into your toes and back up to your head.

Begin making your inhales and your exhales longer. As you do, think about a time when you should have forgiven someone but decided not to. Imagine that whatever feelings come up for you are absorbed into a glowing orb for you to hold. As this happens, replay the situation in your mind's eye and offer your forgiveness. Look up at the last quarter moon and ask it to energetically send this orb of forgiveness to the person you have in mind.

Thank yourself and the person in your mind for sharing space and being patient. Take a deep, slow breath. Let it release slowly, and thank the last quarter moon for its assistance.

Now imagine that the soft light surrounds you like a cloud of loving energy. Continue to focus on your breath. Inhale and exhale. This situation has been energetically resolved and may now show itself to be resolved in your life. Know this is for your highest good. Trust any intuitive feelings and thoughts you may experience. Continue to focus on your breath as you inhale and exhale. Release any control of your breath. Inhale and exhale. Open your eyes, connect with your body, and write down any information you received.

Last Quarter Lunar Focus

As we feel the light from this phase dim, you can start to integrate and process your moon manifesting experiences. Release your doubt and expectation and take a frank view of how everything has settled.

EXERCISE: RELEASE/FORGIVE RITUAL ACTIVATION

This activity can help release any burdens you may be carrying and forgive when needed.

What you need:

3 bay leaves
Blue permanent marker
Medium firesafe dish
Matches/lighter
¼ tsp lavender

Optional:

Moon journal and pen
Tarot deck

What to do:

Gather your ingredients and bring them to your spot in front of your moon altar. Center and ground yourself. Now consider three things you must let go of in this moon cycle. Use whatever comes to mind first. Next, think of three situations you need to forgive. Pick up a bay leaf. Write one thing you will release on one side of the leaf and one thing you will forgive on the other. Write your other things on the remaining leaves. Bay leaves aren't very big, so you can just use a keyword for each as long as you know what they represent.

Now read them over and let your feelings or memories come to the surface. Sprinkle the lavender on the bottom of your firesafe bowl. Take a deep breath. Light each leaf and place in the firesafe bowl. Watch as what you wrote goes up in smoke to be transmuted into something better. Once you've done this with all three leaves, journal or pull a few tarot cards until you feel the ritual is complete.

Now place your bowl on your altar and ground yourself. When you are finished, dispose of the ashes outside if you can. Be sure to say thank you. It is done.

EXERCISE: LAST QUARTER DEVOTIONAL

Let the last quarter moon offer comfort as you start to settle into your moon intention.

What you need:

A method of cleansing your space: smoke, crystals, or sound (for incense and crystal suggestions, see the end of this chapter)
An item that brings you comfort (a piece of clothing, a blanket, or even a stuffed animal)

What to do:

Step outside if possible or be near a window. If you are using smoke to cleanse indoors, be sure the area you are in is well ventilated. Take a few moments to settle into your space, and have your items close by. Take a few deep, cleansing breaths and release them slowly, letting go of any expectations you may currently have. If you cannot physically see the last quarter moon in the sky, imagine its soft, comforting glow cascading over your now-relaxed body.

Pick up the item you chose to cleanse your space and yourself with. Hold it up and say, "May the comfort from the last quarter moon grant me the strength and wisdom to release expectations and reset my energy as I close out this moon cycle. And so it is."

Proceed to cleanse your space, keeping your last quarter moon request at the forefront of your mind. Once completed, settle back into your space. Feel the release activate and allow the potential for change to settle into your energetic self.

Now pick up your comfort item and say, "Now that my energy has been reset, I imbue this energy into my (name of item) as a reminder of and container for this energy in case I need it. Thank you, last quarter moon." If you are working with a specific goddess, you may address her here instead.

Hold your item to your heart and imagine a soft glow of comfort and love being sent to it. Take a few deep breaths, thank the last quarter moon, and journal on your experience.

Lunar Mind

The last quarter moon is the phase in which you take your last actions to wrap up the moon cycle. This includes letting go of some actions or even parts of your intention that were not meant for this cycle. By letting go of these parts of your manifestation, you send them out into the universe to be transmuted into something better for you. Remember that you are not the same person you were at the new moon phase, so you should also release old mindsets and patterns. As you will see, your intention has changed to accommodate the person you are now.

With the release of old thought patterns, you also need to be forgiving to yourself. There is no such thing as an unsuccessful moon manifestation cycle because you have put your trust in your intuition and the universe; everything happened as it was supposed to.

You did an amazing job throughout this cycle and should give yourself a pat on the back for all you have done, the new actions taken, and how you have grown into your magic. Let go of any expectations you may be holding on to; you are now unstoppable.

Enjoy whatever is coming your way right now. You fully deserve it, and stepping into that excitement will help the last bits of your intention surface as you finish this moon manifesting cycle. When you receive the benefits of your intention, a terrific way to show gratitude is to give back to the universe by helping others. Consider all you have learned and think of ways to share this information so that others can benefit from it.

At this point in the moon cycle, as the small light from the moon's last quarter starts to fade, those who will benefit most from your guidance will present themselves. You will recognize their energy and know they are ready to move to a higher vibration of manifesting, just as you were at the beginning of this cycle.

The journaling prompts for this phase focus on giving and receiving, as they go hand in hand when you are ready to expand energetically and others who are ready to manifest with the moon show interest in your journey.

- What parts of your intention do you need to let go of?
- How do you feel about sharing your experience with others?
- Who do you feel would benefit from manifesting with the moon? Would you talk to them about it?
- How do you feel about giving back right now? What can you do to encourage the collective?

- How are you feeling at this moon phase? Is it how you were hoping to feel?

Gratitude Suggestions

Practice acceptance with the following suggested gratitude phrases. When you accept things as they are, you can move forward in your manifestations because it opens you to what needs to be done next.

- Although I may not have reached as many people as I had hoped, the connections I made were wonderful.
- I am grateful I have been authentic on social media even if I did not reach as many people as I had hoped.
- I am thankful I did not rush into making big decisions, and the ones that did not work out taught me to slow down and research more.
- I am thankful my full intention was not realized this cycle; now I have a clearer vision of what I want to manifest in the next cycle.

Affirmations

Try these comforting and validating affirmations.

- I have accomplished what I needed right now, and it feels great.
- The expansive energy I have gained through this experience was life changing.
- I am exactly where I am meant to be.
- I give with love and purpose.
- I am grateful for all I have received.

Lunar Body

You are getting closer to the end of this moon manifestation cycle. You may have experienced physical changes as well as mental and spiritual changes, so take this time to honor your whole self and honor your moon altar, which has been a guiding force and home base throughout this journey.

EXERCISE: LAST QUARTER ALTAR

As you are near the end of your moon manifesting cycle, take time to honor your altar and how it helped guide and focus you. Do you feel a greater connection to this space now? How has that changed your magical practice? Reflect on the changes you made to this space throughout the phases and how doing so changed the energy of your sacred space. Show gratitude to your moon altar as the moon manifesting cycle closes. Simply saying thank you or adorning it with your favorite flower are great ways to show appreciation.

What you need:

Last quarter moon picture or item that represents it
Crystal (see the list at the end of the chapter or choose your own)
4-inch purple taper, plus matches/lighter, and candle snuffer

What to do:

Remove the previous moon picture and replace it with one of the last quarter moon or an item representing the third quarter moon to you. Also, place the items on your altar and remove anything from the waning gibbous moon placed there. Take a moment to connect with your altar and feel the energy shift. Now light your candle and repeat your intention for this moon cycle three times. Snuff the candle out when you are finished so that you can relight it whenever you work at your altar during this phase.

EXERCISE: LAST QUARTER ACTIONS

With the last quarter moon phase, you are starting to slow down in your actions as the night sky darkens. Reflection and assessing where you are now are important. See this reflection on the moon manifesting cycle as if you were reading a business report from the last few weeks. What can you adjust for next time? What did not work that you thought would?

Be gentle with yourself as you move through this reflection process. Ask yourself what worked wonderfully that you will bring into the next moon cycle. As you settle into the darker phases of the moon, it is time to tap into your newfound wisdom. Paying attention to what worked and what didn't during this cycle is important as you move to another intention during the next moon cycle.

What you need:

Moon journal and a pen

What to do:

Head to your moon altar and answer this question in your journal: What ways to release emotions are effective for you? Incorporate at least one action that worked well for you into your routine.

Perform the last quarter phase activities while being mindful of how these new routines have benefitted you.

Create action steps to close out this moon manifestation cycle with the knowledge that you can always create a new intention at the new moon and show gratitude for where your intention is now. Enjoy the benefits of your manifestation this moon cycle.

Tarot: Judgment

The Judgement card wants you to self-reflect but not in an emotional way. Instead, you're invited to review things from more of a business-like perspective to assess exactly how this cycle went without being clouded by emotions. You can then use this information as you move ahead to your next manifesting moon cycle.

In the art of this tarot card, people are rising from the coffins but are not afraid; instead they seem joyful. The symbolism in this card relates to awakening to a new stream of thinking either consciously or subconsciously. As it relates to your manifestation, focus on your mindset in this phase: How has your way of thinking changed since the new moon?

Remember that just like the moon phases, this realization does not come suddenly; it happens over time. Some changes are so subtle that you won't notice them right away. Only when you take the time to reflect can you see the magical changes that have taken place more clearly.

Your fully mature plant/intention may be losing some leaves, but you know how to correct that problem by moving the plant further from the window. The practicality you acquired during the moon cycle can be used toward your intention right now, too. It is never too late to adjust and make corrections where needed.

Think about the theoretical manifesting plant you have nurtured throughout this moon cycle. What sort of shape is it in? Even though a few leaves may have fallen off, buds are starting to sprout from the root area. A small flower may be starting to bud. This cycle may be nearing an end, but the journey is far from over for you. Release what you need to just like the plant lets go of leaves it no longer needs and make space for new ideas, thoughts, and opportunities.

EXERCISE: REFLECT AND RESET TAROT SPREAD

This tarot spread will bring attention to what you need to release gently and what areas you can improve.

What you need:

Tarot deck

Moon journal and pen

What to do:

Shuffle your deck. Place three cards face down and then three more face up on top of the others. The cards facing up are the things you need to not judge yourself so harshly for. The ones face down are solutions to help you move past this and be kinder to yourself.

Flip over each card and journal on the answers you receive. Be sure to go with your first thoughts and feelings, as these are where the answers are most helpful.

From the answers you received, make actionable steps to be kinder to yourself no matter where you are on your manifesting journey. Create reminders on your device about how much you have accomplished. Make a list of what is most important to you right now. Do not get caught up in others' opinions—stand for what makes *you* happy. How can you do this effectively?

SIGIL WORKING: LAST QUARTER

Create a powerful sigil to integrate this phase of your moon manifestation cycle. Using the word "acceptance," we will craft a sigil for this moon phase.

What you need:

Paper and pen or pencils

What to do:

Get comfortable in your sacred space and pick up your paper and pen. Write "acceptance" at the top of the paper. Once you have done this, go through and cross out all the vowels and repeating letters. From these letters we will now craft a symbol.

Start with whichever letter calls to you first and intertwine all of them until you have your sigil. Do not over-scrutinize what you make—just go with the flow of your intuition and see what you create. Remember to leave enough room to draw three clockwise circles around the whole sigil. As you make those circles, say your full intention aloud three times. When finished, say, "This sigil has been activated. And so it is." Now you can leave the sigil on your altar or take a picture of it and use it as the background image for your phone or computer.

RECIPE: LAST QUARTER TEA

This blend of tea at the last quarter moon phase helps you be present in the moment and focus on what this phase has to offer. It is time to fully embrace your new beginnings and dive into your new life. As your new reality settles around you, take some time to release any expectations and enjoy where you are in life right now.

What you need:

1 C water, freshly boiled

1 bag or 1 T loose chamomile tea

3 rose petals (organic) or rose tea

1 small lemon wedge

1 dried orange peel

What to do:

Add all ingredients to the mug and let steep for about five minutes. Sit near your moon altar and take a few breaths. Think about all the positive situations that have happened this moon cycle. With each sip of tea, send love to yourself and those who supported you. Send understanding to those who may not have been extra supportive. When you are finished and the tea bag has cooled, take it outside if you can or to your favorite plant and spread the tea leaves on the soil. Thank the moon for her guidance; now you have sown the seeds for the next cycle.

Last Quarter Moon Closing Thoughts

Taking the time to reflect may not seem like an effective action step, but in fact it is right up there with practicing gratitude. Gratitude is necessary to keep your thoughts and actions aligned and bring you to a successful manifestation. Being available to ground and feel secure in your new magical self is your goal. As you move into the waning crescent/dark moon's theme of self-care, slow your thoughts and focus on the present moment.

Correspondence List

Here are some last quarter correspondences for your moon workings.

Deities: Clementina, Persephone

Herbs: Morning glory, eucalyptus, rue, skullcap, sunflower

Incense: Lemongrass, sage

Crystals: Zoisite, Botswana agate, lepidolite

Oils: Cedarwood, black spruce, bergamot

Colors: Teal, dark purple

Keywords: Evaluation, transformation, surrender

CHAPTER SIXTEEN

WANING CRESCENT MOON

You are so close! You have worked through almost every one of the moon phases except for this one, so it is time to integrate your experiences and feelings from this past moon manifesting cycle with the waning crescent moon. You have come to the phase of your moon manifestation cycle to focus on self-care, a commonly overlooked point in many ritual processes. Manifesting is as much about the work being done as it is about caring for yourself.

Integrating your new mindset and lessons learned is as much a part of manifesting as creating action steps. The importance of self-care during the waning crescent phase relates to both the physical and spiritual self; do whatever helps you relax physically and feel spiritually connected to the universe. You did amazing work and fully deserve this rest and integration phase.

This waning crescent phase, also known as the dark moon phase, calls you to search for the light of wisdom within and see how brightly it shines even though everything outside you may not be shining bright. The reason this phase has two names is because the last stage of the waning crescent moon reaches the point right before the new moon is said to be at its darkest, hence its other name, dark moon.[42]

42. Demetra George, *Mysteries of the Dark Moon: The Healing Power of the Dark Goddess* (New York: HarperOne, 1992), 78.

As the waning crescent appears and the dark moon nestles into the sky, take advantage of this energetically quiet time to focus on the most important magical being: you. You can retreat to your comfortable spaces and just be. Consider connecting to your higher self and meditating a little longer with the focus being on revitalization. The new seeds of your next intention are not going anywhere, so utilize this phase to restore yourself in all ways possible.

You have established a new paradigm of manifestation and magic. Let all your actions, thoughts, and feelings from this past moon manifesting cycle settle where they need to in your energetic body and rest your physical body.

Waning Crescent Moon

Moon Moment

The waning crescent phase is the last moon phase. You can only see a sliver of it in the sky, and it disappears quickly because it is completely in the sun's shadow. This phase lasts for about a week before the new moon cycle begins.[43]

The waning crescent eases into the dark moon just before the new moon, offering only a small window of time. When the moon goes from twenty five percent illumination to zero percent, the dark moon arrives and lasts about a day. The waning crescent is visible just before sunrise and is easy to miss. This phase always faces east (tips of the crescent facing west), in the direction of the sunrise.[44] Because of this phase's calm energy, creativity may heighten and the call to rest is supported by the lull in active moon energy.[45]

43."Phases of the Moon," *Kopernik Observatory & Science Center*, accessed November 25, 2024, https://www.kopernik.org/visitor-info/science-park/phases-of-the-moon/.

44. "Waning Crescent Moon," EarthSky, accessed November 25, 2024, https://earthsky.org/moon-phases/waning-crescent/.

45. "Mental Health, Creativity, and the Lunar Cycles," *PIMSY EHR*, accessed November 25, 2024, https://pimsyehr.com/mental-health-creativity-and-the-lunar-cycles/.

Lunar Spirit

You should be proud of how you have worked with and developed your intuition this moon cycle. Each moon manifestation cycle will bring new insights and developments to your lunar spirit.

EXERCISE: WANING CRESCENT MEDITATION

Receiving love from the moon and letting go of any doubts from this moon cycle is what this meditation is all about.

What you need:

A quiet space
Moon journal and pen

What to do:

Sit in a chair or on the ground with your spine upright. Say aloud: "Dark moon, I ask you to guide me to deep rest so that I can integrate everything that has happened." Quiet your mind and become aware of your breath. Inhale and exhale.

Start sending each inhale deep into your core as you begin making your inhales and your exhales longer. Visualize a dark blue sparkling light from the dark moon meeting you at the top of your head. Imagine that this blue energy is warm and heavy. See this energy gently touch each part of your body, from the top of your head to the tips of your toes, covering you like a warm, heavy blanket.

Notice thoughts that come up, and ask if they need attention. You may have thoughts and feelings that require you to let go of specific emotions. Let your emotions come and go as they need to. Say aloud: "Dark moon, I ask that you help me experience the light energy as I release any emotions that come up right now." Continue to focus on your breath and the warm blanket of energy from the moon. Inhale and exhale.

Stay in this warm, healing space for as long as you need to. Thank the moon for its comfort, healing, and resting energy. Release any control of your breath. Inhale and exhale. Open your eyes, connect with your body, write down any information you received, and rest.

Waning Crescent Lunar Focus

It's now time for a little pampering, and there is no better way to bring balance than a nice magical bath. I am a water person, and bathing always makes me feel rested and happy. You can adjust this exercise as needed to make it work for a shower or even a hot tub. Mindfully taking time to not actively work on something and just focus on yourself during this phase will rejuvenate you for the next moon manifesting cycle.

EXERCISE: FULL BODY EQUILIBRIUM REFLECTION AND ACTIVATION

Float your troubles away in this energetically cleansing ritual bath that will help you achieve a full body equilibrium. Adapt to a shower if bathing isn't an option for you.

What you need:

7 tea light candles (any color)
Large firesafe dish plus matches/lighter
1 C Epsom salts
1 rose quartz crystal
1 T honey
2 handfuls flower petals
2 drops rosemary oil or a sprig of rosemary

Optional:

Moon journal and pen

What to do:

Prepare your bath to your favorite temperature. Gather your candles, firesafe dish, and lighter.

Hold one candle and say, "May this light balance my root chakra at the base of my spine." Light it and place it on the dish. Repeat for each chakra and candle:

"May this light balance my sacral chakra, deep in my belly."

"May this light balance my solar plexus chakra at my diaphragm."

"May this light balance my heart chakra in my heart space."

"May this light balance my throat chakra in my throat area."

"May this light balance my third eye chakra, at the middle of my eyes."

"May this light balance my crown chakra, right at the top of my head."

Make sure your candles are safely burning before proceeding.

Place a handful of Epsom salts in the tub, and say, "May this cleanse any unwanted energies away from me." Now place the rosemary in the tub and say, "May this rosemary purify my intentions to help me succeed." Place the honey in the tub and say, "This honey will sweeten my words so they may be more effective." Lastly, place the flowers in the tub and say, "These flowers bring love and comfort to me and heal what needs to be healed right now."

Get into the tub and think about each energy center, each item you used in this bath, and why. See everything unneeded dissipate into the water and what is needed soak into your skin. When you feel ready, scoop up the flower petals and rosemary and set aside. Let the water out of the tub, visualizing what you do not need going down the drain to be transmuted. Dry off and place the rosemary and flowers on your altar if you feel called. Drink a cool beverage to ground and journal or meditate on how you felt and what thoughts arose.

EXERCISE WANING CRESCENT DEVOTIONAL

Rest and ground with the dark moon energy in this devotional.

What you need:

Eye mask or washcloth

A few drops of your favorite essential oil

A space to lie down on the ground or a plant if you cannot go outside

Moon journal and pen

What to do:

Grab your items and go outside or near a window with space to lie down. Once you are settled into your space, take a few breaths. Put a few drops of essential oil on the outside (the side not touching your skin) of your eye mask or washcloth. Place it on your eyes and relax into the darkness. Feel the weight of your body against the earth or floor. You are grounded and safe.

Imagine a warm, dark, comforting energy coming down from the moon and wrapping around you like a blanket. Now see the earth's energy as a dark green energy wrapping around you like a blanket from below. Take a few breaths and release anything that may come into these energies. You are fully supported.

Say, "Thank you, dark moon and Earth, for your comforting and cleansing energy. I am filled with my power and harness all I am to become with your guidance. May all be at peace and filled with love. And so it is." Stay in this space as long as you feel called to. When ready, slowly move your body and remove the eye covering. Journal on your experiences.

Lunar Mind

You are nearing the end of your moon manifesting cycle. Along the way, you have learned, released, and gained new mindsets and insights. Gratitude supported you through these magical manifesting phases, and now it is time to rebalance your energy and rest. Rest does not come easily to most of us, but that is exactly what this moon phase calls for.

Your intention and new reality are still weaving and becoming real in your universe; now it is time to let them fulfil their purpose. Even though you are not taking physical action, resting and integrating are what you need to focus on now. As you restore and integrate your mind and body, reflect nonjudgmentally on the moon manifestation cycle. Consider your experiences from the last month as if you are playing a movie back in your mind, just observing. Notice the situations, feelings, and thoughts in this mind movie and consider how you have integrated your lunar anima. Now your whole self works magically to easily achieve your intentions.

You will dive a bit deeper into these observations when the time is right, but that time is not now. You may realize that manifesting with the moon is not so much about changing your life, even though that is a plus. It is more about cultivating the life you want and knowing how to use your integrated lunar anima of spirit, mind, and body to bring forth your desires. If you choose to manifest during the next moon cycle, this new perspective will offer many great insights and lessons.

Journaling during this cycle is more laid-back and imaginative. Have fun with it.

- What would it look like if you could create any reality you wanted?
- You have an entire day to yourself with unlimited funds. What will you do?
- Create an imaginary pet; what traits does it have? Magical powers? Does it talk? Write this in detail.
- List all the remarkable things about yourself. Be sure to list at least five but keep going until you cannot think of anything else.
- Have a conversation with the moon. Discuss how you felt collaborating with her and your magic.

Gratitude Suggestions

Try out these gratitude suggestions that are comforting and relaxing. Choose words that give you a sense of calm and peace.

- I am grateful for how determined I am.
- I am thankful I can learn and grow happily through change.
- I am grateful for finding a soft, comfortable spot and allowing myself to rest.
- I am grateful for my body and how I have many ways to nourish it.
- I am thankful for the discernment to let go of what is not serving me right now.

Affirmations

Here are some fun affirmations to add to your waning crescent practice.

- I am a snazzy manifester.
- I am the best at resting and restoring.
- Bedhead is the name of my game.
- I look at myself and think I am the cat's meow.
- Rest is my superpower.

Lunar Body

Now is the time to pamper your physical body, rest, and integrate this past moon manifesting phase.

EXERCISE: WANING CRESCENT ALTAR

Your altar is nearly complete for this manifestation cycle, and it too needs to rest and rejuvenate its magic. Sit with your altar as part of your rest and self-care routine. I like to read while sitting near my altar and just soak up all the energy and magic it's been offering for this lunar cycle. I will use restful scents such as vanilla and lavender and appreciate the magical space I created and how it was so helpful to me throughout my moon manifesting cycle.

What you need:

Waning crescent moon picture or representation
Crystal (see correspondence list at the end of this chapter)
4-inch pink taper candle, matches/lighter, plus candle snuffer

What to do:

Remove the last quarter moon picture and replace it with a waning crescent moon picture or item that represents the waning crescent moon for you. Choose a waning crescent moon crystal that feels the best to you and harnesses that energy. Choose your candle for this phase. I suggest pink but choose what you like best—white works, too. Place the items on your altar and remove anything from the previous phase placed there.

Take a moment to connect with your altar and feel the energy shift. Notice the calm flow of your space. Light your candle and repeat your intention for self-care this moon cycle three times. Snuff out the candle when you are finished and light it whenever you work at your altar during this phase.

EXERCISE: DARK MOON ACTIONS

As you rest and connect with your lunar spirit, mind, and body in a light but profound way, give yourself space to touch the childlike energy of the new moon again and do a few activities you did as a child. Coloring, watching favorite movies, or taking extra naps are great examples of how to step into this energy. You should also focus on self-care actions at this time: try a massage or facial—something you have not done before.

If you notice thoughts of the last moon cycle come up for you, give them passive attention. See them floating away after you acknowledge them.

Mindfully move slower these next few days. How does it feel to do this?

Tarot: The Hermit

When the crescent moves into its final dark moon phase and is tucked away in the heavens, a sweet, calm quiet is upon us. During this phase, it is the time to meditate, contemplate, and rest. You want to offer the waning crescent phase as much attention as the other moon phases; neglecting to do so would be a disservice to your whole moon manifestation process because you are now fully integrating not only your magic but also the last nuances of your lunar intention.

Most times when you rest and integrate your experiences, your most profound inspiration presents itself. Now is the time to strengthen your connection to the Divine, seek the energy of the Hermit tarot card, and find and brighten your inner light.

The Hermit stands alone on a mountaintop but is not lonely or looking for someone to guide him. He holds the light of his inner wisdom. His lantern shines bright because he takes the time needed to recognize and integrate that energy. The Hermit has recognized that he put in the outer work to call in his intentions, and now it is time to focus on his lunar body and how profoundly amazing this can be.

Nurture the flame of your desires by giving your inner world the attention it needs right now. The outer world is not going anywhere and isn't where your attention and energy are needed. Take the extra time to encourage your inner light to shine a little brighter and make space in your world to let that happen. Harnessing Hermit energy is important as you integrate all you have done and created during this moon manifesting cycle.

EXERCISE: THE LIGHT WITHIN TAROT SPREAD

This tarot spread asks for gentle contemplation as you prepare and take solace in your comfortable spaces. It will help you see what self-care you should focus on right now for the greatest vibrational benefit.

What you need:

Tarot deck

Moon journal and pen

What to do:

Shuffle your cards. Find the Hermit card in your deck. Place it face up on the table. Now count to the eleventh card and place it to the right of the Hermit. This is card 1.

Next place the card from the bottom of the deck under the Hermit card. This is card 2.

Shuffle the cards again. Now flip over the top card and place it to the left of the Hermit. This is card 3.

Card 1 (right of Hermit): What divine guidance do you need to give attention to?

Card 2 (bottom card): What aspect of rest is most important right now?

Card 3 (left of hermit): What needs to be put to rest in your life as you end this manifesting cycle?

From the answers you received, sit with the cards and give yourself time to let the answers slowly arise. Rest and mindfully notice what feelings and thoughts come up for you but do not fully attach to them. Pay attention to any dreams during this time; you will be surprised at the messages they hold. Be sure to record this reading and any thoughts in your moon journal.

SIGIL WORKING: THE DARK MOON

Create a powerful sigil to wrap up your moon manifestation cycle. Using a self-care phrase, craft a sigil for the dark moon. For example, I will take an Epsom salt bath.

What you need:

Paper and pen or pencils

What to do:

Get comfortable in your sacred space and pick up your paper and pen. Write your self-care phrase out at the top of the paper. It should not be much longer than a sentence. If it is, shorten to a sentence. Once you have done this, go through and cross out all the vowels and repeating letters. From these letters we will now craft a symbol.

Start with whichever letter calls to you first and intertwine all of them until you have your sigil. Do not over-scrutinize this, just go with the flow of your intuition and see what you create. Remember to leave enough room to draw three clockwise circles around the whole sigil. As you draw the circles, say your full intention aloud three times. When finished, say, "This sigil has been activated. And so, it is." Now you can leave the sigil on your altar or take a picture of it and use it as a screensaver.

RECIPE: WANING CRESCENT TEA

The waning crescent blends harness rest and reflection, just what you need for this moon phase. As you wind down from this moon cycle's activity, it is time to rest and integrate the last few weeks. A restoring, calming blend will not only calm you but also help integrate all the new manifestations.

What you need:

1 C freshly boiled water
½ T Rooibos (loose or bag)
½ T Hibiscus tea (loose or bag)
⅛ t ginger or ginger tea bag
½ T honey, if desired

What to do:

Place all ingredients into your mug of boiled water. Let steep for about eight minutes. Remove the ginger and let steep a few minutes more. If you'd like, add half a tablespoon of honey and stir. Hold the mug in both hands and inhale the aroma of the tea. Feel it fill you up with a comforting, warm energy. Say three times into your mug, "I deeply love and honor myself." Sip your tea and only think loving thoughts about yourself. When finished, do something nice for yourself.

Dark Moon Closing Thoughts

The cycle is complete, and you have been prioritizing yourself. You may feel the pull to start planning for the next cycle or even create new action steps for this one—resist that urge. You will have plenty of time to plan in a few days when the next new moon comes around, so kick your feet up with an enjoyable book and savor this downtime you worked for.

Give yourself time to absorb your magic, incorporate the lessons learned, and celebrate all the successes from this moon cycle. It is time to clean your energetic slate, so you are fresh and ready for improved situations and opportunities in the next moon manifesting cycle.

Correspondence List

Try these suggestions for your dark moon workings.

Deities: Idun, Hekate

Herbs: Allspice, violet, rowan, copal, thyme

Incense: Chamomile, nag champa

Crystals: Tourmaline, black tourmaline, smoky quartz

Oils: Ylang-ylang, vetiver, marjoram

Colors: Soft pink, light yellow

Keywords: Rest, gratitude, reflection

PART THREE

ADVANCED MOON WORK

Now that you have fully harnessed your magical moon practice, here are some other considerations to add to your manifesting work and make it more personalized to you and your intention.

CHAPTER SEVENTEEN

LUNAR ECLIPSES, THE BLUE MOON, AND THE BLACK MOON

Here are some advanced moon workings to incorporate into your practice when you are ready. Using this chapter as a reference will also help you to broaden your moon manifestations as you build your magical practice.

There are meanings and nuances for all the ways the moon transitions through the sky. I am frequently asked about lunar eclipses and collaborating with them. First, I will discuss what a lunar eclipse is, then dive into the energies of these powerful moons. I will provide information about the energies of these potent lunations, and you can decide how and if they are something you want to start working with.

Lunar Eclipses

Lunar eclipses occur during full moon phases and happen when Earth is between the moon and sun. The earth's shadow appears on the surface of the moon, giving it a striking red appearance. During this time, the moon is temporarily blocked from the light and can be considered a cosmic reset. It also aligns with the north and south nodes of your astrological birth chart and are related to karma and fate. If you are familiar with astrology and your birth chart, you can check to see where the nodes are in your chart and see how they affect you depending on their houses and signs. As you get more comfortable with moon cycle work, you can research this more.

There are three types of lunar eclipses: total, partial and penumbral.

Total Lunar Eclipse: Occurs when the moon moves into the innermost corner of Earth's shadow. The number of clouds and the amount of dust in the air determine how red the moon appears.

Partial Lunar Eclipse: The alignment of the moon, sun, and Earth is imperfect, so only a partial shadow of Earth is seen on the moon's surface.

Penumbral Eclipse: The moon only travels on the outer part of the planet, so the shadow is very faint and may be hard to see with the naked eye.[46]

The energy of each type of eclipse is different. I like to use the analogy of a radio. With a total lunar eclipse, the music (energy) is turned up, so your wants and needs are right there in your face. This can be overwhelming, so knowing when a total eclipse is coming and preparing can help you turn the volume down a bit and redirect the energy where it is most needed. As you move to the partial lunar eclipse, the volume is halved. It is a little loud but not so much that you cannot manage it. Here you want to see what comes up and give it some care, but it is not so blaring as during a total eclipse. It's easy to breeze over the penumbral eclipse—the volume is low and you can hear a bit of noise, but at this point it is like white noise. You may get some intuitive tickles but nothing like the other two types of eclipses. This eclipse is easier on you but also gives you time to focus on one aspect that is showing up.

When manifesting, these types of eclipses show up as extra energy and may spark your ego as well. Remember that your ego is built to protect you, but you must not let it stop your actions. Knowing about eclipses and how they work will prepare you for them as they show up during your active manifestation cycles.

Should I Work with Eclipses?

There are many magical people who like to work with eclipses and others to whom do not feel called. Working with eclipse energies can change

46. "Visual Appearance of Lunar Eclipses," NASA, accessed November 25, 2024, https://eclipse.gsfc.nasa.gov/LEcat5/appearance.html.

an intention, so read ahead and then you can decide what is best for your practice. Above all, it's best to work through a few moon cycles and establish your practice before adding eclipses to your moon manifesting rotation. If you feel strongly about a certain eclipse, do what you have been called to do; there may be a specific reason that eclipse called to you. Educating yourself as you move along this process will help you feel more able to determine what will work best for you and your moon manifesting.

Keep in mind that working with these energies is intense, so if you at least know they will amplify everything, you can make them work for you. The situations the eclipses bring up will happen regardless; if you prepare for them, you can shift to harness this energy in a more productive way. Sometimes the plot twists the eclipses bring direct you to your fate. Knowing this lunar energy is coming and making sure to create aligned steps to work with it is better than not acting.

Old limiting beliefs and thought patterns can sometimes creep up and inhibit our moon manifesting flow during eclipses, but this is not a bad thing. You can use this time to rewrite those old narratives and work on past thoughts that may still be nagging you. Asking yourself why they showed up or examining the action you took toward your intention that brought those limiting beliefs to light can help you heal and move past them for good. This is why letting these thoughts surface is not a negative thing. As a society we are taught to push away and bury the thoughts that are not shiny and happy, but there is so much insight in what comes up during an eclipse, and you have the tools you need right here in this book to help you deal with them. The moon represents our emotions, so this is all part of the process. When the moon brings up blocked things, your first thought may be to bury them. It is like the cover of your shadowy portal is cracked open when the moon is darkened for that little sliver of time. If you are ready to do some deep healing, consider working with the lunar eclipses during your moon manifesting and powering your own brand of magic even more.

I incorporate the eclipses into my moon manifesting work if I feel it can benefit my intention or if I am strongly being called to even if I am not sure why. That usually means there is something I need to learn or work on to help move my intention along. If your intuition is saying go for it but you are not sure why, it may be an important piece of your plan for that cycle, so do not ignore it.

If you do decide to go ahead and work with the eclipses, other magical practices such as grounding and sticking to your moon manifesting routine are important. Keeping your energy balanced will help create a vortex of calm as you work with and create big actions for this lunar phase. If you decide to sit this lunar eclipse out, I still suggest grounding and documenting how you felt during this lunation for later reference.

Do not be afraid to try eclipse work—worst case is it does not resonate with you, and you leave it out of your next manifesting cycle. If you have worked with the other phases already, you will also have experience to draw from as you move forward. You will be able to see the differences in working with the eclipses and can make an informed decision the next time one comes around.

Deciding whether to work with eclipses or not really all comes down to what you are ready to incorporate into your magical working and how you feel about eclipse energy. If one happens when you are amid your moon manifesting cycle and you do not harness this extra powerful energy, just pay it no mind. There will not be any negative effects either way; the radio frequency is just a bit louder. I would like to mention that you need to make your own decision about eclipse work based on where you are in your journey. There is a good amount of conflicting advice out there, so using your own inner compass is most important.

How to Harness the Eclipse Energy

If you have decided you are going all in, now is the time to figure out how to work eclipse energy into your practice. The easiest way to determine which eclipse to work with is to ask yourself this: going back to the radio analogy, how loud would you like your wants and needs to become a part of your manifestation?

The best and easiest way to start using eclipses is to incorporate them into your action steps for the phase they occur in. If you are working with a full moon, incorporate the energy into your full moon actions, for example. This extra energy can be used to your benefit and will give your action steps an extra energetic boost. Try using this energy when the eclipse requires a little extra preparation.

The energy of eclipses is usually a fast-moving flow, so be prepared for immediate things to happen when collaborating with them. Once you realize the energy of the eclipse or what is coming up for you energetically, you can then see how it can be integrated with your actions in a way that will bring a bigger and more meaningful result.

The Zodiac and the Eclipse

It is also important to consider what zodiac sign the eclipse is in. For example, if we are coming up on a Taurus eclipse moon, meaning the moon is in the sign of Taurus when the eclipse happens, your base wants and needs will be more pronounced. These would be the core go-to things in your life, things you can always depend on to be there if you need to take time away from the world and seek comfort. Will that help or hinder what you want to manifest? If it will hinder you, then maybe let the Taurus eclipse slide right on by and consider collaborating with it the next time that eclipse moon energy comes around. Keep in mind that the energy of all eclipses is strong, and while it may seem like a lot to add to your manifesting cycle, the result can be fantastic. Momentous changes also mean creating room in your life for improved things. You do not want to overwhelm yourself, but that slight discomfort can be life changing. Let me give you a good, complete example.

If you find yourself in the Libra waxing gibbous moon that will eclipse when full, there will be some limiting thoughts from the past that start to come forward. The energy of the eclipse is building during the waxing gibbous, so you'll want to feel what comes up loudly and work it into your action steps. How can you flip those reemerging thoughts and use them for your action steps in that phase? You can do exactly what that limiting belief tells you is not possible. Is this belief related to your intention? Let's say you were always told you were not good at talking to groups of people. Your intention for this phase is to create a course on vision boards. Take this opportunity to prospect different New Age shops in which to lead a vision board workshop or ask to assist with an existing one. This step not only reverses that limiting belief, but you may also be able to create a new connection, so it is two steps accomplished in one swift action.

The zodiac sign an eclipse occurs in will also determine if the energy you may be working with is pronounced. If an eclipse lands on your moon sign during your manifesting moon phases, then that phase may be one where you are going to have bigger revelations and even break your own glass ceiling. This action can be very expansive for you and affect how you go about the rest of the moon cycle. New avenues of abundance will open for you if you commit to doing the inner work that shows up at this point.

Here's a list of keywords for each zodiac sign's lunar eclipse:

Aries: Impulsive actions or the desire to act impulsively may come up. When this eclipse comes around, be prepared and make sure you are thinking through your decisions and not just doing.

Taurus: Your need to be right may show up strongly during this lunar event. It is important to let others speak and to listen during this time, even if you are correct. Forget about right or wrong—sometimes a unique perspective can provide much-needed insight.

Gemini: You may feel a need to talk everything in circles when it is not necessary when this eclipse comes around. You may have so many thoughts about your actions or manifestations that it can cause confusion. It is important to stick to your moon magic work because it will bring you out of the tumultuous clouds of thought and back down to reality.

Cancer: You may be extra sensitive to situations during this eclipse. You may want to retreat the minute the going gets tough, so having a plan if this starts to happen is key. Reach out to someone and have them check in on you or be in contact with them on a scheduled basis. For instance, a morning or nighttime check-in for a few days to make sure all is well may help.

Leo: Under the roaring Leo eclipse, you may find yourself being a bit too direct, and it may cause some static with people close to you. Not regaining control of your emotions here can cause you to overdo and even halt your manifesting process if you allow your ego to get in the way.

Virgo: Being cautious is not a terrible thing, but when this eclipse shows up you may be taking caution to the extreme. Be mindful of why this energy is showing up for you so it does not keep you from taking the actions needed for your current moon manifesting cycle.

Libra: This eclipse is a gentle one, and it may be more about your creativity than anything else. Take advantage of this and get creative with your daily moon practice and what you are manifesting for that cycle. Dream big and get out of your comfort zone here.

Scorpio: Creativity or wanting to keep valuable information to yourself could show itself here as the energy is about keeping your cards close. While in some cases this can be helpful, make sure you are doing so for the right reasons. If not, assess your worries and work those into your moon magic work.

Capricorn: You may feel you are not doing enough, whether it is about your intention for this cycle, work, or home. This attitude can stall your manifesting flow because you are focusing on the wrong things. Take a deep breath and know it all happens as it is supposed to.

Aquarius: Do not get so caught up in the details of your moon magic that you leave out the emotion of these sacred practices. We want it to be right, but that's not what magic is about—it is about how it makes us feel. Done is better than perfect and in this lunar event that is something to keep in mind.

Pisces: Your intuition or psychic sight will be in overdrive, so be sure to send out what you want returned to the universe and take advantage of these open portals of energy. Grounding is important at this time because you do not want to stay in your spiritual spaces for too long.

Staying tied to your physical reality is important for your magical practice.

As I was working through one of my first moon manifesting cycles, I realized there was an upcoming Aries lunar eclipse. I had not initially planned to work with the lunar eclipse but for some reason I was compelled to look it up. It was a partial lunar eclipse, so if we revisit my radio analogy, it was medium loud. I then realized I had been making fast and furious action steps that were not moving me forward like I expected. When I noticed this lunar event, I tried to slow down and realized the actions I was taking were superficial and really would not move the manifesting scale all that much. I made sure to spend extra time with my daily moon magic and take my time making decisions even though I wanted to just get moving. Doing this taught me a lot, and I realized how this eclipse energy may have been affecting me. Had I not looked it up and just let it pass by, I would not have felt the effects enough to notice. You must invite this energy to fully collaborate with it.

EXERCISE: TO ECLIPSE OR NOT TO ECLIPSE TAROT SPREAD

Use this spread to tap into your intuition to see if working with the eclipse energy is a promising idea for your moon manifesting.

What you need:

Tarot deck
Moon journal and a pen

What to do:

Pull five cards and place them face down in a circle. The first card is placed at the top and the remaining cards counterclockwise.

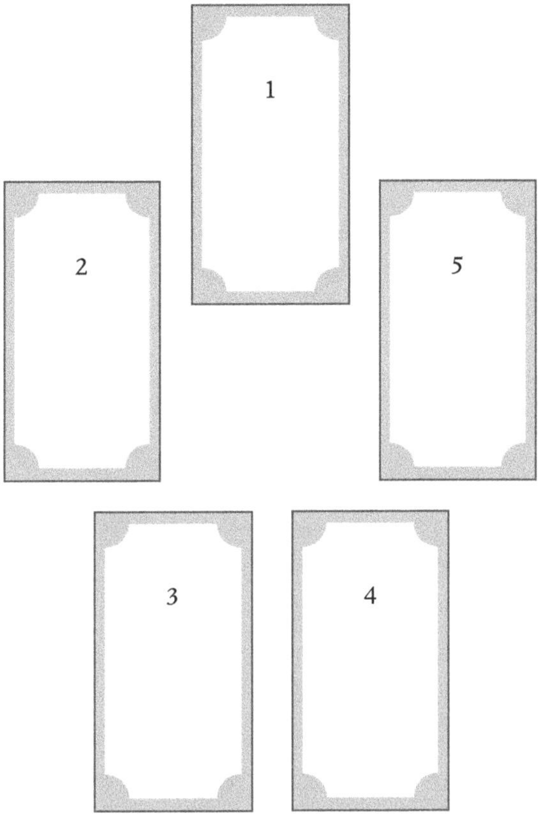

As you read each question, pull the corresponding card, and answer the question with your first intuitive impressions.

Card 1: Am I ready to accept the changes this eclipse presents to me?

Card 2: Will I be able to prepare for and accept the reset of the lunar energy?

Card 3: Will I be okay to just let this eclipse pass by and not bring it into my energetic space?

Card 4: Why do I want to work with the eclipse?

Card 5: What do I expect when working with eclipse energy?

After you have pulled your cards for this tarot spread you will be able to better decide how to manage the upcoming eclipse and how you should proceed in a way that works for you. Since we are working with a more intense energy here, it's important to not rush this tarot spread. I like to pull cards, walk away, and return later to answer the questions. This is great to do anytime you feel a bit overwhelmed when doing spreads.

Blue and Black Moons

You may have heard the phrase "once in a blue moon," but have you ever thought about what that means? A new or full moon usually occurs once per calendar month. Sometimes two moons fall during the same month and that is where the terms "blue" and "black moon" come into play.[47] The second full moon in a calendar month is considered the blue moon, and you can use this extra boost of lunar energy for your manifesting during that cycle. The blue moon adds an extra jolt of energy and allows you space for a big, much-needed change. This moon energy may also illuminate your moon manifesting path just a bit brighter so you can take bigger actions or give you a nudge in the right direction. The black moon occurs when there are two new moons in a calendar month. While calling for bigger change, a black moon may also help you focus on a release that needs to be bigger than you realized. Do not be afraid to dream big during these spiritually supercharged new moons.

Because the blue and black moons are based on the Gregorian calendar we use today, they technically don't hold extra significance. Don't let that stop you from using them to your advantage, however. You can use these moons as a time of extra focus and energy within your own practice. For example, because the black moon is dark in the sky, it may be a great time to use this space for meditating or refocusing on your intention for the moon cycle. The sky is also darker and the stars more pronounced, so meditating with the stars and seeing if you get any intuitive messages from them may be an extra exercise to take advantage of. With the blue moon it usually occurs at the opposite end of the month after the first full moon. You can use these to recommit and rebalance during your manifestation cycle. Our attention and focus on blue and black moons are what harnesses

47. Kirsty Gallagher, *Lunar Living: Working with the Magic of the Moon Cycles* (Hay House, 2021), 151.

this energy. Try working with them to see if these blue and black moons are something you resonate with.

Something else to consider is that the second moon may be in a different zodiac sign, so the energy may shift. You can use that change to your advantage when working with that moon cycle. For example, the blue moon may move into Libra and, at that point during your moon manifesting, you could consider shifting the focus to relationships and how the people around you can assist with your intention.

Whether you decide to work with eclipses and blue or black moon energy, knowing what they bring to the table during a moon cycle is important as you start to navigate your moon manifestation journey. Adding them can also be beneficial during a bigger manifestation cycle to keep you focused on your moon intention. Using the blue and black moons adds another layer to your moon manifesting.

CHAPTER EIGHTEEN

ASTROLOGY AND THE MOON

The zodiac energy of the new and full moons is another way to incorporate specific energy into your moon manifestation practice. After learning how the energy of the zodiac affects you, you can tailor your intentions to the energy of the zodiac sign the moon phase you are working with is in. Then you can decide if you want to include this on your moon manifesting journey. This knowledge will serve as a reference for future moon manifestation workings. Using the moon app on my phone, I check to see what zodiac sign the moon is in every day. Understanding the energy of each sign that the moon enters can help you plan during your moon manifesting cycle.

Moon Signs and Phases

Western astrology has an exceedingly long history. Modern astrology emerged from mathematician and astronomer Ptolemy's *Tetrabiblos*, published about 1,800 years ago. Ptolemy divided Earth's orbit around the sun into distinct thirty-degree sections, each with a different recognition. This led to the twelve zodiac signs we have today.[48] Here are the common glyphs used for each of the signs:

48. "Ancient Zodiac," University of Michigan: Early Astronomy, accessed November 4, 2024, https://early-astronomy.classics.lsa.umich.edu/ancient_ziqpu.

♈	♉	♊	♋	♌	♍
Aries	Taurus	Gemini	Cancer	Leo	Virgo
♎	♏	♐	♑	♒	♓
Libra	Scorpio	Sagittarius	Capricorn	Aquarius	Pisces

At first I did not use any of the zodiac signs in my moon manifesting, but as I started learning more about the zodiac characteristics and looking at what sign the moon was in every day, I began to incorporate them. I am now in the habit of looking every day to see what zodiac energy the moon is in. There is no need to do this when you are still new to moon manifesting, but eventually you may enjoy adding this bit of astrology to your practice. As for now, it's mostly the force of habit for me to check whether I am actively manifesting or not. I started working the zodiac into my moon magic using just my moon sign, as I knew it was extra special. I am an Aries moon so that extra fiery energy was always helpful, and I knew I could harness it in a way that would be beneficial to my moon practice and magic. After a while, I started incorporating all the signs and used those energies to help me along on my journey. We have all signs of the zodiac in our birth charts—all are a part of you somehow.

Your Moon Sign

In a birth chart, each sign has personality characteristics and is used to determine someone's personality traits based on the time they were born. When you go to read your horoscope, you are looking at your Sun sign (sometimes called your "star sign"). Your Sun sign is the exact position the sun was in when you were born. It's common for people to know their Sun sign; when people say, "I'm a Leo" or "I'm a Cancer," they are talking about the placement of the Sun when they were born.

There are also other signs connected to our astrological personality as well, and one of those is your Moon sign. Where the sun sign shows your outer self, or what you want the world to see, the moon sign is more about your hidden self, such as your emotions and deep personal thoughts.

The moon sign shows you how you best process emotions, how your intuition works best for you, the best way you may connect in relationships and how you feel most safe. Your moon sign reflects your inner self and the emotions that drive you to do what you do. Knowing and understanding this part of you will also help you to create intentions and action steps that will be most effective for your moon manifesting.

Most of the time, I will ask people for their moon sign instead of their sun sign because I want to know where they are emotionally, and it helps me to interact with them in a better way. When collaborating with clients, it helps me gauge and better tap into their emotional responses to get a more precise tarot reading or mediumship session for them.

There is so much we do not show the world, unfortunately things we are often taught to hide in our early years. The amount of magic you hold inside and perhaps do not let anyone—sometimes even yourself—see is worth giving attention to and asking to come out of the shadows. You may have hidden talents or even psychic insights just waiting to be brought into the moonlight.

You can do an internet search "what is my moon sign?" to find out which one is yours. I have added a list at the end of the chapter of all the moon signs for reference.

Your Moon Phase

Along with knowing the moon sign at your birth, it is also interesting to find out what phase the moon was in when you were born. This information can help you see how that phase feels for you energetically and prompt you to try diverse ways of working with the phase to best suit your intentions. I was born under a full moon, and no, I was not surprised to find this out because full moons were always incredibly special to me. I could always feel the intensity of a full moon's gaze upon me, and it was hard to ignore. Knowing that I may be a bit more sensitive during the full moon phase helps me plan for that and take it easy on myself. I will make sure to ground more than usual and try to express myself clearly when I am feeling emotional. Since I know this about myself, I can better plan out my full moon action steps for when I am actively moon manifesting.

Knowing which moon phase you were born under also gives you some interesting insight into how you react to situations in your everyday life. For example, if you were born under the waning moon phase you may need a bit more time to process situations. Giving yourself that extra time will help you make better decisions and not feel pressured. Knowing this about yourself will also encourage you to better communicate your needs when sticky situations arise.

Look at the recommended reading section of this book to find websites and books if you'd like to learn what moon phase you were born under.

Moon Phase Keyword List

New moon keywords: Adventurous, creative, impulsive
Waxing crescent keywords: Productive, ambitious, risk avoidant
First quarter keywords: Practical, capable, impatient
Waxing gibbous keywords: Nurturing, calming, perfectionist
Full moon keywords: Sensitive, emotion driven, hesitant
Waning gibbous keywords: Logical, thoughtful, analytical
Last quarter keywords: Loyal, sentimental, devoted
Waning crescent keywords: Imaginative, unorthodox, quiet

Zodiac in Moon Manifestation Practice

Once you have gone through the process of a magical moon manifesting cycle, you can build on your practice by adding the energy of the zodiac signs. Doing so will add extra zest to your magical practice, and you can tailor your moon intention based on the energy of that zodiac sign.

When the moon hits the new and full parts of her cycle, certain characteristics will be amplified depending on what sign she is currently hanging out in, so keep that in mind if you choose to collaborate with them. Integrating astrology can be great when further focusing on your work. The energy of the new moon still focuses on starting something new, but adding the zodiac energy will curate your intention a bit more specific. With the full moon, adding the spice of the signs can steer you in the direction in which your balance needs to be focused.

Collaborating with astrology is like adding an extra shot of espresso in your coffee. If you do not want to harness the energy of that sign, that's fine—it will not affect your magical workings at all. You can also use the energy of the signs for reference when you decide to incorporate them into your own dash of magic. With the addition of the signs into your moon manifestation practices, you will commit all the basic characteristics of each sign to memory in time. From there, you may start being able to recognize peoples' signs just by talking to them, which is an interesting and fun bonus.

Taking the astrological energy of the moon phase you want to work with into consideration can be helpful in shaping your intention in a more detailed way. You can also tap into the elemental energy of the current zodiac sign. For instance, when working with the Virgo moon, you can make sure your intention has a stable, grounded energy or add that element to your moon magic altar, such as a small dish of dirt from outside to symbolize Virgo's earth element. These are all useful tools for you to bring to your magic and harness the energy needed to manifest in the most successful way possible.

You will notice each zodiac sign in the new and full moon differ in focus. Even though most of the time the overall theme is the same for each sign in the phases, these are more directed on how you can use your action steps to best harness the energy.

Why do the Signs Shift Through the Year?

We all tend to take the order and dates of the zodiac signs for granted. But how did they come to be? The idea of one zodiac sign representing a certain time frame goes back to the Mesopotamians, roughly about the second millennium BC. Babylonian priests saw how the stars affected society, namely the king and his kingdom. There is evidence of this in the *Enuma Anu Enli*, a series of seventy cuneiform tablets that hold about seven thousand celestial predictions.[49] And as mentioned earlier, ancient astronomer Ptolemy created the foundation for the zodiac we know and use today, his *Tertrabiblos* focusing on individual astrological interpretations.[50]

Astrological Sign Dates

Aries: March 21–April 19
Taurus: April 20–May 20
Gemini: May 21–June 20
Cancer: June 21–July 22
Leo: July 23–August 22
Virgo: August 23–September 22
Libra: September 23–October 22
Scorpio: October 23–November 21
Sagittarius: November 22–December 21
Capricorn: December 22–January 19
Aquarius: January 20–February 18
Pisces: February 19–March 20

New/Full Moon and Zodiac Correspondences

Here is a list of the new and full moon correspondences so you may incorporate them into your moon manifesting practice. When you are ready to incorporate the zodiac into your manifesting practice, use these to get a general idea of what the energy is and how to best use it.

Aries

Keywords: Brash, creative, and daring

New Moon in Aries: The new moon in Aries wants you to call in things that light you up. What inspires you? What do you have tucked away that

49. Francesca Rochberg, "The Catalogues of Enumā Anu Enlil," in *Assyrian and Babylonian Scholarly Text Catalogues: Medicine, Magic and Divination*, ed. Ulrike Steinert, vol. 9 (2018): 121–36, doi.org/10.1515/9781501504914-006.

50. Catherine Caruso, "The History of Horoscopes," *National Geographic*, July 3, 2024, https://www.nationalgeographic.com/history/article/history-of-horoscopes.

you want to bring forth? Take advantage of this fiery energy and let it ignite a new path within you.

Full Moon in Aries: This full moon wants you to focus on your own wants and needs. This is not a selfish act but one of self-care. What limiting thoughts about yourself can you let go of in the full moon's light? What will you open so that you can receive?

Taurus

Keywords: Stable, pragmatic, and unwavering

New Moon in Taurus: Building your foundation during this sign is a prosperous choice. Know your limits, create new boundaries, and evaluate your strengths. What can you do to make your base stronger? What seeds do you need to sow for success?

Full Moon in Taurus: Do you need to clear some unwanted things in your life—things that are taking up space in your psyche like weeds in a garden? Time to do some mental weeding and see where you may have been a bit stubborn. Where can you ease up?

Gemini

Keywords: Intellectual, communicative, and forward thinking

New Moon in Gemini: Communication is what this air sign is all about. This moon phase/zodiac combination is great to work on open lines of communication and practice saying no to things you do not need to be involved in. This Gemini moon sign can be great when working on a larger manifestation over a few months to help clear the path for wonderful happenings.

Full Moon in Gemini: Are there any communication habits you would like to work on? Now is a wonderful time to work on unpleasant habits that keep you from speaking clearly and truthfully.

Cancer

Keywords: Deep, emotional, and psychic

New Moon in Cancer: Emotion is the name of the game with this sign, so focusing on how you feel about what you want to bring to fruition in your life will be a priority. Make sure to dig deep and really gauge your emotional compass as you start on this new journey.

Full Moon in Cancer: Sometimes letting go of emotions, thoughts, and feelings can be a bit tricky. Holding on to your possessions is a superpower for you. Maybe start small and try to release to make room for bigger and better things to come your way.

Leo

Keywords: Bold, creative, and daring

New Moon in Leo: This new moon is calling to bring out your creative side. It is time for you to shine. What are you good at? This Leo moon wants you to show the world what you are made of. It is time to step up and be proud of all the things you want to accomplish and to build on what you are already good at.

Full Moon in Leo: With that big Leo energy's influence, this moon is asking you to release expectations. Sometimes when you become too embedded in your ego, you need make effort to be mindful and take a step back to reorganize your wants and needs. What can you let go of in your everyday life that was seen through the lens of your ego?

Virgo

Keywords: Stable, pragmatic, and unwavering

New Moon in Virgo: Organization is key for this new moon. Now is a wonderful time to reorder your work or home life. Start new healthy routines and make sure your base is secure. What part of your life can use some reorganizing?

Full Moon in Virgo: Virgo's energy is calling you to be of service. Releasing judgment and helping others with a clear mind is what will be most fulfilling at this time. The full moon in Virgo asks you to let go of what you want to leave energetic space for others to thrive.

Libra

Keywords: Intellectual, communicative, and forward thinking

New Moon in Libra: How are you feeling about the relationships in your life? Do you feel they are stable and harmonious? The moon in Libra calls you to examine stagnant relationships to see if they are still serving you. Nurture those around you and see how it is reciprocated. This can also apply to your relationship with yourself, so take stock in how you feel when you are going through your day. Do you need to be kinder to yourself?

Full Moon in Libra: What relationships have you been letting drag on that may need to be released? The Libra full moon wants you to clear any unhappy emotional attachments you may have right now. By doing this you are creating space for more loving interactions.

Scorpio

Keywords: Deep, emotional, and psychic

New Moon in Scorpio: Your intuition may be off the charts during this new moon. Now is a wonderful time to hone your intuition and trust it more. What new intuitive practice can you start this phase to help you know and trust yourself better?

Full Moon in Scorpio: Have you been holding on to unhealthy habits or limiting beliefs just because that is what you are used to doing? The Scorpio moon is a wonderful time to dig deep and start to shift these patterns that do not help us become our best selves. Decide on at least one not-so-great habit to let go of this deep-feeling full moon.

Sagittarius

Keywords: Brash, creative, and daring

New Moon in Sagittarius: The new moon in Sagittarius is all about luck and having a fun time. Have you been doing anything for fun? Plan that action you have been wanting to take for traveling or at least get the plan in motion during this moon. It is time to let loose and enjoy yourself.

Full Moon in Sagittarius: Taking a good look at the past year would be ideal in this zodiac energy. How does it feel to you? Think about situations, people, or things that may be weighing you down so you can release them.

Capricorn

Keywords: Stable, pragmatic, and consistent

New Moon in Capricorn: As this is the last new moon of the calendar year, you want to wish big. Dig deep and find those hopes and dreams you may have stashed away and start breathing life into them. Organize your life in a way that will leave space for the wonderful opportunities that await you.

Full Moon in Capricorn: Now is the time to clear out all things that no longer serve you. While this may be difficult, it will also bring along some much-needed healing. Time to shift the energy in your favor. Let go and heal.

Aquarius

Keywords: Intellectual, communicative, and forward thinking

New Moon in Aquarius: The current focus is the collective and how you are a part of it. Do you feel you have a community or a friend group? Do you include yourself in activities outside of your home or workspaces? Set a new community action in place this month. Be with those who make you shine.

Full Moon in Aquarius: Evaluate how you show up in the world at this phase. Do you need to practice being more authentic and not worrying about what others think of you? Releasing worry of others' opinions will open you up to new experiences.

Pisces

Keywords: Spiritual, emotional, and intuitive

New Moon in Pisces: Now is the time to lean into your intuition and call in the life that you want. Your magical self is supercharged right now—how can you best use it? Decide what you want and send all your magic to make it happen.

Full Moon in Pisces: Reflection is the name of the game for this moon. Let yourself daydream a little. Daydreaming can also help us realize what we do *not* want; when these things come up for you, let them go. Set them on a little ship in your mind and see it sail away.

New Moon Zodiac Mini Rituals

When you decide to include the zodiac signs in your moon manifesting work, here are some mini new moon rituals based on each sign to include on the new moon you choose to work with. I chose the new moon to focus these on for two reasons. The new moon is a good starting point to start off your moon manifesting with extra energy and secondly these rituals act as a template for you to use to create extra mini rituals for the other phases when you are ready.

EXERCISE: ARIES NEW MOON FIRE AFFIRMATIONS

Try these affirmations to feel and harness fiery Aries energy.

What you need:

Yourself

A mirror

What to do:

Take a few deep, cleansing breaths. Look at yourself in the mirror and say, "I am ambitious and get things done." Take a breath, then say, "I am ready for anything and will adjust accordingly." Pause and say, "I am motivated and ready for what I want or something better." Finish by saying, "And so it is" three times.

Take a few more deep breaths and go about your day. Repeat these affirmations before you begin your moon workings for the Aries moon phase.

EXERCISE: TAURUS NEW MOON PLANT MAGIC

Plant friends make the best friends. See how connecting with plant energy grounds you and how it feels.

What you need:

A small plant in a pot (you can dig one up from outside but ask the plant for permission first)
A small slip of paper and pen
Green crystal (green quartz, aventurine, moss agate, et cetera)

What to do:

Bring your plant and other items to your favorite spot in your home or to your moon altar. Take a moment to get comfortable. On your slip of paper, write what makes you feel most secure and grounded in your moon magic. Read it aloud three times and then place the slip of paper in the soil of your plant.

Now hold your plant to your heart center. Take a few deep breaths and bring up how you feel when you are fully grounded. Let this feeling wash over you and your plant. Place the plant in this space or close to it and nurture it. When you need a grounding boost for your moon manifesting, hold the plant and bring up the feeling of security until you feel better.

EXERCISE: GEMINI NEW MOON CLEARING CLUTTER SPELL

Use this simple spell to release and clear any unneeded energy.

What you need:

1 white birthday candle
1 black birthday candle
Matches/lighter
Medium firesafe dish

4-inch length of jute twine and scissors
Pinch of chamomile
Moon journal and pen

What to do:

Gather your supplies and bring them to your moon altar. Recall any feelings or thoughts that may be hindering your moon manifestation. Now recall any thoughts or feelings about what is going super well in your moon manifesting cycle. Positive thoughts are associated with the white candle and the not-so-positive thoughts are associated with the black candle. Place the jute twine around each candle so they are tied together and cut any remaining twine. Say, "May my thoughts regarding manifesting with the moon be clear and precise." Warm the bottom of both candles with your source of fire and place them in the middle of your dish near each other.

Add the chamomile around the candles and say, "My thoughts are now uncluttered, and my intention is clear to me."

Light the candles and say "And so it is" three times. Let the candles burn down and do not leave them unattended. As they burn, write about this mini ritual in your moon journal.

EXERCISE: CANCER NEW MOON PSYCHIC CLEANSING SCRUB

Scrub away any energy that does not belong to you with this magical concoction for the hands.

What you need:

A medium glass jar with lid
½ C Epsom salt
½ C olive oil
6 drops lavender essential oil
3 drops rosemary or sage oil
Spoon
Black permanent marker

What to do:

Combine all the ingredients in the jar. Pick up your spoon and stir it in the mixture nine times clockwise. As you do this, say, "May this scrub cleanse and clear any energy that doesn't benefit my moon magical manifesting."

Place the lid on and write your name on the top three times. Say, "And so it shall be for as long as I need." Place the jar on your moon altar and use before your moon magic work.

EXERCISE: LEO NEW MOON INTUITIVE DRAWING

Let fiery Leo energy guide you as you tap into your courage and creativity.

What you need:

Three markers or crayons in colors that you relate to Leo energy (yellow, gold, red, etc.)
A piece of blank, unlined paper

What to do:

Tap into a time you felt brave and from this bravery positive change happened for you. Without giving it much thought, pick up any of the drawing media and let your hand draw freely without judgment, letting your intuitive senses take over to guide your hand. Do this for as long as you feel called to. Do not overthink this exercise; if you start to, stop that overthinking train of thought and hop off.

Take a few deep breaths when finished and bring your drawing to your moon altar. Place it there and give yourself a few minutes to observe what you drew without judgment. Leave your creation on your altar for the entire Leo phase; whenever you see it, remember the bravery and strength you possess right below the surface.

Take a picture of your drawing and use it as a phone wallpaper to help you stay brave as you move through your moon manifesting and as a reminder that you have all you need to be successful inside you.

EXERCISE: VIRGO NEW MOON LETTER TO YOUR FUTURE SELF

Grab a pen and your journal, and let your successful future-self know your thoughts.

What you need:

Moon journal and pen
Purple birthday candle
Small firesafe dish
Matches/lighter

What to do:

Gather your items and bring them to your altar. Warm your purple candle and place on your firesafe dish. Light it and as you do so, say, "I write this letter to my future self for insight for continued success."

Pick up your moon journal and write the date at the top. Think about any messages you want to send to your future self or what you hope the future will look like. When you are finished, write at the bottom of your letter, "I send my future self continued love and support." Sign your name.

Set a reminder on your phone to come back to this letter when the moon cycle is over. At that time, read it over and decide how doing this helped your manifestation.

EXERCISE: LIBRA NEW MOON SELF-LOVE SPELL JAR

Create a little portal of self love for when you need an extra boost.

What you need:

Pink tea light candle
Small firesafe dish
Matches/lighter
Small jar with lid (pink if you can find one)
2 pinches dried rose petals
1 t honey
1 t glitter

Full moon water (regular water is fine if you do not have any)
Pinch of rose quartz or sunstone crystal chips

What to do:

Gather your items and bring them to your moon altar. Set your tea light on the dish and light it. Gaze at the flame and feel the warmth of the candle filling you with love.

Place the jar in front of you and pick up the rose petals. Think about something you love about yourself, breathe into your hand, and infuse the petals with this love. Place in jar.

Pick up the honey and place it at your forehead. Ask and answer the question, "How can I be nicer to myself?" Let the answer float in front of your mind and into the honey. Pour into the jar. Now pick up the glitter and ask yourself, "How can I be more playful?" See your answer dance around the glitter and pour it into the jar. Gather the crystal chips, look at them closely, and notice any imperfections or unique qualities about them. Say aloud, "I do not need to be perfect to be loved." Place them in the jar. Now fill the jar three quarters of the way with water and secure the lid on it.

Stand in front of your moon altar with your jar and shake the jar and yourself for about ten seconds. As you do this, say as many times as you can, "I will manifest what I desire in a loving way this moon cycle and have fun doing it."

Place the jar back on your altar, blow out the candle, and say, "The spell is done and sealed to give me extra love during my moon manifestation cycle, and so it is."

Carefully pour the pink wax from the tea light over the top of the jar and let it dry in the firesafe dish.

Carry the jar around or keep it on your altar to approach all your moon magic with love.

EXERCISE: SCORPIO NEW MOON MEETING YOUR DARK SIDE RITUAL

Your darker self tends to get less attention, so why not try this ritual and see how much your darker side has to offer?

What you need:

A pinch of loose-leaf tea (preferably black)
A teacup
Freshly boiled water in a small heatproof container
Small spoon
A dish with a lip to catch a bit of liquid
Moon journal and pen

What to do:

Collect your items and head to your moon altar. Place the pinch of tea in your empty cup and place back on the altar. Pour a small amount of water into the bottom of the cup, just enough to cover your tea leaves. Carefully turn the light off in the room and sit by your altar. (Use your phone light if it helps). Take a few moments to acclimate to the darker room and take a few deep breaths. Think about your traits that you normally do not let others see. Bring up the emotions and stories attached to these traits and choose two in particular to focus on. Think about what your intention is for this moon manifestation cycle. How can you use these darker traits to help you move toward this intention?

Now turn the lights back on and sit near your altar. Journal on these traits and how they can help you manifest successfully. When finished journaling, set your journal aside. Pick up your teacup and swirl it clockwise three times.

Carefully pour the water into the dish, making sure not to pour all the tea leaves out (a few escaping is okay). Look in the cup. What do you see besides a clump of tea leaves? Are there any shapes or even letters or numbers you can make out? Did a swirl of the tea leaves draw your attention? Set down the cup and grab your moon journal again. Write down what you saw and what you think it means in relation to your moon magic practice.

Try to use at least one of these dark traits in your moon phase action steps. Keep in mind that dark does not mean bad—it just refers to what you tend to keep hidden.

EXERCISE: SAGITTARIUS NEW MOON WHERE YOU NEED TO BE SPELL

Use the energy of crystal magic to tell you where you should be.

What you need:

A map (can be printed) of somewhere you want to be
A malachite crystal (quartz is fine if you do not have one)
Spool of thread (any color) and scissors

What to do:

Bring your items to your moon altar. Tie the string around the malachite. Once secure, leave about six inches out from the spool and cut. Set the crystal aside and pick up your map. Why did you choose this place? Will it help your moon manifestation? Place it down on the altar and pick up your crystal on the string. Hold it about two inches above the paper and wait until it is still.

Ask the crystal what a "no" answer looks like. The crystal may go back and forth or in a circle. Whatever movement it makes is your indication. Now do the same for "yes." Whichever way the crystal goes is your yes for this ritual.

Ask yes or no questions about how you can create movement regarding your intention. For example, "Is this place I chose on the map helpful to making my intention successful?" Ask up to three questions and write down your answers. When finished, say thank you for the crystal's help and place on your altar.

Doing this exercise is great to help focus your energy when you are excited and feel pulled in many directions.

EXERCISE: CAPRICORN NEW MOON MINI VISION BOARD

Create a vision board that taps into the balance you need.

What you need:

Sheet of blank paper
Crayons or markers
3 small pictures of things related to your moon intention
Tape and scissors

What to do:

Gather your items and head to your altar. The energy of this sign is very business-like. Look at your chosen items and think of what concrete steps you will need to create to make these things happen. Write those steps on the back of your paper.

Now take the first picture and tape it to the left side of your paper. Draw a line to the right side followed by a big circle connecting the line to the picture and the circle. Do this with each picture and be creative—use assorted colors and remember that the lines do not have to be straight!

On the first picture, write the action step you jotted down before under it, and in the circle write a way you can rest after taking this action step. For example, if your picture is of someone exercising, your rest step may be to not overdo it but to gradually increase your exercise time in a comfortable way.

Do this for each picture. How did it feel writing a way to rest after writing the action step?

Notice these feelings and journal on them later.

Now write on the line how the moon guides you with balance. For example, "The moon guides me about the best time to start a new routine and when to hold off a while." Do the same for each picture.

Now hold the paper in front of you. Fold it in half toward you and say, "My vision for myself is balance with direct action." Turn the paper to the right, fold toward you again, and say, "I learn to ebb and flow like the moon to adjust my actions and rest accordingly." Turn to the right again, fold toward you, and say, "With every action toward my moon manifestation, I will take time to rest, and it shall be." Place your paper, still folded, in your moon journal or on your altar.

EXERCISE: AQUARIUS NEW MOON THE FLOW OF CHANGE RITUAL

A physical representation of how the changes of the moon cycle affect you.

What you need:

Stick of dragon's blood incense plus matches/lighter
2 wine glasses
2 drops red food dye
2 drops blue food dye
1 C moon water (or regular water)
Moon journal and pen

What to do:

This ritual can be done outside or at your moon altar. Wherever you choose, bring your items to that place. Ground and center by taking a few deep breaths. Pick up and light your incense. Hold the incense stick above your head and create three circles in the air above you. Bring your arm down and let the incense settle around you.

Consider your journey working with the moon so far. Decide if you have been embracing the recent changes this moon cycle has brought up for you. If you feel you have been resistant to this change, repeat the circles above your head.

Now place the incense down and add two drops of red dye to one glass and two drops of blue dye to the other. The blue glass represents change, and the red glass represents the resistance to change.

Hold a glass in each hand. Pour the red water into the blue water and say, "I go with the flow of change as I grow and learn from the moon manifesting cycle." Keep going back and forth, pouring the glasses into each other until you feel a shift in your resistance to these changes. Once you feel you've done it enough, place the glasses down and stand up.

Now it is time to shake out that resistance. Literally shake your body and let every part feel those last bits of resistance leave you.

Take a few deep breaths and let them release in a woosh. Journal on this experience if you wish and repeat this ritual when you feel that resistance creep up.

EXERCISE: PISCES NEW MOON HIGHER SELF RITUAL

Call out to your higher-self and receive direct guidance from your higher self with this ritual.

What you need:

4-inch blue taper candle, matches/lighter, medium firesafe dish

A quiet space or your moon altar

What to do:

Gather your items and bring them to your chosen space. Warm the bottom of the candle with your heat source and place it on the firesafe dish. Ground and center.

Now light your candle and sit in front of it. Stare at the flame for about a minute, clearing your mind the best you can. Afterward, close your eyes and focus on your breath for about a minute.

Slowly open your eyes and silently ask to fully connect with your higher self. When you feel you have done so, ask a few questions regarding your moon manifestation journey and what you can do to connect to the energy of the moon in a more profound way.

Sit for as long as you like, until you feel you have received your answers. These answers may show up as pictures, words, colors, or sensations. Just let it happen. When you are finished, thank your higher self and close your eyes again. Take a few more deep breaths before opening your eyes. Journal on your messages, even if they do not make sense right now. Wash your hands or go outside to fully ground back into your body.

Planning what you want to manifest around the energies of the zodiac signs lets you create an incredibly detailed and specific map to make what you want a reality. You choose this adventure, so if zodiac work feels like too much, then just leave it out for now. When something comes up later after you have gained some moon manifesting experience, you will know when the time is right to incorporate the zodiac signs. These tools, tips, and tricks just add to your knowledge, magic, and manifesting cycle mojo.

CONCLUSION

Now that you have completed a magical moon manifesting cycle, take a moment and think about where you started a month ago. How do you feel about how you have grown and changed for the better? Even if you only read this book and did not actively manifest, you still created new pathways of abundance and will be ready to embark on your magical journey when the time is right.

As you move on to the next cycle, take what you have learned and apply it while it is still fresh in your mind and active in your energetic body. Before moving on to the next moon manifesting cycle and creating a new intention, make a list of what you want to bring into the new cycle. By writing it out you are fully integrating it into your being and setting yourself up for success, as you will already be tapping into and communicating with your higher-level self.

My hope for you is to realize the power you hold inside, and I am proud of you for bringing out this magic from within yourself and giving your lunar anima a chance to shine. You are a magical being, and when you choose magic, it chooses you in abundance. So choose magic, stand in your power, and use both to manifest the life you deserve and will love no matter what it looks like to anyone else.

Your Moon Manifesting Cruise Director,
~ Jen xoxo

RECOMMENDED READING

Here are recommended resources that will help as you continue to explore your new moon practice. Books are listed by subject and include notes.

Astrology and the Moon

Cosmic Calendar: Moon Phase. https://astrostyle.com/cosmic-calendar/moon-phase.

Julia Halina Hadas, *The Modern Witchcraft Book of Moon Magick: Your Complete Guide to Enhancing Your Magic with the Power of the Moon.* Adams Media, 2024.

The book includes more than fifty spells and rituals focused to the moon's phases, offering practical tools for anyone looking to deepen their magical practices by aligning with lunar cycles.

Ezzie Spencer, *Lunar Abundance: Cultivating Joy, Peace, and Purpose Using the Phases of the Moon.* Running Press, 2018.

In *Lunar Abundance*, Spencer shares a mindful, intention-setting practice aligned with the moon's eight phases.

Jan Spiller, *New Moon Astrology: Using New Moon Power Days to Change and Revitalize Your Life.* Bantam, 2001.

This book provides practical guidance on harnessing the power of the new moon to set intentions and manifest personal goals.

Crystals

Judy Hall, *The Crystal Bible: A Definitive Guide to Crystals.* Krause Publications, 2003.

This reference book offers detailed descriptions of over 200 crystals, including their properties, uses, and healing applications.

Judy Hall, *The Ultimate Guide to Crystal Grids: Transform Your Life Using the Power of Crystals and Layouts.* Fair Winds Press, 2017.

In this guide, Judy Hall explores the art of creating crystal grids to amplify energy and manifest intentions.

Goddess Work

Lilith Dorsey, *Orishas, Goddesses, and Voodoo Queens: The Divine Feminine in the African Religious Traditions.* Weiser Books, 2020.

Lilith Dorsey dives into the divine feminine within African spiritual traditions, focusing on deities such as Nana Buluku, Oshun, Mami Wata, and Yemaya.

Shelley A. Kaehr, *The Goddess Discovered: Exploring the Divine Feminine Around the World.* Llewellyn Publications, 2023.

Shelley Kaehr introduces readers to over five hundred goddesses from various cultures and time periods.

Stephanie Woodfield, *Dedicant, Devotee, Priest: A Pagan Guide to Divine Relationships.* Llewellyn Publications, 2021.

This book provides information on creating a devotional practice.

Herbs

Emma Callery, *The Complete Book of Herbs: A Practical Guide to Growing and Using Herbs.* Hermes House, 2000.

This book covers the cultivation, harvesting, and various uses of herbs in cooking, health, and home care.

Thomas Easley and Steven Horne, *The Modern Herbal Dispensatory: A Medicine-Making Guide.* North Atlantic Books, 2016.

This book is a valuable resource for anyone seeking to deepen their knowledge of plant-based medicine.

Intuition

Melanie Barnum, *Real Life Intuition: Extraordinary Stories from People Who Listen to Their Inner Voice.* Llewellyn Publications, 2024.

This book explains how to understand and develop the five "clairs" and offers guidance on interpreting dreams, intuitive flashes, and signs.

Astrea Taylor, *Intuitive Witchcraft: How to Use Intuition to Elevate Your Craft.* Llewellyn Publications, 2024.

This practical yet heartfelt book explores how to build your witchcraft and intuition practices together, helping you cultivate personal wisdom.

Sigils

Laura Tempest Zakroff, *Sigil Witchery: A Witch's Guide to Crafting Magick Symbols.* Llewellyn Publications, 2018.

In *Sigil Witchery*, Laura Zakroff offers a fresh, intuitive approach to creating and using sigils in magical practice.

Tarot

Mary K. Greer, *21 Ways to Read a Tarot Card.* Llewellyn Publications, 2006.

Mary Greer presents twenty-one techniques for interpreting tarot cards, encouraging readers to engage deeply with the imagery and symbolism of their decks.

Rachel Pollack, *The New Tarot: Modern Variations of Ancient Images.* Samuel Weiser, 1986.

Rachel Pollack explores the evolution of tarot imagery and symbolism, focusing on contemporary interpretations and decks that expand on traditional archetypes.

BIBLIOGRAPHY

"7 Unusual Myths and Theories About the Moon." History.com, last updated February 7, 2025. https://www.history.com/news/7-unusual-myths-and-theories-about-the-moon.

"A Short History of Writing." Language Insight, March 5, 2019. https://languageinsight.com/blog/2019/a-short-history-of-writing.

"Ancient Zodiac." *University of Michigan: Early Astronomy,* accessed November 4, 2024. https://early-astronomy.classics.lsa.umich.edu/ancient_ziqpu.

"Black Elk," National Park Service, updated August 31, 2020. https://www.nps.gov/people/black-elk.htm.

"Gas Chromatography-Mass Spectrometry (GC-MS)." EAG Laboratories, accessed November 25, 2024. https://www.eag.com/techniques/mass-spec/gas-chromatography-mass-spectrometry-gc-ms/.

"Gem-A Gemstone & Mineral Collection: Understanding Selenite." GemA: The Gemmological Association of Great Britain, April 18, 2019. https://gem-a.com/gem-hub/gem-knowledge/understanding-selenite.

"The Greek Zodiac." Greece.com, accessed 2023. https://www.greece.com/info/general/greek_zodiac.

"The Moon and Eclipses." NASA, accessed 2023. https://moon.nasa.gov/moon-in-motion/phases-eclipses-supermoons/eclipses.

"Phases of the Moon." Kopernik Observatory & Science Center, accessed November 25, 2024. https://www.kopernik.org/visitor-info/science-park/phases-of-the-moon/.

"Visual Appearance of Lunar Eclipses." *NASA*, accessed November 25, 2024. https://eclipse.gsfc.nasa.gov/LEcat5/appearance.html.

"Water Science School: The Water in You: Water and the Human Body." U.S. Geological Survey, May 22, 2019. https://www.usgs.gov/special-topics/water-science-school/science/water-you-water-and-human-body.

"What is a Waxing Gibbous Moon?" EarthSky, January 1, 2023. https://earthsky.org/moon-phases/waxing-gibbous/.

Akaṣpāda *The Analects of Rumi*. Independently Published, 2019.

Alexander, Jane. *The Smudging and Blessings Book*. Sterling Press, 2009.

Arroyo, Stephen. *Chart Interpretation Handbook*. CRCS Publications, 1989.

Boeckmann, Catherine. "A Guide to Traditional Full Moon Names and Their Meanings." Almanac.com, last updated March 12, 2025. https://www.almanac.com/full-moon-names.

Boland, Yasmin. *Moonology: Working with the Magic of Lunar Cycles*. Hay House, 2016.

Boyle, Rebecca. "Ancient Humans Used the Moon as a Calendar in the Sky." *ScienceNews*, July 9, 2019. https://www.sciencenews.org/article/moon-time-calendar-ancient-human-art.

Caruso, Catherine. "The History of Horoscopes." *National Geographic*, July 3, 2024. https://www.nationalgeographic.com/history/article/history-of-horoscopes.

Cascio, Christopher N., Matthew Brook O'Donnell, Francis J. Tinney, Matthew D. Liberman, Shelley E. Taylor, Victor J. Strecher, Emily B. Falk. "Self-affirmation activates brain systems associated with self-related processing and reward and is reinforced by future orientation." *Social Cognitive and Affective Neuroscience* 11, no. 4 (2015): 612–29. doi.org/10.1093/scan/nsv136.

Casiraghi, Leandro, Ignacio Spiousas, Gideon P. Dunster, Kaitlyn McGlothlen, Eduardo Fernández-Duque, Claudia Valeggia, Horacio O. de la Iglesia. "Moonstruck sleep: Synchronization of human sleep with the moon cycle under field conditions." *Science Advances* 7, vol. 5 (2021): 1–8. doi:10.1126/sciadv.abe0465.

Chandler, Adam. *99% Perspiration: A New Working History of the American Way of Life*. Pantheon Books, 2025.

Chen, Pamela. *Enchanted Crystal Magic: Spells, Grids & Potions to Manifest Your Desires*. Llewellyn Publications, 2021.

The Complete A–Z Reference of Essential Oils for Health and Healing. Fall River Press, 2015.

Darwin, Charles. *The Descent of Man, and Selection in Relation to Sex*. 1st ed. John Murray, 1871. Last updated October 2022. https://darwin-online.org.uk/converted/published/1871_Descent_F937/1871_Descent_F937.1.html.

Deloria Jr., Vine. *God Is Red: A Native View of Religion*. Fulcrum Publishing, 1992.

Dickinson, Emily. *Collected Poems of Emily Dickinson*. Gramercy, 1988.

Emmons, Robert. *Thanks! How Practicing Gratitude Can Make You Happier*. Houghton Mifflin Harcourt, 2008.

Erdoes, Richard, and Alfonso Ortiz, eds. "Navajo Stories of the Moon and Stars," in *American Indian Myths and Legends* Pantheon Books, 1984.

Farber, Monte. *Quantum Affirmations: The New Energy Science of Conscious Manifestation*. Schiffer Publishing, 2012.

Feldt, Laura. "Total devotion in the ancient world: emotions and narrative in radical religion." *Religion* 53, vol. 1 (2023): 1–23. doi.org/10.1080/0048721X.2022.2150405.

Frazier, Karen. *Crystals for Beginners: The Guide to Get Started with the Healing Power of Crystals*. Althea Press, 2017.

Frazier, Karen. *Crystals for Healing: The Complete Reference Guide with Over 200 Remedies for Mind, Heart & Soul*. Adams Media, 2016.

Gallagher, Kirsty. *Lunar Living: Working with the Magic of the Moon Cycles.* Hay House, 2021.

Galejs, Janis. "Schumann Resonances 1." *Radio Science Journal of Research* 69D, 8 (1965). Accessed at: https://nvlpubs.nist.gov/nistpubs/jres/69D/jresv69Dn8p1043_A1b.pdf.

George, Demetra. *Mysteries of the Dark Moon: The Healing Power of the Dark Goddess.* HarperOne, 1992.

Gillett, Roy. *The Secret Language of Astrology.* Watkins Media, 2012.

Graham, Loren. "The Power of Names: Religion & Mathematics." Philoctetes Center, November 11, 2009. http://philoctetes.org/news/the_power_of_names_religion_mathematics.

Greer, Mary K. *Tarot for Your Self: A Workbook for Personal Transformation.* 2nd ed. Weiser Books, 2002.

Hall, Judy. *The Crystal Bible: A Definitive Guide to Crystals.* Krause Publications, 2018.

Hall, Judy. *The Ultimate Guide to Crystal Grids: Transform Your Life Using the Power of Crystals and Layouts*. Fair Winds Press, 2017.

Hawthorn, Hannah. *The Magic of Birthdays: Rituals, Spells, and Recipes for Honoring Your Solar Return.* Witchy Books, 2021.

Hayden, Brian. *The Power of Ritual in Prehistory: Secret Societies and Origins of Social Complexity.* Cambridge University Press, 2018.

Helfrich-Förster, Charlotte, Stefanie Monecke, Ignacio Spiousas, Thomas Hovestadt, Oliver Mitesser, and Thomas A. Wehr. "Women Temporarily Synchronize Their Menstrual Cycles with the Luminance and Gravimetric Cycles of the Moon." *Science Advances* 7, no. 5 (2021): eabe1358 .doi.org/10.1126/sciadv.abe1358.

Idris, Zamzuri, Zaitun Zakaria, Ang Song Yee, Diana Noma Fitzrol, Abdul Rahman Izaini Ghani, Jafri Malin Abdullah, Wan Mohd Nazaruddin Wan Hassan, Mohd Hasyizan Hassan, Asrulnizam Abdul Manaf, and Raymond Ooi Chong Heng. "Quantum and Electromagnetic Fields in Our Universe and Brain: A New Perspective to Comprehend Brain

Function." *Brain Sciences* 11, vol. 5 (2021): 558. doi.org/10.3390/brainsci11050558.

Kramer, Samuel Noah. *History Begins at Sumer: Thirty-Nine Firsts in Recorded History.* Doubleday, 1956.

Lieber, Arnold L. *The Lunar Effect: Biological Tides and Human Emotions.* Anchor Press, 1978.

Long, Kim. *The Moon Book: Fascinating Facts about the Magnificent, Mysterious Moon.* Johnson Books, 1998.

Mankey, Jason. *Transformative Witchcraft: The Greater Mysteries.* Llewellyn Publications, 2019.

"Mindfulness." American Psychological Association, accessed 2023. https://www.apa.org/topics/mindfulness.

Mulhern, Kathleen. "What Are the Sabbats?" *Patheos* (blog), accessed 2023. https://www.patheos.com/answers/what-are-the-sabbats.

Naylor, Ernest. *Moonstruck: How the Lunar Phases Affect Life.* Oxford Press, 2015.

Ornstein, Robert. *The Evolution of Consciousness: The Origins of the Way We Think.* Simon & Schuster, 1991.

Patton, John-Paul. *Lightning Bolts and Dew Drops: A Cauldron of Poesy.* Independently published, 2015.

Von Petzinger, Genevieve. *The First Signs: Unlocking the Mysteries of the World's Oldest Symbols.* Atria Books, 2016.

Pearson, Nicolas. *Crystal Basics: The Energetic, Healing, and Spiritual Properties of 100 Gemstones.* Healing Arts Press, 2015.

Pollack, Rachel. *The New Tarot Handbook: Master the Meanings of the Cards.* Llewellyn Publications, 2017.

Pollack, Rachel. *Seventy-Eight Degrees of Wisdom: A Tarot Journey to Self-Awareness.* 2nd ed. Thorsons, 1997.

Raible, Florian, Hiroki Takekata, Kristin Tessmar-Raible, "An Overview of Monthly Clocks and Rhythms," *Frontiers in Neurology* 11, no. 8, (2017): 189. doi.org/10.3389/fneur.2017.00189.

Rochberg, Francesca. "The Catalogues of Enūma Anu Enlil." In *Assyrian and Babylonian Scholarly Text Catalogues: Medicine, Magic and Divination* vol. 9 (2018): 121–36. Edited by Ulrike Steinert. doi.org/10.1515/9781501504914-006.

Röösli, Martin, Peter Jüni, Charlotte Braun-Fahrländer, Martin W. G. Brinkhof, Nicola Low, Matthias Egger. "Sleepless night, the moon is bright: longitudinal study of lunar phase and sleep." *Journal of Sleep Research* 15 (2006):149–153. https://blog.surf-prevention.com/wp-content/uploads/2012/01/Sleepless-night-the-moon-is-bright-longitudinal-study-of-lunar-phase-and-sleep.pdf.

Scialla, Janelle. "A Brief History of Crystals and Healing." Crystal Sage, accessed 2023. https://www.crystalage.com/crystal_information/crystal_history/.

Sjöblom, Margareta, Kerstin Öhrling, Maria Prellwitz, and Catrine Kostenius. "Health throughout the Lifespan: The Phenomenon of the Inner Child Reflected in Events during Childhood Experienced by Older Persons." *International Journal of Qualitative Studies on Health and Well-Being* vol. 11, 1 (2016): 34186. doi:10.3402/qhw.v11.31486.

Snider, Amber C. "Learning to Surrender: The Sacred Lessons of Yemayá," Atmos, last updated June 21, 2022, https://atmos.earth/ocean-conservation-santeria-yemaya-lessons/.

Wen, Benebell. *Holistic Tarot: An Integrative Approach to Using Tarot for Personal Growth*. North Atlantic Books, 2015.

Wintner, Bakara. *WTF is Tarot & How Do I Do It?* Page Street Publishing, 2017.

Wix, Angela A. *The Secret Psychic: Embrace the Magic of Subtle Intuition, Natural Spirit Communication, and Your Hidden Spiritual Life*. Llewellyn Publications, 2021.

Whitt, Kelly Kizer. "The Moon's Terminator Line Divides Night and Day. Earthsky.org, January 29, 2023. www.earthsky.org/astronomy-essentials/definition-moon-planet-terminator-line-twilight-zone/.

Yirka, Bob. "Cave Paintings Show Ice Age Hunter-Gatherers Used a Lunar Calendar," *Phys.org*, January 5, 2023, https://phys.org/news/2023-01-cave-ice-age-hunter-gatherers-lunar.html.

Zakroff, Laura Tempest. "Tending to Your Spiritual Cauldrons." Llewellyn Worldwide website, May 22, 2017. https://www.llewellyn.com/journal/print.php?id=2629.

Zakroff, Laura Tempest. *Sigil Witchery: A Witch's Guide to Crafting Magick Symbols*. Llewellyn Publications, 2018.

To Write to the Author

If you wish to contact the author or would like more information about this book, please write to the author in care of Llewellyn Worldwide Ltd. and we will forward your request. Both the author and the publisher appreciate hearing from you and learning of your enjoyment of this book and how it has helped you. Llewellyn Worldwide Ltd. cannot guarantee that every letter written to the author can be answered, but all will be forwarded. Please write to:

Jen Sankey
℅ Llewellyn Worldwide
2143 Wooddale Drive
Woodbury, MN 55125-2989

Please enclose a self-addressed stamped envelope for reply, or $1.00 to cover costs. If outside the U.S.A., enclose an international postal reply coupon.

Many of Llewellyn's authors have websites with additional information and resources. For more information, please visit our website at https://www.llewellyn.com.

NOTES

NOTES